"Lloyd-Jones would surely have Christian life requires an unders~~........~~ ~~...~~ ~~..........~~ ~~..~~ ~~...~~ ~~......~~ ~~......~~, ~~..~~e whole gospel, and the whole body of Christian doctrine. Meyer is to be congratulated on his remarkable achievement of giving us a clear and concise portrait of Lloyd-Jones and his ministry, wisely grounded in a splendid summary of his exposition of the gospel."

Sinclair B. Ferguson, Chancellor's Professor of Systematic Theology, Reformed Theological Seminary

"My few personal meetings with 'the Doctor' before he entered what he called 'the Glory' in March 1981 were marked by personal encouragement. That spring, at a conference of several hundred pastors who were asked to bear witness to the life and ministry of the late Dr. Lloyd-Jones, a strong majority of those who spoke fastened onto the countless kindnesses the Doctor had displayed to them. Jason Meyer rightly and capably emphasizes the extraordinary unity of doctrine and experience in Lloyd-Jones's life. This Christian vitality in his life was other-focused: the outworking of the gospel of the triune God in the life of the believer was not pursued in an individualist fashion, but sought the good of other believers, the benefit of the church, and the glory of God."

D. A. Carson, Research Professor of New Testament, Trinity Evangelical Divinity School; Cofounder, The Gospel Coalition

"Both for those already familiar with the published works of Martyn Lloyd-Jones and for those taking them up for the first time, Meyer's work will be prized. From a thorough knowledge of the sources, he highlights and clarifies the truths which Lloyd-Jones preached, and, most importantly, he does it with the same heartbeat. It has done me good to read this book."

Iain H. Murray, author, *Jonathan Edwards: A New Biography* and *Evangelical Holiness*; Founding Trustee, Banner of Truth Trust

"When I was a young boy, my father took me to hear Martyn Lloyd-Jones speak. I remember little of the occasion, except my father's deep desire that I hear 'the Doctor' preach while he was still alive. My mother was a regular at his Friday night lectures on Ephesians. Lloyd-Jones was a major influence on my parents and, through them, on me. So it is a joy to welcome this book on his understanding of the Christian life. Read it to discover what drove this titan of the twentieth-century church. But better still, let the Doctor examine your Christian life, diagnose its ailments, and prescribe a God-centered remedy."

Tim Chester, Pastor, Grace Church, Boroughbridge, United Kingdom; Faculty Member, Crosslands Training

"Martyn Lloyd-Jones stood out in two compelling ways: theological depth and spiritual power. 'The Doctor' therefore represents what we most need afresh in our generation, especially as we pastors long to preach the biblical gospel under the anointing of the Holy Spirit. This wonderful new book by Jason Meyer meets our need, not by idealizing a man but by drawing us into deeper personal reality with the living God."

Ray Ortlund, Lead Pastor, Immanuel Church, Nashville, Tennessee

"In our day, popularity is easy to come by, but enduring significance is not. Many people who are liked and retweeted today will be forgotten tomorrow. However, there are some people who have been significant but are not well known. In this volume, Meyer introduces us to a man whose name may not be trending but whose effect on countless Christians and pastors is far more noteworthy than many realize. It is my hope that Meyer's book will expand the influence of Martyn Lloyd-Jones to a new generation of Christians who are in desperate need of his voice."

C. J. Mahaney, Senior Pastor, Sovereign Grace Church of Louisville

"I wrote in the Director's Statement for the documentary *Logic on Fire* that it is as important for our generation to understand why Martyn Lloyd-Jones made the choices he did in life and ministry as it is to understand him on Romans, Ephesians, the Sermon on the Mount, or spiritual depression—and that is saying quite a lot. Jason Meyer's excellent book navigates the reader *ad fontes*, to the Doctor's own understanding of the Scriptures, and proves that his unshakable confidence in them was the fuel to his fire. Lloyd-Jones's life is still giving light and heat to the church today, and I pray this book will be a conduit that brings much illumination to our day and generation. I commend this book to you heartily and enthusiastically."

Matthew Robinson, Director, Media Gratiae; Director, *Logic on Fire: The Life and Legacy of Dr. Martyn Lloyd-Jones*

LLOYD-JONES

on the Christian Life

THEOLOGIANS ON THE CHRISTIAN LIFE

EDITED BY STEPHEN J. NICHOLS AND JUSTIN TAYLOR

Augustine on the Christian Life:
Transformed by the Power of God,
Gerald Bray

Bavinck on the Christian Life:
Following Jesus in Faithful Service,
John Bolt

Bonhoeffer on the Christian Life:
From the Cross, for the World,
Stephen J. Nichols

Calvin on the Christian Life:
Glorifying and Enjoying God Forever,
Michael Horton

Edwards on the Christian Life:
Alive to the Beauty of God,
Dane C. Ortlund

Lewis on the Christian Life:
Becoming Truly Human in the Pres-
ence of God,
Joe Rigney

Lloyd-Jones on the Christian Life:
Doctrine and Life as Fuel and Fire,
Jason Meyer

Luther on the Christian Life:
Cross and Freedom,
Carl R. Trueman

Newton on the Christian Life:
To Live Is Christ,
Tony Reinke

Owen on the Christian Life:
Living for the Glory of God in Christ,
Matthew Barrett and
Michael A. G. Haykin

Packer on the Christian Life:
Knowing God in Christ,
Walking by the Spirit,
Sam Storms

Schaeffer on the Christian Life:
Countercultural Spirituality,
William Edgar

Spurgeon on the Christian Life:
Alive in Christ,
Michael Reeves

Warfield on the Christian Life:
Living in Light of the Gospel,
Fred G. Zaspel

Wesley on the Christian Life:
The Heart Renewed in Love,
Fred Sanders

LLOYD-JONES

on the Christian Life

DOCTRINE AND LIFE AS FUEL AND FIRE

JASON MEYER

FOREWORD BY SINCLAIR B. FERGUSON

WHEATON, ILLINOIS

Lloyd-Jones on the Christian Life: Doctrine and Life as Fuel and Fire

Copyright © 2018 by Jason C. Meyer

Published by Crossway
    1300 Crescent Street
    Wheaton, Illinois 60187

Cover design: Josh Dennis

Cover image: Richard Solomon Artists, Mark Summers

First printing 2018

Printed in the United States of America

Unless otherwise indicated, the author's Scripture quotations are from the ESV® Bible (The Holy Bible, English Standard Version®), copyright © 2001 by Crossway, a publishing ministry of Good News Publishers. Used by permission. All rights reserved.

Scripture quotations marked KJV are from the King James Version of the Bible.

All emphases in Scripture quotations have been added by the author.

Trade paperback ISBN: 978-1-4335-4527-6
ePub ISBN: 978-1-4335-4530-6
PDF ISBN: 978-1-4335-4528-3
Mobipocket ISBN: 978-1-4335-4529-0

Library of Congress Cataloging-in-Publication Data

Names: Meyer, Jason C. (Jason Curtis), 1976– author.
Title: Lloyd-Jones on the Christian life: doctrine and life as fuel and fire / Jason Meyer; foreword by Sinclair B. Ferguson.
Description: Wheaton: Crossway, 2018. | Series: Theologians on the Christian life | Includes bibliographical references and index.
Identifiers: LCCN 2017042373 (print) | LCCN 2018007066 (ebook) | ISBN 9781433545283 (pdf) | ISBN 9781433545290 (mobi) | ISBN 9781433545306 (epub) | ISBN 9781433545276 (tp)
Subjects: LCSH: Lloyd-Jones, David Martyn. | Reformed Church—Doctrines. | Christian life.
Classification: LCC BX4827.L68 (ebook) | LCC BX4827.L68 M49 2018 (print) | DDC 285.8092 [B] —dc23
LC record available at https://lccn.loc.gov/2017042373

Crossway is a publishing ministry of Good News Publishers.

VP   28   27   26   25   24   23   22   21   20   19   18
15   14   13   12   11   10   9   8   7   6   5   4   3   2   1

*To the elders
at Bethlehem Baptist Church:
One of the greatest joys of my life
is the partnership we share
in the greatest cause.*

CONTENTS

SERIES PREFACE

Some might call us spoiled. We live in an era of significant and substantial resources for Christians on living the Christian life. We have ready access to books, DVD series, online material, seminars—all in the interest of encouraging us in our daily walk with Christ. The laity, the people in the pew, have access to more information than scholars dreamed of having in previous centuries.

Yet, for all our abundance of resources, we also lack something. We tend to lack the perspectives from the past, perspectives from a different time and place than our own. To put the matter differently, we have so many riches in our current horizon that we tend not to look to the horizons of the past.

That is unfortunate, especially when it comes to learning about and practicing discipleship. It's like owning a mansion and choosing to live in only one room. This series invites you to explore the other rooms.

As we go exploring, we will visit places and times different from our own. We will see different models, approaches, and emphases. This series does not intend for these models to be copied uncritically, and it certainly does not intend to put these figures from the past high upon a pedestal like some race of super-Christians. This series intends, however, to help us in the present listen to the past. We believe there is wisdom in the past twenty centuries of the church, wisdom for living the Christian life.

Stephen J. Nichols and Justin Taylor

FOREWORD

It is an honor and privilege to write a foreword for this carefully researched and well-crafted study of Lloyd-Jones on the Christian life. Most of what has been written about Dr. Lloyd-Jones has come from those who knew him or belonged to the generation he immediately influenced, to whom he was a living voice. Jason Meyer, however, belongs to the next again generation, born in the latter part of the twentieth century. Members of his generation were at most children when "the Doctor" (as he was universally known) went to be with the Lord. Inevitably, those who knew and heard him may think that they have the advantage, and in many ways this is true. But it is surely encouraging to find someone from the next generation again commending Dr. Lloyd-Jones's life and work. And Dr. Meyer does this not in the interests of a regressive hagiography but to stress the perennial principles of David Martyn Lloyd-Jones's life and ministry.

In this context, Meyer is particularly well suited. He is himself esteemed as a pastor and preacher with considerable intellectual gifts (more important even than academic credentials—which he also possesses in abundance). This well equips him to pinpoint what was so central to Lloyd-Jones's life and ministry—doctrine on fire transforming lives—just as the Doctor believed that it is logic on fire that transforms preaching.

The story of Lloyd-Jones's early life is a unique one. He was called to the ministry from his early career as a rising star in the British medical world. Then followed his first ministry in South Wales, marked by his fresh discoveries of the depth of the gospel and by great fruitfulness and the long ministry at Westminster Chapel in London, along with the wide reach of his preaching throughout the United Kingdom.

It was in this last connection that I first heard his name. Memory is an interesting phenomenon—how it is that we can recall the very place we were when we heard a significant piece of news (the death of President Kennedy or the attack on the Twin Towers). I was sixteen years old, going to the local dairy in the morning to collect milk and bread before school lessons began. I met a young lady from the church I attended whose soon-to-be fiancé had taken her (on a date!) to hear Dr. Lloyd-Jones preach the night before in my native city of Glasgow. She answered my question "What was it like?" with the never-to-be-forgotten answer: "He preached on the destruction of Dagon in 1 Samuel 5. I felt that the building was about to collapse." I remember thinking, "I must hear this man for myself!" A year or so later I devoured his two-volume study *The Sermon on the Mount*. Occasionally, the opportunity arose to hear him preach. Another five years or so would pass before his multivolume expositions of Romans and Ephesians began to appear, and then *Preaching and Preachers*. By that time, I was a young minister and, like many others, eagerly devoured each volume as soon as it appeared. Here indeed was logic on fire.

I suspect I was not the only young minister who could write about his first more personal encounter with Martyn Lloyd-Jones, and of his encouragement. But I had a special reason to be taken aback by it. In 1975 I was living on the most northerly inhabited island in the United Kingdom, in the Shetland Islands far off the north coast of the Scottish mainland. The mail that arrived one Friday at lunchtime included a letter in a none-too-legible hand (medical doctors in the UK have a reputation for bad handwriting, but that connection was very far from my mind as I opened the envelope and began to read). Having the habit of trying to take in the contents of a letter at a glance, I could not make sense of the words that seemed to leap off the page. And then came the stunning realization: this was a personal letter from the Doctor. How could he know *who* I was, far less *where* I was? Later, of course, it would dawn on me that this—the encouragement of young ministers—was part and parcel of his model of biblical ministry. Even so, his reach had extended to *ultima Thule*!

The correspondence that ensued was marked by grace and encouragement on his part (not least since I was a comparative child in the ministry), especially his emphasis on both heat and light in the preaching of the Word—the great combination, as he regarded it. Looking back now, I suspect that he engineered little ways of testing my mettle, none more so than in 1978 when an invitation came to give two addresses at a ministers' conference in Wales. As it turned out, the other speaker (for "other" read "main"!) was, yes, D. Martyn Lloyd-Jones. He gave one of the most remarkable addresses I have ever heard, entitled "Extraordinary Phenomena in Revivals of Religion." It was thrilling and an extraordinary phenomenon in its own right! Being of a shy disposition I found the whole experience somewhat daunting—more so, because, when I stood up to preach, Dr. Lloyd-Jones was sitting in the center of the front row! It was an occasion to remember that no matter who is in the congregation, we always preach before the face of God. But here again, the connectedness between what Lloyd-Jones urged on Christians and his own practice was evident. As I made my way from the meeting, a strong hand gripped my arm from behind, and turning around I found myself looking into his face and hearing him say, "My dear brother . . ." What struck me then—I can still feel the sense of it—was how whole-souled his encouragement was.

All this is said by way of introducing *Lloyd-Jones on the Christian Life*, to underline that it was what the Lord made Dr. Lloyd-Jones as a man and as a Christian that shaped his ministry. He did not live to preach; he lived for Christ. All preachers are differently wired; there is a wide variety in gifts and temperaments, in experience and understanding. But when a man is given over to the love of Christ in his living, it cannot be hidden in his preaching; just as sadly, if he is given over to love of self, it will also eventually show. Lloyd-Jones was an exemplar of the gospel, not only a preacher of it.

There is, therefore, a fittingness to Jason Meyer's approach in these pages. The Doctor would have approved of his emphasis on *understanding* Christian doctrine being a major key to *living* the Christian life. Not light without heat, however; but burning light that enflames.

Lloyd-Jones's grasp of Christian doctrine was surely a key to his skill as a spiritual diagnostician and physician of the soul, whether in public or in private. Only the person who understands the whole body of divinity can hope to be able to deal with the many dysfunctions in the body of Christ and its members. Dr. Meyer aptly alludes in these pages to Sir Arthur Conan Doyle's fictional detective Sherlock Holmes (who first met his associate Dr. Watson in a lab at London's St Bartholomew's Hospital, where the young Martyn was a medical student). A pedant might complain that any analogy between an opium-taking detective and a great pastor-preacher breaks down at too many points. But Meyer puts his finger on a key similarity—the use of reason, logic, and analysis to understand the significance of evidence, be it the evidence of a crime or the presenting symptoms of spiritual sickness and death. It was—at least in my own view—not his medical training alone that shaped Lloyd-Jones's preaching style (illustrated by the way he often analyzes the human condition, moves through false explanations of the symptoms to the true cause, and then continues from spiritual diagnosis to gospel remedies and prognosis). Rather, it was what was enshrined in this logical, stage-by-stage examination of the presenting symptoms in the human condition and rich understanding of anatomy—whether physical or spiritual. This is not gained merely by the study of medical facts, any more than the mere study of theology makes a student a great preacher and a superb pastor. Here is where an acute logical mind, biblical understanding, and spiritual giftedness were combined in Martyn Lloyd-Jones.

In one of his adventures, Sherlock Holmes comments on the fact that many detectives can engage in synthetic thinking. (The rarely succeeding detectives of Scotland Yard belong to this category in the world of the amateur detective!) They can follow the trail sometimes. What is much rarer—and, of course, the ability Holmes possesses in superabundance—is the ability to think analytically and to reason backward from the crime to the cause, the motive, the means, the opportunity, and therefore to the culprit. "There is a strong family resemblance about misdeeds," asserts Holmes, "and if you have all the details of a thousand at your finger ends, it is odd if you can't unravel the thousand and first."[1]

Here there is more than an echo spiritually in Lloyd-Jones, whose ability to analyze the human condition was exceptional. In his case he had at his "finger ends" such a knowledge and understanding of the Scriptures and what they say about the human condition that he could give unusual help to people. His analysis led him back from the symptom to the cause, and his knowledge of the gospel enabled him to prescribe the antidote, the gospel pharmaceuticals to be found in the riches of God's grace in Jesus Christ. To use a different detective analogy, G. K. Chesterton's priest-sleuth, Father Brown solved crimes because of his knowledge of the sinfulness of the human heart, not least his own. Lloyd-Jones's skill in spiritual diagnosis and cure were no doubt learned at the cost of the discovery of his own need of Christ and the wonder of Christ's all-sufficiency for him.

---

[1] Arthur Conan Doyle, *A Study in Scarlet* (London: Penguin, 2001), 21.

There is so much more to say (especially to preachers) by way of encouragement to read every page Meyer has written, but two observations must suffice. The first is the challenge represented by a comment made by Mrs. Lloyd-Jones (herself a medical doctor): no one would ever be able to understand her husband without first knowing he was "an evangelist and a man of prayer." The second is this: Lloyd-Jones's preaching took three forms essentially—Friday night instruction, Sunday morning preaching to believers, and Sunday evening evangelistic sermons. When some of his sermons in this third category were published, I remembered how older Christians had spoken about how they looked forward to "the deep teaching Dr. Lloyd-Jones gives us when he comes north to Scotland." In fact, however, he was preaching reworked versions of *his Sunday night evangelistic sermons!* The lesson? The same preaching that God uses to convert sinners he is well able to use to build up saints. The reason? The exaltation of God in Christ. Everything we need for salvation, from its beginning in our lives to its consummation in glory, is to be found in Jesus Christ. In this respect too, Lloyd-Jones modeled what it means to be determined to preach Christ crucified, to know nothing except Jesus Christ and him crucified, to publicly portray him as crucified, and to boast in nothing except the cross of our Lord Jesus Christ (1 Cor. 1:23; 2:2; Gal. 3:1; 6:14).

Martyn Lloyd-Jones was sometimes seen as a *controversial* figure. In some quarters he still is. That would not have troubled him, even if snide criticism can be very sore. For error calls for opposition, and he was not slow to expose it. Like the early fathers of the church (themselves no strangers to controversy), he well knew that not even physical persecution can destroy the church of Jesus Christ, but false doctrine always will. It is striking now, decades after his death, to hear well-known Christian leaders reflect on ways in which some of his views have been substantiated by later history.

A late colleague, a professor at Westminster Theological Seminary in 1969 when Dr. Lloyd-Jones delivered the lectures later published as *Preaching and Preachers*, once told me how much his family had enjoyed hosting the Doctor for a meal. His comment was revealing: "He was a big man; he filled the room." But the Doctor was not in fact a big man. His filling of the room was not so much physical as metaphysical! My colleague's words were reminiscent of J. I. Packer's comment that he had never heard a preacher with "so much of God" about him. Size is spiritual as well as physical, as the example of our Lord suggests (Luke 2:52).

But it would be a mistake for us to compare ourselves with Lloyd-Jones, and a misstep to berate others because they cannot do what he did. Hagiography can very easily turn into an instrument to demean and to be blind to the gifts and graces Christ distributes to his people in different places and times. Jason Meyer avoids this error. But by the same token, we ought to learn as much as we can from the gift that Dr. Lloyd-Jones was to the whole Christian church—and here *Lloyd-Jones on the Christian Life* is a wonderful help.

Surely no twentieth-century preacher more deserves to share the testimony that David Clarkson gave to another "Doctor"—John Owen:

> I need not tell you of this who knew him, that it was his great Design to promote Holiness in the Life and Exercise of it among you. . . . It was his Care and Endeavour to prevent or cure spiritual Decays in his own Flock: He was a burning and a shining Light, and you for a while rejoyced in his Light. . . . It was but for a while; and we may Rejoyce in it still.[2]

Thankfully, through the recommendation of his ministry by well-respected contemporary preachers, because of the recordings of his preaching made freely available by the MLJ Trust, and by the widespread availability of his books, we can continue to benefit from Dr. Lloyd-Jones's ministry.

My own favorite photograph in Iain H. Murray's thrilling biography of Lloyd-Jones is of the Doctor being introduced to Queen Elizabeth II by Marjorie Blackie, a member of his congregation and herself a physician to the Queen. The expression on his face one can only describe as modesty and pleasure combined. Perhaps he would feel the same about being mentioned in the same breath as the great Puritan divine. Those who knew or heard Lloyd-Jones rejoiced in his light. It was but for a while—but we may rejoice in it still.

So I for one warmly welcome this study and pray that these pages will not only introduce new readers to Martyn Lloyd-Jones—as well as encourage Jason Meyer's own generation to grow as preachers in accordance with the apostolic exhortation—but also challenge the new and rising generation of preachers to aspire to be God-exalting, Christ-glorifying,

---

[2] David Clarkson, *A Funeral Sermon on the Much Lamented Death of the Late Reverend and Learned Divine John Owen, D.D.*, in *The Life of the Late Reverend and Learned John Owen, D.D.* (London: Marshall, 1720), lxxi.

Spirit-filled ministers of the Word of God. And may it also inspire those who are not preachers to live Christ-filled Christian lives and to pray that God will raise up a new army of men to preach the Word with grace and power, light and heat, and to live Christian lives which manifest the fruit of doctrine on fire.

Sinclair B. Ferguson

INTRODUCTION

The Thesis

The Thesis Stated

Doctrine and life are fuel and fire, not oil and water. The combustible combination of doctrinal precision and experiential power creates an explosion called the Christian life. No theologian explains the explosion better than Martyn Lloyd-Jones. The thesis of this book is that according to Lloyd-Jones, *the Christian life is doctrine on fire.*[1]

The Thesis Clarified

This thesis requires three further points of clarification: (1) doctrine and life should be inseparable; (2) the right order is essential; and (3) criticism is inevitable.

Doctrine and Life Should Be Inseparable

First, Lloyd-Jones stresses that doctrine and life belong together. What are biblical doctrines according to Lloyd-Jones? Biblical doctrines are "particular truths" that the Bible "wants to emphasize and to impress upon the minds of us all."[2] He holds that knowing biblical doctrines

---

[1] Discerning readers may notice the similarity between what I am calling "doctrine on fire" and the familiar expression "logic on fire," which is how Lloyd-Jones himself defined preaching. "What is preaching? It is theology on fire. And a theology which does not take fire, I maintain, is a defective theology; or at least the man's understanding of it is defective. Preaching is theology coming through a man who is on fire" (D. Martyn Lloyd-Jones, *Preaching and Preachers* [Grand Rapids: Zondervan, 1971], 97). This similarity is intentional. I am proposing that his theology of preaching is seamlessly interwoven within his approach to all of the Christian life. He sought to practice the blessed union of doctrine and life in all realms—the pulpit included. In both preaching and living, doctrine must always be served hot!

[2] D. Martyn Lloyd-Jones, *Great Doctrines of the Bible: God the Father, God the Son* (Wheaton, IL: Crossway, 1996), 2.

should not be isolated from experiencing these truths in everyday life. As a specific example, the resurrection of Jesus is a core biblical doctrine not only to be understood, embraced, and defended, but also to be experienced. Paul declares and defends the resurrection in 1 Corinthians 15, but he goes even further in Philippians 3:10. The apostle has an experiential ambition to "know him and the power of his resurrection" (Phil. 3:10). In other words, Paul is interested not merely in the *truth* of the resurrection but also in the *power* of the resurrection. Why stop short at doctrinal knowledge of the resurrection? Scripture reveals the *resurrection of the Lord* so that we will encounter and experience the *resurrected Lord* himself.[3]

Therefore, Lloyd-Jones often makes the case that doctrine and life belong together. He says he is concerned with doctrine because "it helps me most in the living of the Christian life."[4] "I spend half my time telling Christians to study doctrine, and the other half telling them that doctrine is not enough."[5] The tendency to divorce doctrine and life is a perennial problem because people are "creatures of extremes." It is always easier to take the extreme position, and it is "most difficult to avoid going either to one extreme or the other."[6]

"Either–or" positions on doctrine and life are a recipe for half-baked Christian living. Why stress head *or* heart, light *or* heat, doctrine *or* life? All head and no heart would make someone a stoic egghead. All heart and no head would make someone a squishy, shallow sentimentalist. The abundant life comes only from a fully baked "both–and" combination of head *and* heart, light *and* heat, doctrine *and* life.

It is important to note that Lloyd-Jones uses the terms *doctrine* and *life* to refer to three-dimensional living. He does not reduce the Christian life to head and heart (two dimensions) but speaks about the mind, heart, and will (three dimensions). Doctrine should start in the head, catch fire in the heart, and create a life aflame with true obedience in the will. The Christian life as doctrine on fire must have all three realities.

The gospel captivates and satisfies the whole person (mind, heart, and

---

[3] "Paul does not say that he is anxious to have a greater knowledge about Christ. . . . He tells us that he longs for a greater and more intimate personal knowledge of the Lord himself" (D. Martyn Lloyd-Jones, *Life of Peace: An Exposition of Philippians 3 and 4* [Grand Rapids: Baker, 1993], 69).

[4] D. Martyn Lloyd-Jones, *Great Doctrines of the Bible: God the Holy Spirit* (Wheaton, IL: Crossway, 1997), 95.

[5] D. Martyn Lloyd-Jones, quoted in Dick Alderson, compiler, "The Wisdom of Martyn Lloyd-Jones: Selections of Sayings," *Banner of Truth*, no. 275 (August/September 1986): 7–12.

[6] Lloyd-Jones, *God the Holy Spirit*, 244.

will). Lloyd-Jones calls this complete capture "one of the greatest glories of the gospel."[7] The following paragraph easily ranks somewhere in my top ten favorite Lloyd-Jones quotations:

> The Christian position is three-fold; it is the three together, and the three at the same time, and the three always. A great gospel like this takes up the whole man, and if the whole man is not taken up, think again as to where you stand. "You have obeyed from the heart the form of doctrine delivered unto you." What a gospel! What a glorious message! It can satisfy man's mind completely, it can move his heart entirely, and it can lead to wholehearted obedience in the realm of the will. That is the gospel. Christ has died that we might be complete men, not merely that parts of us may be saved; not that we might be lop-sided Christians, but that there may be a balanced finality about us.[8]

The Doctor stresses more than the mere inseparability of doctrine and life; he also emphasizes the order of them. When it comes to doctrine and life, he constantly states that doctrine must come first.

The Right Order Is Essential

Second, Lloyd-Jones never tires of saying one must begin with doctrine (the mind):

> In New Testament teaching we are first of all given the doctrine, the teaching; then we are told that we have to apply that to our personal circumstances. Obviously, if we do not know the doctrine we cannot apply it; if we lack an understanding of the teaching we cannot put it into operation. First of all we have the instruction; we must receive it and understand it; then we say, "Now in the light of this, this is what I have to do." That is the New Testament doctrine of sanctification.[9]

This is a divinely inspired order because it stands as the clear and consistent teaching of Scripture. "The New Testament always lays down its doctrine first, and then, having done so, says, 'If you believe that, cannot you see that this is inevitable?'"[10]

---

[7] D. Martyn Lloyd-Jones, *Spiritual Depression: Its Causes and Its Cure* (Grand Rapids: Eerdmans, 1965), 56.
[8] Ibid., 60.
[9] D. Martyn Lloyd-Jones, *Life in the Spirit in Marriage, Home and Work: An Exposition of Ephesians 5:18–6:9* (Grand Rapids: Baker, 1974), 308. Here and throughout this book, the placement and form of quotation marks within Lloyd-Jones quotations have been Americanized for consistency of appearance.
[10] D. Martyn Lloyd-Jones, *The Life of Joy: An Exposition of Philippians 1 and 2* (Grand Rapids: Baker, 1989), 174.

Given Lloyd-Jones's three-dimensional view, the order also matters with the three parts of the Christian life. He maintains that (1) doctrine comes to the mind, and then (2) the truth captures the heart, which then (3) moves the will to act. The Doctor argues that this order mirrors the authoritative order established by the apostle Paul (cf. Rom. 6:17).

Is there a way to tell if we are holding these things together in proper balance? There is a test of balance, but it is a surprising one. Other people can unwittingly help us maintain our balance through their criticism.

Criticism Is Inevitable (and Even Helpful!)

Third, criticism should not be shunned or unexpected, but should be expected and welcomed! The reason is obvious upon reflection. Extreme "either–or" people will by definition criticize attempts to be "both–and." Lloyd-Jones actually regards criticism as a reassuring sign when it comes from people on opposite poles.

> It seems to me that we have a right to be fairly happy about ourselves as long as we have criticism from both sides. . . . For myself, as long as I am charged by certain people with being nothing but a Pentecostalist and on the other hand charged by others with being an intellectual, a man who is always preaching doctrine, as long as the two criticisms come, I am very happy. But if one or the other of the two criticisms should ever cease, then, I say, is the time to be careful and to begin to examine the very foundations.[11]

Having stated and clarified the thesis of this work, I need to intensify it by showing its importance. How does Lloyd-Jones himself regard this issue? Is it a high priority or simply one problem among many that the church faced in his day?

The Thesis Intensified

Two years before his death, the Doctor diagnosed the "greatest trouble" in the church of his day: "If I were asked to name the greatest trouble among Christians today, including those who are evangelical, I would say that it is our lack of spirituality and of a true knowledge of God."[12] This deficit was

---

[11] D. Martyn Lloyd-Jones, *The Love of God: Studies in 1 John* (Wheaton, IL: Crossway, 1994), 18.

[12] D. Martyn Lloyd-Jones, *The Unsearchable Riches of Christ: An Exposition of Ephesians 3* (Grand Rapids: Baker, 1979), 6. The sermons on Ephesians 3 were preached in 1956. These quotes concerning the greatest danger in the church come from the Doctor's preface to the sermons. The Doctor wrote this preface in 1979.

the direct result of divorcing doctrine and life. An example of the exact opposite was Paul, whose very life modeled the marriage of doctrine and life. "No man had a greater theological and intellectual understanding than the Apostle Paul, but, at the same time, no man had a deeper, personal and experimental knowledge."[13]

Lloyd-Jones therefore put his finger on the pulse of the problem— either–or thinking: "To put our entire emphasis on the one or the other, or to over-emphasize either is the prevailing danger today."[14] But how dangerous is this problem? What is the aftermath of this great divorce of doctrine and life? Divorcing doctrine and life is not a minor misstep but a deadly departure from the Bible.

> There is nothing which I know of which is more unscriptural, and which is more dangerous to the soul, than to divide doctrine from life. There are certain superficial people who say, "Ah, I cannot be bothered with doctrine; I haven't the time. I am a busy man, and I have not the time to read books, and have not, perhaps, the aptitude. I am a practical man. I believe in *living* the Christian life. Let others who are interested in doctrine be interested!" Now there is nothing that every New Testament epistle condemns more than just that very attitude.[15]

The stakes are high at this point because right doctrine is the prerequisite for right living. Lloyd-Jones sees this as a systemic problem that impacts every area of life.

Impure living flows downstream from polluted doctrine. "It is no use your saying, 'We are not interested in doctrine; we are concerned about life'; *if your doctrine is wrong, your life will be wrong*."[16] Our conduct heralds the content of our doctrine.

> All of us by our conduct and behavior are proclaiming our views, our philosophy of life. It is inevitable. Our behavior is determined by our thinking; even if it is lack of thinking it comes out in our conduct. "As a man thinks, so he is." Very well, as a Christian thinks, and he thinks in terms of his doctrines, so he behaves. Inevitably our conduct is determined by our doctrine.[17]

---

13 Ibid.
14 Ibid.
15 D. Martyn Lloyd-Jones, *The Gospel of God: An Exposition of Romans 1* (Carlisle, PA: Banner of Truth, 1985), 169.
16 Lloyd-Jones, *The Love of God*, 23; my emphasis.
17 D. Martyn Lloyd-Jones, *Darkness and Light: An Exposition of Ephesians 4:17–5:17* (Grand Rapids: Baker, 1982), 302.

Therefore, Lloyd-Jones often warns about the disaster that awaits someone who divorces doctrine and life. Here are five things that happen when this great divorce takes place.

1. *We dishonor God.* The great divorce of doctrine and life means we deny him with our lives and insult the living God. "There is nothing which is more insulting to the holy Name of God than to profess Him with your lips and deny Him in your life."[18]

2. *We quench the Spirit and hinder the work of God.* The great divorce of doctrine and life leads to a situation in which "the Spirit is always quenched" and the work of God "is always hindered."[19]

3. *We destroy holiness and joy.* The great divorce of doctrine and life not only dishonors God; it also destroys holiness and joy. It destroys holiness because it removes the direct association of doctrine to life. Holiness is like a cut flower apart from the soil of doctrine. Lloyd-Jones says that there "is no holiness teaching in the New Testament apart from this direct association with doctrine; it is a deduction from the doctrine."[20]

In the same way, Paul fought hard against false doctrine because joy was at stake. He called Christians to "rejoice in the Lord always" (Phil. 4:4). Paul made it clear to the Philippians that "false doctrine makes joy in the Lord impossible."[21] Great doctrines should lead to deep experiences of great joy. Those who neglect doctrine relegate themselves to a shallow and miserable life.

> The way to a rich subjective experience is, in the first instance, a clearer objective understanding of truth. People who neglect doctrine rarely have great experiences. The high road to experience is truth, and to concentrate on experience alone is generally to live a Christian life which is "bound in shallows and in miseries."[22]

The divorce of doctrine and life weakens the entire foundation of the Christian life, which makes the whole structure susceptible to shaking and swaying.

---

[18] D. Martyn Lloyd-Jones, *Evangelistic Sermons at Aberavon* (Carlisle, PA: Banner of Truth, 1983), 145.
[19] D. Martyn Lloyd-Jones, *Revival* (Wheaton, IL: Crossway, 1987), 61.
[20] D. Martyn Lloyd-Jones, *The New Man: An Exposition of Romans 6* (Carlisle, PA: Banner of Truth, 1972), 271.
[21] Lloyd-Jones, *The Life of Joy*, 19.
[22] D. Martyn Lloyd-Jones, *God's Ultimate Purpose: An Exposition of Ephesians 1* (Grand Rapids: Baker, 1978), 436. The final part of Lloyd-Jones's quote is from Shakespeare's *Julius Caesar*, act 4, scene 3.

4. *We become flimsy and shaky.* If only those who endure to the end are saved (Matt. 24:13), then Christians will put a premium on a pattern of life that will last and stand the test of time. The whole purpose of doctrine is to help us endure by making us unmovable and unshakable; "not merely to give us intellectual understanding or satisfaction, but to establish us, to make us firm, to make us solid Christians, to make us unmovable, to give us such a foundation that nothing can shake us."[23]

A weak doctrinal foundation will cause the entire building of the Christian life to shake. "The man whose doctrine is shaky will be shaky in his whole life. One almost invariably finds that if a man is wrong on the great central truths of the faith, he is wrong at every other point."[24] A weak Christian life built on a minimal and fragile foundation is in constant danger of crashing to the ground.

5. *We are highly susceptible to disaster.* A shaky Christian life is susceptible to disaster because of the high winds of false teaching and temptation.

> If we go astray in our doctrine, eventually our life will go astray as well. You cannot separate what a man believes from what he is. For this reason doctrine is vitally important. Certain people say ignorantly, "I do not believe in doctrine; I believe in the Lord Jesus Christ; I am saved, I am a Christian, and nothing else matters." To speak in that way is to court disaster, and for this reason, the New Testament itself warns us against this very danger. We are to guard ourselves against being "tossed to and fro and carried about with every wind of doctrine" [Eph. 4:14], for if your doctrine goes astray your life will soon suffer as well.[25]

The great divorce of doctrine and life will destroy the Christian life. Imagine that the Christian life is like a plane that must fly between two massive mountains. This plane needs both wings (doctrine and life) to avoid a fatal crash. We could label these two mountains as two dangerous *isms.* Doctrine by itself is not enough because the plane will veer off and crash into the mountain of *intellectualism.* Experience by itself is not enough because it causes the plane to crash into the mountain of *emotionalism.* Therefore, Lloyd-Jones wisely sees that it is foolish to have an either–or debate about which wing of the plane we need. We must have both.

---

23 Lloyd-Jones, *God's Ultimate Purpose,* 302.
24 Lloyd-Jones, "The Wisdom of Martyn Lloyd-Jones," 7–12.
25 Lloyd-Jones, *God's Ultimate Purpose,* 118.

The Rest of This Book

Part 1 of this book introduces the life and times of Lloyd-Jones. There I succinctly tell his story and paint a brief backdrop of the times in which the
Doctor lived and the false doctrine that he faced.

Parts 2 and 3 form the heart of this volume. The flow of the book follows Lloyd-Jones's conviction that doctrine is the direct key to holiness.
Doctrine (part 2) must come before life (part 3).[26] Therefore, part 2 explores
the doctrinal framework of the Christian life first. It also stresses the organic connection between knowing the doctrines and the application that
should naturally follow.

Part 3 looks at the Christian life in greater detail, especially the difficulty of applying the doctrines. Each chapter follows the same format. The
Doctor defines a constituent part of the Christian life, diagnoses the difficulty of application, and then prescribes a way to overcome the difficulty.

Part 4 closes the book with a brief look at the legacy of Lloyd-Jones. I
consider his place in the history of the church and examine why his life
and ministry continue to speak to us today.

I have labored to give readers ample opportunity to hear the voice of
Lloyd-Jones himself in the pages that follow. His writings have a distinctive style, and it may help at the outset to point out a couple of patterns
that characterize his writings. First, Martyn Lloyd-Jones never technically
"wrote" a book. All his books began as sermons or addresses that were later
put into print. This fact gives his writings a distinctive tone of exhortation.
The heraldic quality of his writing means that one will often feel directly
addressed when reading Lloyd-Jones.

Second, Lloyd-Jones often says things like "this is the most important"
point or text or thing to remember. These comments reflect the passion of
a preacher who was so gripped by the truth he was preaching that it really
was the most important point, text, or thing to him in that moment.

We begin by getting to know Lloyd-Jones a little better and discovering
why he was affectionately called "the Doctor."

---

[26] "We must always put these things in the right order, and it is Truth first. It is doctrine first, it is the
standard of teaching first, it is the message of the gospel first" (Lloyd-Jones, *Spiritual Depression*, 61).

PART I

"THE DOCTOR"

CHAPTER I

THE LIFE AND TIMES OF MARTYN LLOYD-JONES

Lloyd-Jones asked a friend to preach at his funeral on the themes of the loveliness of Christ and obtaining an abundant entrance into the eternal kingdom. As the minister was getting ready to leave, Lloyd-Jones called him back and said, "Come here, my boy. I want you to remember one thing. I am only a forgiven sinner—there is nothing more to me than that. Don't forget it."

VERNON HIGHAM [1]

Introduction

If Sherlock Holmes had been a pastor instead of a private investigator, he would have looked a lot like Martyn Lloyd-Jones. Dr. Lloyd-Jones was trained in medicine at St Bartholomew ("Barts") Hospital in London. Sir Arthur Conan Doyle patterned the fictional Sherlock Holmes after a medical doctor who was Doyle's teacher in the Edinburgh Infirmary (Dr. Joseph Bell). Holmes's assistant, Dr. Watson, was a student at Bart's, and the two first met in the lab there.

Both Sherlock Holmes and Martyn Lloyd-Jones exhibit fine-tuned diagnostic acumen. In fact, the preaching ministry of the one affectionately

---

[1] In *Logic on Fire: The Life and Legacy of Dr. Martyn Lloyd-Jones* (documentary), directed by Matthew Robinson (New Albany, MS: Media Gratiae, 2015), DVD.

known as the Doctor reflected all the marks of a medical cast of mind. His preaching would start with symptoms in society and then diagnose the root disease (i.e., the sin) and prescribe a gospel cure. The third section of this book will use the Doctor's diagnostic method as a format for diagnosing and overcoming the difficulties of the Christian life (define the doctrine, diagnose the difficulty, and prescribe the cure).

The story of Martyn Lloyd-Jones sounds like something from a Hollywood script. He gave up fame and a lucrative medical profession in London in exchange for a pulpit in a poor area of Wales. Why? Lloyd-Jones's life served as a canvas upon which God painted a bright and bold portrayal of the surpassing power of the gospel. God put this power on display in the Doctor's conversion, and then many times over in the Doctor's ministry.

Think of Lloyd-Jones's conversion and his call to ministry. Why did God save him and call him to ministry in the most unlikely place? God loves to choose the most unlikely people from the most unlikely places so that "no human being might boast in the presence of God" (1 Cor. 1:29). No one would expect that Bart's would be a fertile field for growing ministers of the gospel. Iain Murray calls it the "last place imaginable" as a training ground for gospel ministry because it was like a temple to scientific rationalism.[2] Murray sees the same historical pattern of poetic providence at work with Lloyd-Jones as with other gospel ministers: "When the true idea of the minister is lost, God has often restored it by calling individuals to the office in unlikely ways. Amos was called from being a farmer; John Knox from his post as a church lawyer; and Lloyd-Jones from the hospital and the consulting room."[3]

The rest of his life and ministry put God's glorious grace on display in amazing ways. In what follows, I offer a thumbnail sketch that structures the Doctor's life around five distinct movements.[4] The first three movements follow a journey from Wales to London (from birth to Barts), London to Wales (conversion, call, and ministry in Wales), then Wales back to London (ministry at Westminster Chapel). The fourth journey is a broader move, from London to the wider world (retirement). The last trip is a higher move, from London to heaven (final days and "the glory").

[2] Iain H. Murray, Lloyd-Jones: Messenger of Grace (Carlisle, PA: Banner of Truth, 2008), 5.
[3] Ibid.
[4] I am happily indebted to Iain Murray and Philip Eveson for many biographical details in what follows. See Iain H. Murray, The Life of Martyn Lloyd-Jones, 1899–1981 (Carlisle, PA: Banner of Truth, 2013); Philip H. Eveson, Travel with Martyn Lloyd-Jones (Leominster, UK: Day One, 2004). See also Steven J. Lawson, The Passionate Preaching of Martyn Lloyd-Jones (Sanford, FL: Reformation Trust, 2016).

Trip I: Wales to London—from Birth to Barts (1899–1925)

The story of Martyn Lloyd-Jones begins in South Wales, where he was born on December 20, 1899. His parents, Henry and Margaret, had three boys: Harold, David Martyn, and Vincent. Harold was two years older than Martyn, and Vincent was two years younger. Harold died an untimely death at the age of twenty with the outbreak of Spanish influenza in 1918 (twenty million people died worldwide). Vincent grew up to be a highly respected high court judge and lived to be eighty-six (five years longer than Martyn).

Henry Martyn owned a grocery shop at 106 Donald Street in Cardiff, a cosmopolitan, English-speaking town in South Wales. Six years later, Henry sold the business and headed back to the heart of southwest Wales to the smaller, Welsh-speaking village of Llangeitho.

Martyn grew up with a fondness for horses. He loved to spend summer holidays with his grandfather Evans, who had horses. "He enjoyed carrying buckets of water and horsemeal and leading some of the quieter horses to the railway station and helping to put them into horseboxes for their journey to some large show in the West of Carmarthen, the West of England or London."[5]

His carefree life would go up in flames at the age of ten. Philip Eveson describes the experience:

> Farmers had come to his father's shop to pay their outstanding bills with gold sovereigns [coins] on Wednesday evening, January 19, 1910. They had stood talking and smoking in the clothing section of the store and some tobacco ash had obviously fallen on fabric and lay smouldering; it ignited in the early hours of Thursday morning when everyone was asleep. Martyn was rescued by his father who threw him from an upstairs window into the arms of three men standing below. The whole house and shop went up in flames. One of the few items retrieved from the fire were the sovereigns, which were now reduced to a solid mass of gold.[6]

The fire was a crushing blow. The financial losses would plague the Lloyd-Jones family for a long time, even though they tried to hide it from their children. These financial troubles, however, did have one positive outcome in that they provided the impetus for Martyn to take his studies more seriously.[7] Martyn was playing football (i.e., soccer) in the village square

5 Eveson, *Travel with Martyn Lloyd-Jones*, 14.
6 Ibid., 15.
7 Murray, *The Life of Martyn Lloyd-Jones*, 14.

one day, and a student assistant named Edmund Jones (who later joined the school as a teacher) saw him. He decided to pull young Martyn aside and offer him some straightforward guidance for the future. "He warned him that unless he put his mind to his work he would not gain a scholarship to the County Secondary School like his brother." These words hit home, because Martyn knew that the family's financial situation precluded further schooling without a scholarship. He heeded the warning and devoted himself to his studies, earning second place in the scholarship exams of 1911 (scoring even higher than his brother Harold had done two years earlier).[8]

Perhaps even more devastating than the fire of 1910 was the day Henry Lloyd-Jones had to declare bankruptcy in 1914. His real financial position was exposed and put on public display when all that the family owned was auctioned off to the highest bidder over the course of two days at Jubilee Hall.[9] Martyn's father left to look for work in Canada for a few months, but nothing materialized. In July 1914, Henry boarded a ship to look for work in London, and Martyn joined his father when the ship reached London on August 3. It was a stirring and tumultuous time to be in London, because the next day the British declared war on Germany.

Henry bought a dairy business, and the family was reunited in London in October 1914. The dairy business was so successful that all of Henry's debts were eventually repaid. Martyn and Vincent were then able to go to St Marylebone Grammar school (January 1915), where Martyn excelled. In his senior examination in the summer of 1916, he passed all seven subjects and gained distinction in five.[10] He applied to the medical school of St Bartholomew's Hospital in London and was accepted at the "unusually young age of sixteen."[11]

Martyn was a standout student at "Barts." In particular, his diagnostic ability attracted the attention of one of the most distinguished teachers there, Sir Thomas Horder (the king's physician). On one occasion, Lloyd-Jones made a diagnosis based on his claim that he could feel an enlarged spleen in the abdomen of the patient. This was something that even Horder's own examination had missed. Horder was so impressed that he chose Martyn to be his junior house physician (even before the results of

---

8 Eveson, *Travel with Martyn Lloyd-Jones*, 17.
9 Murray, *The Life of Martyn Lloyd-Jones*, 18.
10 Eveson, *Travel with Martyn Lloyd-Jones*, 32.
11 Ibid.

the qualifying exam were announced). Martyn later became Horder's chief clinical assistant.[12]

One of Martyn's most important tasks was to go through the case notes of Horder's patients in order to catalog and index all the diseases Horder had treated. Lloyd-Jones was shocked to see "the kinds of conditions suffered by some of the dignitaries of the land, including members of the royal family and cabinet ministers."[13] The Doctor began to note that the problems were deeper than medical or intellectual. He diagnosed that the real problem was "moral emptiness and spiritual hollowness."[14] Murray comments perceptively, "Horder's card index was to him almost what the vision of a valley of dry bones was to the prophet Ezekiel."[15]

At age twenty-three (1923), Martyn received a London University MD (doctor of medicine degree). He then was awarded research scholarships in 1923–1924 to study a form of Hodgkin's disease called Pell Epstein disease, as well as a heart disease known as infective endocarditis. At the young age of twenty-five (1925), he became a member of the Royal College of Physicians (MRCP). Lloyd-Jones had a private practice at 141 Harley Street, the same place where Horder had his offices. Only the "cream of society" could afford the services of a Harley Street doctor.[16] Sir Thomas Horder introduced Martyn to a whole new social stratosphere. And it was an eye-opening experience for the young doctor to witness the wickedness, excess, and jealousy that characterized the elites of London.[17]

Trip 2: London to Wales—Conversion, Call, and Ministry in Wales (1925-1938)

During this climb to the top of his profession, something else began to stir within Martyn's soul. In 1923 he began to listen to the preaching of Dr. John Hutton, the minister at Westminster Chapel. A spiritual power in this man's preaching arrested Martyn's soul and made him aware of the amazing power of God to save and change lives.[18] He had never experienced this power at any other church he attended (despite having attended church his whole life).

---

12 Horder's highest book recommendation was of W. S. Jevon, *The Principles of Science: A Treatise on Logic and Scientific Method.* Horder's high esteem for Martyn became clear when he gave his personal copy of the book to Martyn.
13 Eveson, *Travel with Martyn Lloyd-Jones*, 41.
14 Murray, *The Life of Martyn Lloyd-Jones*, 48.
15 Ibid.
16 Eveson, *Travel with Martyn Lloyd-Jones*, 43.
17 Ibid.
18 Murray, *The Life of Martyn Lloyd-Jones*, 46.

Lloyd-Jones later described his conversion this way:

> For many years I thought I was a Christian when in fact I was not. It was
> only later that I came to see that I had never been a Christian and became
> one. . . . What I needed was preaching that would convict me of sin. . . .
> But I never heard this. The preaching we had was always based on the as-
> sumption that we were all Christians.[19]

During the same period, Lloyd-Jones was shocked to see the moral conditions of both ends of London's social scale. He saw the ravaging effects of
drunkenness and sexual immorality among the poor, and he saw the equally
destructive impact of drunkenness and illicit sex among the social elites who
seemingly had everything. "The case histories of seventy percent of those
who came to Thomas Horder's private practice revealed they had nothing
more physically wrong with them than that they ate or drank too much."[20]

Martyn became troubled by the thought that he was helping people
get well so that they could simply go back to sinning with more abandon.
Medicine could not address the real disease. Only the gospel had the power
to change people at the core. From the spring of 1925 to the summer of
1926, Lloyd-Jones was in tremendous turmoil of spirit as he considered
moving from medicine to a preaching ministry. He lost twenty pounds in
this period of serious wrestling. By June of 1926 he was convinced that God
had called him to be a preacher of the gospel.

June 1926 was also important because Martyn made another momentous decision. He proposed to the girl of his dreams, Bethan Phillips (also
a physician). In the first two months of 1927, Martyn experienced three of
the most stressful yet joyful things in life: (1) he got married, (2) moved to
a new place, and (3) changed jobs. He and Bethan moved to South Wales
and accepted a call to the Bethlehem Forward Movement Hall at Sandfields,
Aberavon. The Forward Movement was a mission work among the Welsh
Calvinistic Methodists.

The Lord moved mightily through Lloyd-Jones's ministry at Aberavon.
People from every walk of life experienced the life-changing power of the
gospel. The most foul-mouthed, quick-tempered men, like Mark McCann,[21]

---

[19] Iain H. Murray, *D. Martyn Lloyd-Jones: The First Forty Years, 1899–1939* (Carlisle, PA: Banner of Truth, 1982), 58.
[20] Eveson, *Travel with Martyn Lloyd-Jones*, 50.
[21] See Mark McCann's remarkable story in Bethan Lloyd-Jones, *Memories of Sandfields* (Carlisle, PA: Banner of Truth, 2008), 69–83.

and the most outwardly religious women (like Martyn's own wife) both became converted during his ministry. Bethan confessed that she sat under her husband's ministry for two years before she came to the point where the light of the gospel dawned upon her soul:

> I tried to do all a "Christian" should do in such duties as church atten-
> dance and I accepted the Bible as the Word of God. But I had no inner
> peace or joy and I knew nothing of the glorious release of the gospel.
>
> I rejoiced to see men and women converted . . . and I envied them and
> sometimes wished, when I saw their radiant faces and changed lives,
> that I had been a drunkard or worse, so that I could be converted! I never
> imagined that I needed to be converted, having always been a "Christian"
> or that I could get any more than I had already! . . . God graciously used
> Martyn's morning sermons to open my eyes and show me myself and
> my need.[22]

The gospel had the power to save drunkards, prostitutes, and good religious Welsh chapel girls. A spiritist medium attended the chapel after she saw many people passing by her house on their way to the hall. She came under the power of God's Word and was converted. She testified that the power she experienced at the hall was much different than she had known as a spiritualist. Unlike the power she was accustomed to, this was a "clean power."[23]

One should not lose sight of how vital these results were to the valida-tion of Lloyd-Jones's ministry. The prevailing view of the time was that modern men and women would no longer listen to preaching (that was the "old time" religion). Churches needed more of what modern men and women wanted (drama, music, etc.). And people wanted less preaching.

The Doctor felt the strong winds of prevailing public opinion but did not yield to them. He stepped right into them and kept to the ancient path of the apostle Paul, who resolved "to know nothing among [them] except Jesus Christ and him crucified" (1 Cor. 2:2). That was the text for his first sermon, and he never drifted from it as his guiding principle. He suspended the church's drama society, and musical evenings were canceled. He simply preached Christ as the church's only attraction. He replaced the so-called

---

22 Lynette G. Clark, *Far above Rubies: The Life of Bethan Lloyd-Jones* (Fearn, Ross-shire, UK: Christian Focus, 2015), 55. Iain Murray believes that Mrs. Lloyd-Jones was already converted but lacked assurance (per-sonal correspondence with the author, August 4, 2017).
23 Eveson, *Travel with Martyn Lloyd-Jones*, 68.

modern attractions with the timeless attraction of Christ. His sermon on Psalm 34:8 (June 28, 1931) testifies to this conviction: "The business of preaching is not to entertain, but to lead people to salvation, to teach them how to find God."[24]

Eveson estimates are that over five hundred people were converted and joined the church in the eleven years that Lloyd-Jones ministered at Sandfields.[25] The Doctor had a cupboard full of liquor bottles that his converts gave him after being set free from a life of addiction, a tangible testimony to the changed lives in this poor area of Wales often decimated by drunkenness.

Trip 3: Wales to London—Ministry at Westminster Chapel (1938-1968)

After eleven years of ministry, Martyn began to feel the effects of fatigue. He even experienced vocal failure on occasion and was unable to finish his sermon. Eveson notes that this was later attributed to an error in vocal production.[26] In 1938, he resigned from his church. The very weekend he announced his resignation, he providentially received a letter from Dr. Campbell Morgan, the minister at Westminster Chapel in London, to share the preaching there for six months. At the end of 1938, the Lloyd-Jones family moved to London.

Lloyd-Jones regarded his time at Westminster as a temporary arrangement. He fully expected to return to Wales. In 1938–1939, he awaited word on the possibility of becoming the principal of Bala Theological College in Wales. A controversy broke out over his nomination, and Lloyd-Jones regarded this as God's providential work to keep him at Westminster. On April 23, 1939, he accepted the call to become associate pastor at Westminster.

Lloyd-Jones's previous move from Wales to London was on the eve of the First World War. A few months after accepting the pastorate at Westminster, the Second World War broke out in September 1939. During the war, the numbers at the chapel dwindled from two thousand to a hundred and fifty. Sunday offerings no longer could meet church expenses, and the salaries of both Campbell Morgan and Lloyd-Jones were drastically reduced. Morgan retired in 1943.

Westminster Chapel faced far more than financial disaster. During the

---

[24] Murray, *The First Forty Years*, 130.
[25] Eveson, *Travel with Martyn Lloyd-Jones*, 69. Some of the sermons from this period are found in D. Martyn Lloyd-Jones, *Evangelistic Sermons at Aberavon* (Carlisle, PA: Banner of Truth, 1983). All of the sermons at Aberavon were preached in English.
[26] Eveson, *Travel with Martyn Lloyd-Jones*, 72.

bombing raids of 1941, the chapel was hit three times, but each time fire-fighters were able to save the building. In June of 1944, a V-1 flying bomb (called a doodlebug) landed on the Guards Chapel (a few hundred yards away) and shook Westminster. The entire congregation stood at attention. After a brief pause, Lloyd-Jones "continued his prayer as though nothing had happened and the congregation sat down again." He was covered in white dust from the ceiling, but the secretary came and dusted him down and the service continued.[27]

The Doctor faced the same pressure at Westminster that he had felt while in Wales. At the end of the war, many influential people at Westminster Chapel wondered whether the current service configuration (no choir or organ recital) could draw people back to the chapel.[28] But the Doctor preached the Word of God, and once again the Lord built his church. By 1948 the first gallery opened again. And in 1951, the second gallery reopened.

These results once again validated his philosophy of ministry, however out of step it was with the dominant ideology of his day. People were concerned about declining numbers in church attendance. Many sensed that the church had a diminishing influence in the modern world. What should be done to counteract these trends? In the name of relevance, many people thought that the church had to become more like the world in order to reach the world. The old doctrines were no longer popular because modern man had a distaste for the supernatural. Therefore, mainline churches surrendered to the world's skepticism about the Bible and succumbed to liberal theology or modernism.[29]

Even theologically conservative churches were tempted to downplay doctrines that were deemed controversial (like the virgin birth of Christ) in the name of unity. The ecumenical movement was a powerful force in the Doctor's day because it was seen as a solution to the growing influence of secularism. If the church was going to grow strong in influence once again, then it would have to make a big showing to the world. The ecumenical movement intended to make it hard for the world to ignore the church. The church would make the world take notice because of its large unified front.

---

[27] Ibid., 81. Iain Murray disputes Eveson's account that Lloyd-Jones was dusted down. Murray says that the church secretary came to the pulpit for a brief announcement after the long prayer as he always did. He may have carried a duster and dusted off the pulpit desk, but nothing more (Iain Murray, personal correspondence with the author, August 4, 2017).

[28] Eveson, *Travel with Martyn Lloyd-Jones*, 84.

[29] J. Gresham Machen powerfully addressed these same points in 1923 with the publication of *Christianity and Liberalism*. A new edition was published in 2009 with a foreword from Carl R. Trueman: Machen, *Christianity and Liberalism* (Grand Rapids: Eerdmans, 2009). See especially chap. 2, on doctrine.

Lloyd-Jones regarded this so-called cure as proof that churches were confusing the symptoms with the root disease. The root disease in the world was still sin. The world did not need the church to water down its doctrinal distinctives in the name of becoming larger and more visible. The world needed greater clarity on the differences between Christianity and the world. The church did not need to become like the world to win the world; it needed to stand out more clearly so that it could offer the world a clear alternative. The problem with the church was that it had lost trust in the truth of the Bible and no longer believed in the saving power of the preaching of the gospel.

The Doctor spoke out clearly and forcefully against these trends:

> The gospel of Jesus Christ confronts and challenges the modern world with the statement that it alone has the answer to all man's questions and the solution to all his problems. In a world that is seeking a way out of its tragedy and its troubles, the gospel announces that the solution is already available. In a world that is feverishly looking to the future, and talking about plans for the future, the gospel proclaims that the search is not only mistaken in direction, but is also quite unnecessary.[30]

There is nothing new under the sun. The same drama had played out upon the stage of the previous century in Great Britain. The Lord raised up Charles Spurgeon to confront that downward spiral into liberalism. It became known as the Downgrade controversy. R. C. Sproul insightfully says that "Martyn Lloyd-Jones was to twentieth-century England what Charles Spurgeon was to nineteenth-century England."[31]

Lloyd-Jones believed in the saving power of the gospel preached. He developed a consistent preaching pattern at Westminster Chapel. His Sunday morning sermons were more pastoral in nature, while the Sunday evening sermon was strongly evangelistic. He also believed that it was a mistake to water down the great doctrines of the faith. So in 1952, he began a Friday night lecture series on Christian doctrine, which outgrew the main hall where it first met and needed to move into the main chapel building. After this three-year series on great Christian doctrines, Lloyd-Jones began his epic series of expository sermons/lectures on the book of Romans, which

---

[30] D. Martyn Lloyd-Jones, *Truth Unchanged, Unchanging* (Wheaton, IL: Crossway, 1950), 105.
[31] Endorsement of *The Christ-Centered Preaching of Martyn Lloyd-Jones*, ed. Elizabeth Catherwood and Christopher Catherwood (Wheaton, IL: Crossway, 2014).

ran for thirteen years (1955 to 1968). He never finished the book of Romans. When he retired in 1968, he had reached Romans 14:17.

Trip 4: London to Wider World—Retirement (1968–1981)

At the age of 68, Lloyd-Jones was diagnosed with colon cancer. When he preached at Westminster Chapel on March 1, 1968, no one knew it would be his last sermon there. After successful surgery, he suddenly announced his retirement. His ministry would go on to reach further than ever before as he edited his sermon manuscripts for publication and accepted invitations to preach both near and far. A special emphasis during those days was to encourage younger ministers.[32] One especially notable trip involved sixteen lectures on preaching at Westminster Theological Seminary in Philadelphia in the spring of 1969. These lectures became his landmark book *Preaching and Preachers*. He preached his last sermon at age eighty at Barcombe Baptist Church on June 8, 1980.

As noted earlier, the Doctor never actually wrote a book. All of his books are edited sermons or lectures he gave. His retirement was a fruitful time of preparing his sermons for publication. He edited many volumes during 1968–1981 (especially his sermons on Ephesians and Romans), and his family members have continued this labor of love after his death.

Trip 5: London to Heaven—Final Days and "the Glory" (March 1, 1981)

Two days before his death, Lloyd-Jones wrote a note with a trembling hand to his wife and children: "Do not pray for healing. Do not hold me back from the glory." That was the Doctor's special phrase for heaven: "the glory." His elder daughter, Elizabeth, says that the glory was a golden thread in the tapestry of his life: "It was essentially part of him. Because of the greatness and glory of God, it made salvation so much grander—that this great God was coming down so low to save us. This love for God's glory and greatness—it was his greatest characteristic and quality."[33]

The Doctor never got over how far down the Most High God came to save him. He knew himself to be a sinner saved by grace. He asked Vernon Higham to preach at his funeral on the themes of the loveliness of Christ and an abundant entrance into the eternal kingdom. As Higham was

---

[32] For example, Sinclair Ferguson once told Stephen J. Nichols about the encouraging notes he received from Lloyd-Jones (Nichols, personal correspondence with the author, May 19, 2017).
[33] Elizabeth Catherwood, in *Logic on Fire*, DVD.

leaving the room, Lloyd-Jones suddenly called him back and said, "Come here, my boy. I want you to remember one thing. I am only a forgiven sinner—there is nothing more to me than that. Don't forget it."[34] Even to his dying day, the Doctor never lost sight of that unforgettable fact. He wanted others to remember it as well.

Another man noted that the Doctor's message and the Doctor's experience in the end coincided. This man was listening to one of Lloyd-Jones's sermons while in the hospital. When the man received word from his wife that Lloyd-Jones had just passed away, he said: "What a remarkable thing. I was just listening to a sermon from him. In that sermon, he has just been telling me about the glory . . . and now he knows it."[35]

The day of his heavenly home going was March 1, 1981—thirteen years to the day after he preached his last sermon at Westminster. His earthly body took one more trip from London to Wales. He was buried at Newcastle Emlyn, near Cardigan, West Wales. Lloyd-Jones chose this burial place because of his great affection for Bethan, whose family was buried there.

In that Welsh graveyard a simple gravestone with an inscribed message sums up his ministry with the very words of the text he preached in his first sermon at Aberavon fifty-five years earlier, from 1 Corinthians 2:2:

> In Loving Memory of
> D. Martyn Lloyd-Jones,
> The beloved Doctor,
> 1899–1981.
> For I determined not to know
> anything among you,
> save Jesus Christ, and him crucified.

The Doctor was certainly a preacher, but he was so much more. He testified to this very truth at the end of his life: "I did not live for preaching."[36] He had a higher love. Being a Christian was the most wonderful thing in the world to him.[37] His life and his message challenge us to ask ourselves if we can testify to that same truth.

---

[34] Vernon Higham, in *Logic on Fire*, DVD.
[35] Andrew Davies, in *Logic on Fire*, DVD.
[36] Iain Murray, in *Logic on Fire*, DVD.
[37] See Murray, *Messenger of Grace*, xi. The Doctor says it in his own words: "Is there anything in the world which is comparable to the privilege of being a Christian?" (D. Martyn Lloyd-Jones, *Darkness and Light: An Exposition of Ephesians 4:17–5:17* [Grand Rapids: Baker, 1982], 312).

PART 2

THE DOCTOR'S DOCTRINE

As mentioned above, the Doctor gave a series of Friday night lectures on biblical doctrines from 1952 to 1955, later published as *Great Doctrines of the Bible*. These lectures serve as the foundation for the next six chapters on doctrine. Chapters 2–4 focus on (1) God the Father, (2) God the Son, and (3) God the Holy Spirit, following the work of the Trinity in planning (the Father), achieving (the Son), and applying (the Holy Spirit) redemption. Chapters 5–7 follow the outworking of redemption in justification and sanctification, the church, and the consummation. In many places, I will provide a bare bones summary of the very full treatment of those doctrines found in the book. I follow the same three-fold format for each chapter: (1) introducing the doctrine, (2) defining the doctrine, and (3) applying the doctrine.

Lloyd-Jones made it very clear that his aim in his lectures was not merely theological but also doxological. He emphatically stressed that he was not giving his people intellectual knowledge to puff them up. The atmosphere was not to be that of the classroom. There were no examinations, no diplomas. The sole aim was to know God in pure worship. God reveals himself in the Bible in order to be worshiped in Spirit and truth. The Doctor's aim was to promote such worship. If we don't understand what God reveals about himself in the Bible, then "our worship can never be real."[1] Therefore, every "consideration of the Bible is worship," and "there is nothing so dangerous as to approach the Bible and its teaching as you approach any other text book."[2]

The Doctor would have us pray that the Lord himself would breath life into the study of these doctrines so that "we may all come to know Him, the only true and living God, and Jesus Christ whom He has sent—and as a result may all be revived. And so . . . the whole Church may be revived, and . . . we may witness again in our midst the manifestation of God's glorious power."[3]

[1] D. Martyn Lloyd-Jones, *Great Doctrines: God the Father, God the Son* (Wheaton, IL: Crossway, 1996), 57.
[2] Ibid., 10.
[3] Ibid.

CHAPTER 2

GOD THE FATHER ALMIGHTY

The Person and Work of the Father

Strangely enough, the Christian gospel—let me say this with reverence, lest I be misunderstood—the Christian gospel does not start even with the Lord Jesus Christ, it starts with God the Father. The Bible starts with God the Father always, everywhere and we must do the same—because that is the order in the blessed Trinity: God the Father, God the Son, God the Holy Spirit.

D. MARTYN LLOYD-JONES [1]

Introducing the Doctrine

What is theology? The Doctor argues that theology must be defined in relation to the fact that God cannot be exhaustively defined. In other words, theology must first concede that the finite cannot fully know the infinite. Therefore, theology is sometimes an exercise in negation. Lloyd-Jones pictures theology as the act of building a fence around the incomprehensible mystery of God. We cannot define God in an ultimate and exhaustive sense, but we can fence off the false from the true by saying what he is not (e.g., *in*finite means fencing off the fact that he is *not* finite).

Lloyd-Jones begins his study of biblical doctrines with a study of biblical inspiration because that doctrine defines our approach to doctrine

---

[1] *The Assurance of Our Salvation: Studies in John 17* (Wheaton, IL: Crossway, 2000), 44.

in general and functions as our frame of reference. The Doctor believes that general revelation is a genuine source of knowledge concerning God, but general revelation is incomplete without the fullness of God's self-disclosure in Scripture.

> We started at the very beginning with the whole concept and category of revelation. We know nothing apart from that. I do not put forward theories and philosophies; I start on this premise—that what I am announcing is what God has done, what God has revealed. I know nothing apart from what I find in the Bible. I am entirely shut up to it; I am utterly dependent upon it. And therefore it is my business to come to it as a little child. "The world by wisdom knew not God" (1 Cor. 1:21); so, if that was true and is still true, then I must depend upon this book, I must accept its authority, I must receive its statements, even though my little mind cannot always understand them.[2]

Lloyd-Jones recommends approaching God's self-revelation in a specific order. One should start with God's infinity, incomprehensibility, and inaccessibility. From that exalted vantage point, one will look in wonder at the way this transcendent God draws near to us in the revelation of his attributes. Once those *general attributes* are seen and savored, then God draws even nearer to us with the revelation of *specific names* so that we can know and adore him more than ever.[3] We will begin by defining the doctrine of God before applying the doctrine of God.

Defining the Doctrine

The Infinity of God

The Bible does not debate the existence of God but declares it.[4] Since God exists, the question must be asked, "Can He be known?"[5] The Doctor argues that God is incomprehensible in that he can never be known in the "ultimate, final and complete sense."[6] His incomprehensibility flows from his infinity. The Bible reveals that God is an infinite, absolute, ultimate being. One can know the meaning of "infinite" in a preliminary way through de-

---

[2] D. Martyn Lloyd-Jones, *Great Doctrines: God the Father, God the Son* (Wheaton, IL: Crossway, 1996), 260–61.
[3] Ibid., 58.
[4] Ibid., 48.
[5] Ibid., 50.
[6] Ibid., 51.

claring what it does *not* mean. Infinite means that there are no borders or boundaries with God. He is "free from all restrictions and all bounds; there is no limitation whatsoever where God is concerned, He is everything, everywhere, unlimited."[7]

God's infinity and incomprehensibility also relate directly to his gracious self-disclosure. God is true. It is impossible for him to lie (Titus 1:2). It follows then that if God has chosen to reveal himself, the recipients of that revelation can know him. God's gracious self-disclosure makes it possible to know him *truly,* but his infinity and incomprehensibility make it impossible to know him *fully.* In theology, we must confess our limits. We are not only finite but also fallen, and we see in a glass dimly (1 Cor. 13:12). Our partial knowledge of God is real knowledge, but it falls far short of comprehensive or exhaustive knowledge.

This infinite God is also an absolute being. God's "absoluteness" refers to far more than his underived self-existence. It is true that God does not depend upon anything or anyone for existence (Acts 17:25a). But the Bible goes further. Everything that exists owes its existence to God (Acts 17:25b). The glorious fact that God is absolute and ultimate means that he is "not derived from something else nor conditioned by anything else."[8] Rather, he himself is the cause of everything.[9]

Scripture exults in the exaltedness of God, the majesty of God, the transcendence of God.[10] God alone is

> Holy, holy, holy, . . . Lord God Almighty,
>   who was and is and is to come! (Rev. 4:8)

The supreme scope of God's exaltedness and transcendence means that he is not only incomprehensible but also inaccessible. He is utterly separated in exaltation and elevation far above the rest of his creation. No one has seen God (John 1:18); he is immortal and invisible, and dwells in light inaccessible (1 Tim. 1:17).[11]

---

[7] Ibid., 53.
[8] Ibid.
[9] Ibid.
[10] Ibid.
[11] God is also a unity (Deut. 6:4) and has personality. Lloyd-Jones says that the term "personality" does not appear in the Bible, but it is implied everywhere. "Personality exists where there is mind, intelligence, will, reason, individuality, self-consciousness and self-determination" (ibid., 55). Why does this point matter? Lloyd-Jones says that this point is "vitally important" in demolishing the error of pantheism, which says everything is God and God is everything. Pantheism denies that God has personality. It says that God is simply a force or unconscious energy. "The Bible says that God is a person and this is abso-

Now, the Doctor follows the movement from the infinity and inaccessibility of God to the gracious self-disclosure of God found in the revelation
of his attributes.

The Attributes of God

The attributes of God are "things about God, certain aspects of His great
and glorious eternal nature, which He has been pleased to reveal to us,
and which, in a measure, we can lay hold of."[12] The Doctor distinguishes
between the attributes that God does and does not share with humanity.

1. *The attributes that belong to God alone.* God is (1) eternal, (2) unchanging, (3) all-present, (4) all-wise, (5) all-powerful, (6) perfect in every
way, and (7) glorious. The first two attributes are best understood together.
God's *eternality* means that he is without beginning and end.

> Before the mountains were brought forth,
> > or ever you had formed the earth and the world,
> > from everlasting to everlasting you are God. (Ps. 90:2)

God is eternal and he is also absolutely *unchangeable.* "God is always ever-
lastingly the same. It is never possible that God should differ in any respect
from what He always is and always has been."[13] James 1:17 declares God's
unchanging nature (often called his "immutability"): "Every good gift and
every perfect gift is from above, coming down from the Father of lights,
with whom there is no variation or shadow due to change." The Doctor glories in this verse, saying, "He is not only without change but utterly without
even the possibility of change."[14]

The next three attributes (God is omnipresent, omniscient, and om-
nipotent) are also best viewed together. First, God's *omnipresence* means
that he is present everywhere, though not necessarily present in the same
way in every place. God's presence is everywhere, but the Bible also de-

---

lutely vital to any true sense of worship, and to our having a feeling of confidence about ourselves and
about the world" (ibid.).

[12] Ibid., 59.

[13] Ibid., 60.

[14] Ibid. If someone asked why the Bible says that God repented of certain things (see Gen. 6:6 KJV), Lloyd-
Jones had a simple, yet profound answer. "God's character never changes, but His dealings with people
change" (ibid., 61). God varies his procedure according to whether they repent or not. When talking about
immutability, we must not separate it from God's personality. It is not the immutability of lifeless objects
like a machine or a stone. His is the immutability of absolute perfection. "Because God is personal in His
dealings with men and women, He varies His actions" (ibid.).

clares that heaven is God's dwelling place in a unique way.[15] Second, God's *omniscience* means that he perfectly knows everything completely and absolutely.[16] His omniscience also extends to the distinction between knowledge and wisdom. God has perfect knowledge and the perfect ability to apply all of that knowledge. God has no deficiency in knowledge or discernment.[17] Third, God's *omnipotence* means that he is all-powerful. Lloyd-Jones stresses that God's power "surpasses our power of expression" and "our power of comprehension."[18]

The last two attributes (God's perfection and glory) should also be discussed together. God's absolute *perfection* refers to "the sum total of all excellency." God is "exalted above all shortcomings and all limitations." Nothing exists either actually or possibly that is higher or greater or better than God. "God's own perfection is the object of God's own knowledge and of His own love. He rejoices in Himself. He delights in Himself and is perfectly and absolutely self-sufficient. God is, according to the Scriptures, well-pleased within Himself and His glorious being: the blessedness of God."[19] The Bible most often refers to this greatness and splendor as the *glory* of God.[20]

2. *The attributes God shares with humanity.* The second category consists of attributes that God has perfectly and humanity (made in the image of God) has partially. Four attributes fit this category: (1) holiness, (2) righteousness/justice, (3) goodness/love, and (4) faithfulness.

God's *holiness* refers to his absolute separation from sin and evil and his absolute moral purity.[21] The doctrine of God's holiness is not theoretical but practical, because it teaches sinners how to approach him "with reverence and awe" (Heb. 12:28).[22] The holiness of God also makes it possible to grasp the wretched nature of sin. And without a right understanding of sin, one cannot have a right understanding of God's holiness.

The second attribute in this category is the *righteousness* or *justice* of God. This attribute follows inescapably from the first one, because God's righteousness is God's "holiness manifested in God's dealings with us."[23]

---

15 Ibid., 62.
16 Ibid., 63.
17 Ibid., 66.
18 D. Martyn Lloyd-Jones, *God's Ultimate Purpose: An Exposition of Ephesians 1* (Grand Rapids: Baker, 1978), 397.
19 Lloyd-Jones, *God the Father, God the Son*, 68.
20 Ibid., 68.
21 Ibid., 69.
22 Ibid., 71.
23 Ibid., 72.

Righteousness is the quality in God that ensures that he always does right and is incapable of doing anything wrong.[24] God's righteousness comes to us through his holy and just laws (legislative holiness), while God's justice often finds expression in exacting penalties upon those who are guilty of breaking his law (judicial holiness). So "the righteousness of God is God's love of holiness, and the justice of God is God's abomination of sin."[25]

The third attribute in this category is the *goodness* or *love* of God. "The goodness of God is that perfection of God which prompts Him to deal bounteously and in a kindly way with all His creatures."[26] The psalmist says,

> The LORD is good to all,
> and his mercy is over all that he has made. (Ps. 145:9)

God's goodness is an attribute describing his bounteous nature, but God's love is an attribute highlighting his self-giving nature. "God's love is that attribute in God by which He is eternally moved to communicate Himself to others."[27] "The love of God is something that communicates itself; God is eternal, and God is eternal love."[28] This is the entry point into the doctrine of the Trinity. "Because God is eternal and is eternal love, there must have been someone whom He always loved."[29]

God's goodness and love come to his creatures in four ways: (1) a general sense, (2) grace, (3) mercy, and (4) patience. In his goodness he showers everyone with a *general* sense of his love; he causes his rain to fall and sun to rise on the righteous and unrighteous (Matt 5:45; Acts 14:27). God's goodness and love also come to us through his *grace.*

> There is no more glorious word than the word "grace." Grace, this great word that you find so constantly in the Scriptures, is the goodness or the love of God towards those who do not in any way deserve it. It is the unmerited goodness or love of God towards those who have forfeited every claim upon Him and His love, and who deserve judgment and condemnation.[30]

---

[24] Ibid.
[25] Ibid.
[26] Ibid., 74.
[27] Ibid.
[28] Ibid.
[29] Ibid.
[30] Ibid., 75.

In addition, the goodness and love of God come to the world in the form of his *mercy*. Mercy is "defined as the goodness or the love of God towards those who are in misery or distress as the result of their sin, and irrespective of their deserts."[31] Finally, God brings his goodness and love to the world through his *patience*, his long-suffering forbearance shown to those who continue to sin against him.[32] This is another glorious expression of God's goodness. Lloyd-Jones told his Friday night hearers, "Not one of us would be here tonight were it not for this!"[33]

The fourth moral attribute is the *faithfulness* of God. The fact that God is faithful means that "he is one upon whom you can safely lean. It means one on whom you can absolutely rely; one upon whom you can depend; one upon whom you can stay yourself, without ever being in any doubt [about whether] He will suddenly let go and let you go."[34]

God applies all of these attributes, both shared and not shared with humanity, to all of his works in creation, providence, and redemption.[35] The Doctor also offers the stunning reminder that all of God's attributes are indivisible:

> The will of God is sovereign—it is not determined by anything but God Himself. It is the expression of His Lordship, His absolute being. But remember, His will is never arbitrary. It is never exercised except in perfect harmony with all the other attributes of God's great and glorious being. It is the same God who is omniscient, who is omnipresent. It is the same God who is glorious and wonderful. It is the same God who is love and compassion and mercy. We must not divide these things, though we distinguish them for the purposes of thought and understanding.[36]

God's attributes are essential for our knowing him, but he has done so much more. God graciously draws nearer still by disclosing his name and essential nature.

The Names of God and the Blessed Holy Trinity

The Doctor surveys thirteen different names for God in his doctrinal lectures.[37] Each name is an expression of an aspect of God's character, because

---

31 Ibid., 76.
32 Ibid.
33 Ibid.
34 Ibid., 76–77.
35 Ibid., 66.
36 Ibid., 67.
37 Ibid., 79–83.

a name stands for "who the person really is; his character, his propensities, and perfections."[38] "To declare the name of God is to tell the truth about God."[39] The biblical names for God put "this great truth about God's being in a form that men and women can grasp and apprehend."[40]

But the greatest, most mysterious, and most difficult doctrine is the doctrine of the blessed Holy Trinity.[41] No other doctrine proves our absolute dependence upon God's revelation as much as the Trinity. "It comes directly from the Bible and from nowhere else at all. Men and women have thought of God; they have their gods; but no one has ever thought of the Trinity. . . . There is no question at all but that the doctrine of the Trinity is the most distinctive doctrine of the Christian faith."[42]

The doctrine of the Trinity rejects the false notion of three Gods (i.e., tritheism). It also shuns the heretical idea that the Father, Son, and Spirit are mere modes in which God appears (i.e., modalism).[43] The Doctor appeals to the Athanasian Creed and affirms the fences that it establishes: there are three persons, not three Gods.[44] Therefore, we confess that God is *one* in terms of his "innermost nature," and he exists as *three* persons.[45] The difficulty at this point is the "inadequacy of language" when we use the word "persons." We tend to think of individuals when we think of persons, which can create a false sense of separation. But the Bible speaks of the members of the Trinity in a profoundly unified sense. Our inadequacy of language leads to the Doctor's humble confession: "Now I do not pretend to understand. Nobody understands."[46]

There is not only a profound unity in the persons of the Trinity; there is a beautiful harmony in the unified plan of salvation. One cannot separate the coequal, coeternal members of the Trinity, but one can distinguish a division of labor for the purposes of salvation.[47] One should talk about this division of labor and unified plan with a reverent sense of awe.

---

38 Ibid., 79–80.
39 Ibid., 80.
40 Ibid.
41 Ibid., 83.
42 Ibid., 84. The Doctor declares that the church has neglected the doctrine of the Trinity because of sheer laziness. There is no excuse for laziness because this is the "most amazing and astonishing thing that God has been pleased to reveal to us concerning Himself" (ibid.).
43 Ibid., 88.
44 Ibid., 90.
45 Ibid., 85–86. The Doctor admits that there is no direct statement that says God exists in three persons. Rather the Old and New Testaments together demand that doctrine through the cumulative effect of their testimony (ibid., 85).
46 Ibid., 86.
47 Ibid., 90.

Now that is a staggering thought. That these three blessed Persons in the blessed Holy Trinity for my salvation have thus divided up the work. The Son has put Himself at the disposal of the Father, and the Spirit has put Himself at the disposal of the Father and the Son. The Spirit does not speak of Himself, but testifies to the Son. The Son did not speak of Himself, but received His words and His works from the Father, though He was equal and eternal—the economic Trinity. So that while, in a sense, we can say that it was the Father who sent the Son, and the Son who came and did the work, and the Spirit applied it, we must at the same time say this: God was in it all. "God was in Christ reconciling the world unto himself, not imputing their trespasses unto them" (2 Cor. 5:19). There was a kind of division of labor and yet a unity in purpose and a unity in doing it all.[48]

This plan of salvation is part of the eternal purpose of God, which leads naturally to the topic of the decrees of God.

The Eternal Decrees of God

The eternal decrees of God are "things which God determined and or-dained before He had done anything at all."[49] The Doctor admits that this doctrine is difficult because it deals primarily with "the mind of the Eternal," which is beyond "our finite understanding and the grasp of our puny and pygmy intellects."[50] But if this doctrine is so difficult, why study it? The Doctor gives four reasons. First, the decrees are revealed in the Bible, and we must be whole-Bible Christians. Second, the decrees reveal fresh aspects of the glory of God. Third, studying the decrees will save us from many errors. Fourth, studying the decrees will give great consolation.[51]

The Doctor then describes the doctrine of decrees in six propositions: (1) "From eternity God has had an unchangeable plan with reference to His creatures." (2) "The plan of God comprehends and determines all things and events of every kind that come to pass." (3) "All the decrees of God are unconditional and sovereign." (4) "The decrees of God are efficacious." (5) "The decrees of God are in all things perfectly consistent with His own most wise, benevolent, and holy nature." (6) "The salvation of men and

---

48 Ibid., 90–91.
49 Ibid., 93.
50 Ibid.
51 Ibid., 94.

women and of angels, and of certain of them in particular, was determined by God before the foundation of the world."[52]

Applying the Doctrine

This whole chapter on the doctrine of God functions as the Doctor's prescribed cure for the greatest weakness of the church.

> I think the greatest weakness in evangelical Christianity today is that it forgets God. We are interested in experiences, we are interested in happiness, we are interested in subjective states. But the first need of every soul, as we shall see, is to be right with God. Nothing matters but that. The gospel starts with God, because what is wrong with everybody is that they are in a wrong relationship to Him.[53]

Therefore, the cure for forgetting God must include a more rigorous application of the doctrine of God. Applying this crucial doctrine should have at least three far-reaching effects. The doctrine of God should lead to (1) a greater sense of awe, (2) a greater depth of repentance, and (3) a greater ability to hear and heed the comforts and warnings of Scripture.

A Greater Sense of Awe

These truths about God are not mere facts to grasp with the intellect; they must capture the affections and reawaken our awe. Once the heart is awake again to the majesty of God, we ascribe the glory back to God with fresh wonder. We must be "more anxious than ever before to fall at His feet, to yield ourselves utterly and unreservedly to Him, realizing that the greatest privilege that has ever come to us is to worship Him and to commune with Him.[54] If our study of the doctrine of God does not lead to worship, then we have spent our time in vain.[55] All of these doctrines are windows that expansively open up to us "a greater and a grander conception of God" that should lead to a greater reverence for God.[56]

Therefore, the attributes of God ought to confront the attitudes of the heart. "If ever you feel tempted to say that God is not fair, I advise you to

---

[52] Ibid., 96–101.
[53] D. Martyn Lloyd-Jones, *Great Doctrines of the Bible: God the Holy Spirit* (Wheaton, IL: Crossway, 1997), 127.
[54] Ibid., 68.
[55] Ibid.
[56] Ibid., 94.

put your hand, with Job, on your mouth, and to try to realize of whom you are speaking."[57] Grasping God's greatness should be immediately reflected in our humility.[58] If we are at the point of "doubting God" or asking why God does "allow this" or why he doesn't "do that," then we should "wait for a moment" and realize that we "are going to express an opinion about the eternal, almighty, everlasting Being who said, 'Let there be light,' and there was light (Gen. 1:3)."[59]

The doctrine of God should directly impact our communion with God in prayer. Small views of God lead to puny prayers.[60] The Doctor stresses that "great prayer is always the outcome of great understanding."[61] As our vision of God expands, the scope of our prayers will expand. "There is no limit, we are praying to the eternal and the illimitable God."[62]

A Greater Depth of Repentance

A right understanding of this doctrine of God is also essential for a right assessment of ourselves. Lloyd-Jones believes in a certain type of examination that avoids too much self-introspection. Rather, he places the stress on spending "sufficient time" with the doctrine of God and his holiness in order to see our sin rightly. The way to see sin is not primarily through self-introspection and self-examination, but by "going into the presence of God" and seeing ourselves in comparison to his absolute purity.[63] The Doctor teaches that the "nearer a man gets to God the greater he sees his sin."[64]

Repentance comes from "a change in our view of and thoughts concerning God." The very moment we really see "the holiness and the greatness of God," we *have* repented.[65] When we see God truly, we repent of our unbelief. Unbelief is foolishness because people who do not believe in God invariably believe in something, which Isaiah identifies as idols (Isa. 40:19). The problem is not a failure to believe; it is a failure to believe the right thing. Our modern idolatry is just as foolish, because we put our trust in wealth or status or science or human leaders.

---

[57] Lloyd-Jones, *God's Ultimate Purpose*, 16.
[58] Lloyd-Jones, *God the Holy Spirit*, 135.
[59] D. Martyn Lloyd-Jones, *The All-Sufficient God: Sermons on Isaiah 40* (Carlisle, PA: Banner of Truth, 2005), 84.
[60] "Shame on us for our puny prayers" (Lloyd-Jones, *Revival* [Wheaton, IL: Crossway, 1987], 314).
[61] Ibid., 293.
[62] Ibid., 314. He says, "There is no limit to what you should pray for, no limit at all" (ibid., 313).
[63] Lloyd-Jones, *God the Father, God the Son*, 71.
[64] D. Martyn Lloyd-Jones, *Spiritual Depression: Its Causes and Its Cure* (Grand Rapids: Eerdmans, 1965), 70.
[65] Lloyd-Jones, *God the Holy Spirit*, 134.

The main reason for these moments of unbelief is that "we do not appreciate the truth concerning the being and character of God."[66] The Doctor offers this profound diagnosis for unbelief:

> It is this failure that accounts ultimately for all our other troubles. We will persist in thinking of God as one of ourselves, as but a man, and we look at his actions as if they were the actions of a human being. We always start with ourselves, with our measures, with our judgments and assessments; and our most fatal error is that even when we come face to face with God, we bring all these measurements with us. Then, because God does not fit into our categories, we say we cannot believe and we reject the message of the gospel.[67]

Essentially one could say that repenting is resizing. We start in the wrong place; we size up the things we see with our standards of measurement. We should start with God as our standard of reference and then resize all that we see in relation to him. For example, we might look at the nations of the world, with all their power, and justifiably feel intimidated, but everything changes when we compare them not to ourselves but to God. The Doctor expounds on Isaiah 40:15 to illustrate this principle:

> All these great nations with their might and their tanks and their armies and their atomic and hydrogen bombs and all their great schemes, what are they? It is like this to God: you have emptied the dust that is on your balance in order to get it cleaned, to get an accurate measurement, but there is a little speck left; or you have poured the water out of the bucket, and think you have poured it all out, but there is a little drop left. That is the nations to God: a drop in the bucket; a speck of dust.[68]

The doctrine of God confronts all our tendencies both to overestimate what humanity can do and to underestimate what God can do. Therefore, knowing God ought to lead to a greater experience with the comforts and warnings of Scripture.

A Greater Ability to Hear the Comforts and Warnings of Scripture

The doctrine of God functions like a megaphone that amplifies the comforts and terrors of Scripture. The tremendous comfort and terrifying warn-

---

[66] Lloyd-Jones, *The All-Sufficient God*, 80.
[67] Ibid., 80–81.
[68] Ibid., 85.

ings of Scripture should sound out louder and clearer if we understand the attributes and character of God.[69]

Take the omnipresence of God as an example. It is a "wonderfully comforting thing" to have an omnipresent Father when we realize "that it does not matter where your circumstances may put you, God is still with you." However, God's omnipresence also warns us about the folly of trying to run from God. "If you have sinned against God, you will find it impossible to get away from Him."[70]

God's unchanging nature also comforts and chastens us. "I know nothing, in a sense, in my Christian life and experience which is so comforting as the doctrine of the eternity and immutability of God. Of course, to the sinner it is one of the most terrifying of all the doctrines."[71]

Furthermore, all of God's attributes combine to give a grand sense of the veracity of his Word. If he swears in his anger that the wilderness generation will not enter his rest, he keeps his oath. If he promises to preserve his people, then nothing can snatch them from his almighty hand. One can trust the promises of God because of the "unchanging will of God."[72]

Sinners can even take great comfort in the justice of God. We are comforted as forgiven sinners because justice has now changed sides. Before our sins were forgiven, the justice of God stood against us as lawbreakers deserving eternal destruction. But now in Christ, God's promise to forgive our sins is based upon his faithfulness and justice. The apostle John says, "If we confess our sins, *he is faithful and just to forgive us our sins* and to cleanse us from all unrighteousness" (1 John 1:9). What does that mean? "Having prepared the way of forgiveness, if we conform to it, the justice of God comes in, and by His justice God forgives us."[73] The Doctor brings this point home to our hearts: "So let us be clear about this. It is no sign of humility, no mark of saintliness, to go into the presence of God doubting whether God is forgiving you."[74] It is not humble but audacious to suggest that the God who promises forgiveness may in fact be a liar!

The sending of the Son of God into the world is the greatest manifestation and vindication of the total truthfulness of God. The Father of Lies had been questioning God's greatness and glory. What was at stake

---

69 Lloyd-Jones, *God the Father, God the Son*, 62–63.
70 Ibid.
71 Ibid., 61.
72 Ibid.
73 Ibid., 73.
74 Ibid., 355.

in salvation brings the glory of God to the forefront of the discussion of what salvation is.

> Salvation, the whole purpose and object of salvation in the first instance, is to vindicate God, is for God again to manifest the truth concerning Himself. The devil is described in the Scripture as "a liar and the father of lies"; and the apostle John tells us in the third chapter of his first Epistle that God sent His Son into this world in order to destroy the works of the devil. That is the first object, that the whole character of God should be vindicated. Of course, the devil in an ultimate sense did not, and cannot and could not, affect the being and the nature and the character of God, but in the sight of created beings he could, and he most certainly did. He succeeded in the case of all the fallen angels; he succeeded in the case of Adam and Eve and the whole of their posterity. And the whole problem in the world today is the attitude of man towards God. So God has initiated this great movement of redemption and of salvation primarily in order to declare and to manifest and to vindicate again His own glory, His own greatness and the truth about Himself. Why has He done it? He has done it "that in the ages to come he might show (display) the exceeding riches of his grace in his kindness toward us through Christ Jesus" [Eph. 2:7].[75]

Many people have sadly never thought of salvation in those terms. The Doctor laments the "sentimental" way people talk about salvation: "God forbid" that the church would be blind to the vindication of God in the cross of Christ. If we miss this fact, we fail to see that the cross is "the grandest theodicy of the ages."[76]

Conclusion: Do We Thirst for God?

Lloyd-Jones believes that knowing God is the first need of the soul and the great call upon the church. The church grows weak as its love grows cold. The church will be weak to the extent that it forgets its God. Our response to the doctrine of God is a measure of our spiritual health. If eternal life is knowing him (John 17:3), then do we hunger and thirst to know him?

> The most vital question to ask about all who claim to be Christian is this: Have they a soul thirst for God? Do they long for this? Is there something

---

[75] D. Martyn Lloyd-Jones, *God's Way of Reconciliation: An Exposition of Ephesians 2* (Grand Rapids: Baker, 1972), 110–11.
[76] Ibid.

about them that tells you that they are always waiting for His next manifestation of Himself? Is their life centered on Him? Can they say with Paul that they forget everything in the past? Do they press forward more and more that they might know Him, and that the knowledge might increase, until eventually beyond death and the grave they may bask eternally in "the sunshine of His face"?[77]

This essential question cannot fully be answered without the next chapter. No one can see the "sunshine" of the Father's face apart from Christ. Scripture bids us gaze upon the "glory of God in the face of Jesus Christ" (2 Cor. 4:6). That is where we turn next.

---

77 Lloyd-Jones, *God's Ultimate Purpose*, 349.

CHAPTER 3

CHRIST AND HIM CRUCIFIED

The Person and Work of Christ

While this is obviously not the starting point of biblical doctrine, it is certainly its center. The truth concerning the Lord Jesus Christ is the central and the most stupendous fact in the history of redemption. It stands out as the unique event in all history. This truth concerning Him is the biggest and most astounding event of all.

D. MARTYN LLOYD-JONES[1]

Introducing the Doctrine

Lloyd-Jones spent twelve weeks lecturing on the person and work of Christ. He put great stress on the *order* of the doctrines and why that order was necessary to understand the *meaning* of the doctrines.[2] He did not lecture on God the Father and immediately move to God the Son. Prior to his twelve weeks on God the Son, he spent twelve weeks lecturing on angels, creation, providence, the fall, original sin and pollution, redemption, and the covenant of grace.

The specific progression of thought the Doctor followed flowed from the previous lectures on the fall and the covenant of grace. Because of the fall, God must do something if man is ever to be saved. The covenant of grace

---

[1] *Great Doctrines of the Bible: God the Father, God the Son* (Wheaton, IL: Crossway, 1996), 245.
[2] "I do trust that we are all observing the order in which we are taking these truths. I conceive it to be my main function in these addresses to show you that order as it is worked out in the Scriptures; the details, the facts, you can derive from the Scriptures themselves" (ibid., 259–60).

gives assurance that God will do what must be done to save his people. Specifically, the covenant of grace points to a singular Savior: the Lord Jesus Christ.

Defining the Doctrine

The Doctor explores the doctrine of God the Son in an orderly manner. In general terms, the most basic distinction is between the person of the Son and the work of the Son. One cannot possibly grasp the work of Christ without first embracing the revelation of the person of Christ.[3]

The Person of the Son

1. *General reasons for studying the Son in detail.* Lloyd-Jones begins with a general exposition of several reasons why the Bible forces us to consider the Lord Jesus Christ as the center of biblical revelation. Then he proceeds to look more closely at the details of this truth and why it had to be that way. He then probes the details in even more depth concerning Christ's virgin birth, deity, and humanity before observing how all of these things are reconciled fully in the doctrine of the God-man.[4]

The Doctor's preliminary remarks set the tone for the rest of the lecture. He opens with a strong warning against those who think the subject of the Lord Jesus is too great and mysterious to study in detail. One must not somehow think that these theological details belong only to professional theologians. Such an attitude is "utterly unscriptural." The New Testament Epistles came in response to "simple Christians" succumbing to false teachings. Therefore, one must come to grips with the way the apostles spoke such "stern warnings against the terrible danger to the soul of believing these wrong teachings and false ideas concerning our Lord and Savior Jesus Christ."[5]

Furthermore, the New Testament itself interrogates the reader with a series of questions he or she must answer about Jesus.

It is not enough to say, "I believe in Jesus Christ." The New Testament asks you questions when you say that. It asks, "What do you believe about Him? Is He man only? Is He God only? Did He really come in the flesh or

---

[3] Ibid., 290.
[4] Ibid., 254.
[5] Ibid., 247. Lloyd-Jones also stresses that heresies about Jesus kept sneaking into the church in the first four centuries. If we care at all about our salvation and the salvation of others, we must be clear about these details concerning the Lord Jesus (ibid., 248).

did He not? What did He do? What is the meaning of His death?" The New Testament is concerned about definitions, and there is nothing, I suggest, that is further removed from its teaching than to say, "It is all right; so long as you believe in the Lord Jesus Christ it does not matter very much what you say in detail." The "detail," as I am hoping to show you, is all-important and absolutely vital.[6]

In answer to those essential questions, the Doctor begins with four reasons why we must take this study seriously: Jesus is (1) the fulfillment of all the Old Testament prophecies and promises, (2) the only one by whom we can be reconciled to God and come to know God, (3) the one who holds all things in his hands, and (4) the Judge of all.[7]

2. *The incarnation.* Lloyd-Jones constructs a fence around the mystery of the incarnation with a general guideline and eight specific propositions. The guiding declaration is "that the eternal second Person in the blessed Trinity entered into time and into the world, took unto Himself human nature, was born as a babe, lived a life as a man, and appeared in 'the likeness of sinful flesh' (Rom. 8:3)."[8] This statement guards against the "rank heresy" that wrongly believes that "the one who was born" came into being and started his "existence as a person."[9] A new personality did not come into being; it was the eternal person himself, the Son of God, "who now assumed this form and entered the life of man in the world."[10]

The Doctor's eight propositions fence the mystery against heresy and error: (1) the doctrine of the incarnation is a key piece of the doctrine of the Trinity;[11] (2) the second person of the triune God became flesh;[12] (3) the second person of the Trinity came in the flesh in reality, not just in appearance;[13] (4) the second person of the Trinity, the person himself, became flesh;[14]

---

6 Ibid., 247.

7 Ibid., 248–52.

8 Ibid., 253.

9 Ibid.

10 Ibid.

11 "Someone who does not believe in the Trinity cannot be a Christian because he cannot believe in the doctrine of redemption. Therefore as we talk about the person of the Son we see how important it is always to realize that God exists in three Persons—Father, Son and Holy Spirit" (ibid., 256).

12 It was "not that the eternal triune God became flesh, but that the second Person in the triune God became flesh." The Word became flesh (John 1:14), not the Father (ibid.).

13 "The third statement is that the doctrine of the incarnation does not say that it was merely an appearance or a form that was taken on by the second Person in the Trinity, but that it was indeed a true incarnation; He did come in the flesh" (ibid.).

14 "Point number four is again a negative one. The doctrine of the incarnation does not say that it was merely the divine nature that somehow became united with human nature and so formed a person. It is not that; it was the second Person Himself, the Person, who became flesh" (ibid., 257).

(5) the incarnation did not change the personality of the second person of the Trinity,[15] just the state in which he manifested himself; (6) the Son of God took on true humanity, not the mere appearance of humanity;[16] (7) the Son of God took on a full human nature;[17] and (8) the Son of God took on a complete human nature from the Virgin Mary.[18]

3. *The virgin birth.* Lloyd-Jones then addresses the question raised by the previous discussion: "How did all this come to pass?" That question leads invariably to the doctrine of the virgin birth.[19] The Doctor appeals to the Apostles' Creed as an apt summary: "He was conceived of the Holy Ghost and born of the Virgin Mary."[20] The first order of business is to fence the mystery by stressing that "the male human being did not enter into the question of His conception."[21] The second order of business is to point to the positive affirmation of the miraculous supernatural "instrumentality" of the Holy Spirit.[22]

Some find this doctrine difficult to accept. The Doctor's outlook is exactly the opposite. He says concerning the babe in the manger as the second person of the Trinity, "I would find myself in much greater difficulty if I did not have the doctrine of the virgin birth to believe."[23] The incarnation and the virgin birth are so inseparable that the virgin birth could be called "the sign of the mystery of the incarnation."[24]

4. *The humanity and the deity of Jesus.* The Doctor makes a lengthy case for embracing the deity and humanity of Jesus. He provides eight arguments for Jesus's deity and then eleven for his humanity.

The Scriptures afford these eight strands of evidence for Jesus's deity:

---

[15] "There was a change in the form in which He appeared, there was a change in the state in which He manifested Himself, but there was no change in His personality, He is the same Person always. In the womb of the virgin Mary, and lying as a helpless babe in the manger, He is still the second Person in the Holy Trinity" (ibid.).

[16] The Doctor here distinguishes theophany and incarnation. The Son of God made appearances as the angel of the Lord, but these pre-incarnate manifestations of the Son of God represent a theophany, not an incarnation. "Theophany means that an angelic or a divine person appears in this form for the time being, but the doctrine of the incarnation asserts that the Lord Jesus Christ has taken on human nature itself—not its appearance but real human nature" (ibid., 258).

[17] Here the Doctor says that the incarnation was complete, not partial (ibid.).

[18] "Some people have taught that God created a new human nature for His Son, and that this human nature merely passed, as it were, through Mary. That is wrong. The doctrine states that He derived His human nature from His mother, the Virgin Mary. It was not a new creation. He did not bring His human nature with Him. He received it from her" (ibid., 259).

[19] Ibid.

[20] Ibid., 260.

[21] Ibid., 262. The Doctor shares something he heard from someone else that captured the dual truth well: "As the Lord's divine nature had no mother, so His human nature had no father" (ibid.).

[22] Ibid., 262.

[23] Ibid., 263.

[24] Ibid.

(1) divine *names* are ascribed to Jesus;[25] (2) divine *attributes* are ascribed to Jesus;[26] (3) he is said to hold and fill divine *offices*;[27] (4) statements about Yahweh in the Old Testament are applied to Jesus in the New;[28] (5) the names of the Father and the Son are coupled together;[29] (6) divine worship is ascribed to Jesus;[30] (7) Jesus claimed to be God;[31] and (8) the virgin birth and the resurrection are proof of his deity.[32]

The rest of the lecture highlights eleven arguments for the humanity of Jesus: (1) the virgin birth;[33] (2) the names of Jesus;[34] (3) the true human nature of Jesus;[35] (4) Jesus grew and developed;[36] (5) Jesus was subject to limitations of knowledge;[37] (6) Jesus was subject to physical limitations;[38] (7) Jesus was subject to temptations;[39] (8) Jesus needed to pray;[40] (9) Jesus needed and was given the power of the Holy Spirit;[41] (10) Jesus referred to God as his God;[42] and (11) Jesus was truly human in every respect.[43]

5. *The doctrine of the God-man.* The Doctor stresses that Jesus is one person with two natures (truly God and truly man).[44] He also fences this mystery by clarifying that the two natures are not mixed, not fused, and not intermingled.[45] He warns his people against the false teaching of those who deny

---

25 Ibid., 266. The Doctor surveys sixteen different names (e.g., Son of God, only begotten Son, first and last, Alpha and Omega, beginning and end, the Holy One, the Lord, the Lord of glory, and God blessed forever) (ibid.).

26 Ibid., 267–68. These attributes include omnipotence, omniscience, omnipresence, and eternality.

27 Ibid., 269. These offices include creating the world, forgiving sins, raising the dead, subduing all things, bringing judgment upon all, and bestowing eternal life.

28 Ibid. Ps. 102:24–27 (cf. Heb. 1:10–12); Isa. 6:1, 3, 10 (cf. John 12:37–38); Isa. 8:13–14 (cf. 1 Pet. 2:7–8); Isa. 40:3–4 (cf. Matt. 3:3; Luke 1:76).

29 Ibid. Matt. 28:19; Rom. 1:7; 2 Cor. 13:14; 1 Thess. 3:11; James 1:1.

30 Ibid., 270. Matt. 28:9; Luke 24:52; John 5:23; 1 Cor. 1:2; 2 Cor. 12:8–9; Acts 7:59; Phil. 2:10.

31 Ibid. Matt. 3:14–15, 17; 5:21–37; 11:27; Luke 2:41–52; John 8:58; etc.

32 Ibid., 271.

33 Ibid.

34 Ibid. For example, Jesus refers to himself as "Son of Man" in the Gospels, and Paul refers to him as "the man" Christ Jesus (1 Tim. 2:5).

35 Ibid., 272. John 1:14 gives proof of this point.

36 Ibid., 272–73. Jesus grew (Luke 2:40). He increased in wisdom, in stature, and in favor with God and man (Luke 2:52). Heb. 5:8 also speaks of his learning obedience through suffering.

37 Ibid., 273. Mark 13:32.

38 Ibid.. He grew weary; he slept; he experienced hunger, thirst, and death.

39 Ibid., 273–74. He was tempted in every way as we are, yet without sin (Heb. 4:15).

40 Ibid., 274.

41 Ibid.

42 Ibid. Jesus said "to my God and your God" (John 20:17).

43 Ibid. The author of Hebrews stresses the totality of his humanity: "He had to be made like his brothers in every respect" (Heb. 2:17).

44 Lloyd-Jones begins the lecture by giving evidence that the Scriptures clearly teach the subordination (economical, not ontological) of the Son to the Father. The Doctor provides thirteen lines of evidence, but he also establishes a qualification for the subordination. None of the thirteen mention subordination before his birth and incarnation. Not one of them says any of these things about him before his birth, before his incarnation (ibid., 279).

45 Ibid., 282.

Jesus's deity (e.g., the Unitarians) or humanity. And he exposes the error of denying the integrity of the natures or denying the unity of the person (e.g., saying Jesus is two persons or saying that there is one mixed nature).

The Work of the Son

The Doctor moves next to a series of eight lectures on the work of the Son. He uses the threefold grid of Prophet, Priest, and King to summarize the Son's work. These three aspects of his work provide a unique window through which one can see the unparalleled glory of Christ. In the Old Testament, these three roles were always filled by separate people. "But the glory of the Lord Jesus Christ is that He in Himself alone combines all the offices—three functions in the one person, and this is something which makes us realize the grandeur, greatness and majesty of the person of our blessed Lord."[46]

1. *Prophet.* The Doctor stresses that sinners need Jesus as Prophet to save them from the *ignorance* of sin. The apostle Paul accents the futility and darkness and ignorance of the Gentiles as they walk in alienation from God (Eph. 4:17–18). Those walking in darkness need the light of revelation.

A prophet is different from a priest. A priest "represents us with God," while a prophet represents "God with us."[47] In the Old Testament, a prophet would speak the words of God—in the sense of both foretelling (what would happen) and forthtelling (rebuke and judgment for what had happened).[48] The Old Testament also foretold of *the* Prophet to come (Deut. 18:15). The New Testament declares that Jesus is the Prophet who was foretold (John 6:14; Acts 3:19–26). Jesus himself claimed to be a Prophet (Luke 13:33) who spoke only the words of the Father (John 8:26; 12:49–50).[49]

The Doctor specifies that the Son of God served as a Prophet before the incarnation (1 Pet. 1:11).[50] The Son continues to fulfill the role of a Prophet after the incarnation while on earth through his teaching (John 8:12) and life (John 10:37–38),[51] and after his ascension as he still speaks through the Holy Spirit (1 Cor. 2:12).[52] One cannot stress his prophetic role

---

[46] Ibid., 291–92.

[47] Ibid., 297.

[48] Ibid., 292.

[49] Ibid., 293.

[50] Ibid., 294. The Doctor says that Christ was the Prophet teaching the prophets and giving them their message. He draws this inference from 1 Pet. 1:11, where Peter points out that all the prophets before Christ spoke as the Spirit of Christ signified to them.

[51] Ibid. One should not think of the prophetic role as a reference only to speaking. Jesus fulfilled the role of prophet on earth through his teaching *and* by his life example.

[52] Ibid., 295.

too strongly, because on the last day we will be judged according to his word (John 12:47–48).

2. *Priest.* Lloyd-Jones also emphasizes that sinners need Jesus as Priest to save them from the *guilt* of sin. The prophet comes with a message from God to man; the priest goes from man to God and approaches God on behalf of man.[53] The priest is a mediator between God and man and in that role does two main things: (1) propitiates God by sacrifices and (2) intercedes on behalf of the people.[54] Jesus is a greater Priest than all who came before for many reasons, but one of the greatest contrasts is that the priest must find a sacrifice (e.g., a lamb), while Jesus offers himself so that the Priest and the sacrifice are now the same. This combination is another example of how Jesus brings together in his person all the things that were separated in the Old Testament (Prophet, Priest, and King).[55]

Jesus, as the Priest and sacrifice, offers himself as a substitute. This doctrine is the target of many of the Devil's attacks because nothing is as central to understanding our salvation. The Doctor says, "If I understand the New Testament aright, there is no place where we should be more careful to go with our minds fully operating as to the cross on Calvary's hill.[56]

Therefore, the Doctor carefully puts forward eight propositions concerning Jesus's substitutionary sacrificial death: (1) Jesus's death was in line with the Old Testament teaching on sacrifices;[57] (2) Christ saves us by his death;[58] (3) the range of New Testament terms for what Christ did proves the truth of this doctrine (*ransom, redemption, propitiation, reconciliation*).[59] Many texts testify to (4) substitution,[60] (5) union with Christ,[61] (6) deliverance from the penalty of the law through Jesus,[62] (7) God's plan and will at work at the cross,[63] and (8) the necessity of the atonement.[64]

What are the effects of Jesus's sacrificial death? Christ's work on the cross did not change God (i.e., his character), but his sacrifice did cause a

---

[53] Ibid., 297.
[54] Ibid., 299.
[55] Ibid., 303.
[56] Ibid., 308.
[57] Ibid., 317.
[58] Ibid., 319.
[59] Ibid., 321.
[60] Lloyd-Jones refers to the various Old Testament types, and of texts that speak of Jesus giving himself "for our sins" (1 Cor. 15:3; 1 Pet. 3:18; 1 John 2:2; etc.).
[61] Ibid., 324.
[62] Ibid.
[63] Ibid., 326.
[64] Ibid., 330.

threefold change in the way God relates to sinners in Christ. Jesus's death served as (1) a *propitiation* to satisfy the wrath of God, (2) an *expiation* to remove the guilt of sin, and (3) an *atonement* to restore the relationship between God and sinner so they are set at one.[65]

Additional light on the impact of Jesus's death shines through the theme of Christ as Victor. The Doctor refers to the view of Martin Luther at this point: "Man, in this life and born in sin, has five main enemies: Satan, sin, death, the law and the wrath of God, and, according to Luther, before a man can be saved those five enemies have to be dealt with."[66] The Doctor maintains that Christ as Victor adds to the grand theme of his substitutionary atonement, rather than subtracting from it. The doctrine of Christ as Victor is inseparable from the doctrine of Christ's resurrection. One must "always be filled with a sense of triumph as we think of the resurrection" because the resurrected Christ is the Victor over death and Satan and his whole dominion of darkness.[67]

Jesus's death also brought about a change *in heaven*. Noting the comparison between the earthly and heavenly tabernacles, the Doctor observes that Hebrews regards both as cleansed with blood (Heb. 9:22–24). The earthly "patterns were purified by blood of bulls and goats."[68] However, the blood of bulls and goats could not purify the heavenly tabernacle. Something better was needed and was provided. "And it has been purified by something better. It has been purified by the blood of the Son of God Himself. He offered His own blood."[69]

Jesus's death also has an effect *upon the world* in general, not just the church in particular. The Doctor says that without the anticipation of the work of Jesus on the cross, God would have certainly destroyed the world when Adam fell into sin. The implication is that every blessing that comes to unbelievers ultimately derives from the cross.[70]

Jesus's blood also has an impact *upon the church* by purchasing all the blessings of the new covenant for us. The Doctor identifies these

---

65 Ibid., 302.
66 Ibid., 339.
67 Ibid., 340.
68 Ibid., 347.
69 Ibid. What caused the need for this cleansing or purification? Lloyd-Jones theorizes that the fall of Satan introduced impurity in heaven: "This vile, this foul thing that first caused the fall of Satan, and then caused the fall of man has, if one may use such language, introduced a kind of impurity even into heaven—into the heavenly tabernacle, at any rate. And according to this teaching, as I understand it, it was necessary for our Lord to purify and to purge the heavenly tabernacle of that taint, and the statement here is to the effect that He has done so" (ibid.).
70 Ibid., 363.

blessings as (1) forgiveness of sins, (2) new access to God, (3) being no longer under law but under grace, and (4) the guarantee that he will save to the uttermost.[71]

3. *King.* We have seen that Jesus as Prophet saves us from the *ignorance* of sin because we sinners walk in darkness and ignorance and need the light to shine on us. And Jesus as Priest saves us from the *guilt* of sin. Now the Doctor also stressed that we sinners need Jesus as King to save us from the *dominion* of sin. In salvation, we are transferred from the dominion of darkness into the dominion of his beloved Son (Col. 1:13). As King, Jesus sets us free and makes us citizens of his gracious kingdom.

The second person in the Trinity has always shared in the dominion over all of creation. However, a special kingship is now at work in Jesus's existence as the God-man. It is often called his kingship as Mediator, which Lloyd-Jones defines as "His official power to rule all things in heaven and earth for the glory of God and for the execution of God's purpose of salvation."[72]

The Doctor distinguished between Jesus's *appointment* as King and his *functioning* as King. His appointment as King happened before the foundation of the world, but he began to operate in this capacity after the fall.[73] God gave a promise in Genesis 3 about this coming King. The second person of the Trinity was already at work throughout the plan of salvation in the Old Testament. He made appearances as the angel of the Lord during that period. Yet he was not formally and publicly installed as mediatorial King until after his ascension (Acts 2:29–30; Phil. 2:9–11).[74]

What are the aspects or dimensions of his kingship? The Doctor begins with a definition: "Wherever the rule of Christ is acknowledged and delighted in, there is Christ's kingdom, and there Christ is King."[75] His kingship has three dimensions: First, there is a spiritual rule as he reigns over the church as Head and King. Second, there is a general rule over everything with all authority and power (Ps. 2:8; Matt. 28:18; Eph. 1:20–23; Heb. 2:8–9). Third, the final consummation will usher in the new heavens and new earth. At that time, Christ will deliver "the kingdom to God

---

71 Ibid., 350–58.
72 Ibid., 368.
73 Ibid.
74 Ibid., 369.
75 Ibid.

the Father after destroying every rule and every authority and power" (1 Cor. 15:24).

Applying the Doctrine

These doctrinal details should lead to doxological explosions of praise, thanksgiving, outreach, and obedience. The impact on us should be felt in at least three areas: (1) a greater sense of wonder and adoration, (2) a greater passion for evangelism, and (3) greater growth in Christlikeness.

A Greater Sense of Wonder and Adoration

The details of the doctrine of Christ should lead to wonder and awe. We were created to worship; we are meant to marvel. Can we truly claim to understand the doctrine of God the Son without a deep sense of reverence and awe? Sometimes the awakening of awe is the best application of this doctrine as we come face-to-face with the mystery of God in the flesh. Lloyd-Jones calls the coming of Christ in the flesh "the strangest, the most amazing thing that has ever happened—indeed, I do not hesitate to say, the supreme act of God."[76]

The Doctor points out that delight in saying the name of Jesus is a practical proof that we have grasped the glory of these doctrinal details. Do we savor the name of the Lord Jesus Christ? This question is like a stethoscope to our spiritual heartbeat. One of "the best tests of our whole position as Christians" is whether we are "as fond of the Name as the Apostle Paul was."[77] Do we love repeating the name? Do we savor the sweetness of it? We should speak the name with a heart aflame with the realization that he is "the Alpha and the Omega, the beginning, the end, the All and in all."[78]

Another proof that the gospel of Christ's glory has gripped us is that we meditate on the mystery of Christ rather than skipping over it lightly. Lloyd-Jones believes that there is nothing "more wonderful for us to contemplate and consider." These truths are soul-stretching and mind-blowing. The Doctor asks, do we "feel that it is a great privilege to be allowed to look into such wondrous mysteries and glorious truths?" God has revealed each of these things in his Word, "not that we might skip over it lightly, but that we might delve into it and try to grasp what has happened."[79]

---

[76] Ibid., 264–65.
[77] D. Martyn Lloyd-Jones, *Assurance: Exposition of Romans 5* (Carlisle, PA: Banner of Truth, 1998), 8.
[78] Ibid.
[79] Lloyd-Jones, *God the Father, God the Son*, 287–88.

If we cannot be still and study what Christ did for us on the cross, we have little hope for a humble grasp of who we are in Christ. The accomplishment on the cross decisively demolishes our pride. The Doctor even says that if we believe our becoming Christians gives us any grounds for boasting, then we have not become Christians.[80] The apostle Paul argues in Romans 3:27 that human pride is so decisively excluded that, in the Doctor's words, it is "put out through the door and the door locked on it; there is no room for it here at all."[81]

Humility is not an accomplishment; it is a worshipful response to what Christ has done. The Doctor explains why meditating on the mystery of Christ is essential for humility:

> A friend was asking me the other day, "How can I be humble?" He felt there was pride in him, and he wanted to know how to get rid of it. He seemed to think that I had some patent remedy and could tell him, "Do this, that, and the other and you will be humble." I said, "I have no method or technique. I can't tell you to get down on your knees and believe in prayer because I know you will soon be proud of that. There's only one way to be humble, and that is to look into the face of Jesus Christ; you cannot be anything else when you see him." That is the only way. Humility is not something you can create within yourself; rather, you look at him, you realize who he is and what he has done, and you are humbled.[82]

A Greater Passion for Evangelism

Understanding the doctrine of Christ will not only cause Christians to savor the name of Jesus; it should also cause them to share the name of Jesus with others. Lloyd-Jones goes so far as to say that once "a man has the love of Christ in his heart you need not train him to witness; he will do it."[83]

The details of the doctrine of Christ will impact our evangelism because true evangelism is "highly doctrinal."[84] Evangelism is not sharing stories and "playing on people's emotions." Biblical evangelism lays out the "form of doctrine," as Paul himself states in Romans 6:17 (KJV).[85] Sharing

---

80 Ibid., 132–33.

81 Ibid., 132–33.

82 Martyn Lloyd-Jones, *Living Water: Studies in John 4* (Wheaton, IL: Crossway, 2009), 710.

83 D. Martyn Lloyd-Jones, *The Unsearchable Riches of Christ: An Exposition of Ephesians 3* (Grand Rapids: Baker, 1979), 253.

84 D. Martyn Lloyd-Jones, *Knowing the Times: Addresses Delivered on Various Occasions* (Carlisle, PA: Banner of Truth, 1989), 58.

85 D. Martyn Lloyd-Jones, *The New Man: An Exposition of Romans 6* (Carlisle, PA: Banner of Truth, 1972), 214.

the gospel must involve teaching. The profound doctrines of the book of Romans all fall under the heading of "the gospel of his Son" (Rom. 1:9). These doctrines are part of the good news and must not be left out.[86]

A Greater Growth in Christlikeness

The doctrines of Christ are also essential for growth in Christlikeness. The Doctor never tires of stressing that holiness teaching in the Scriptures is always a matter of doctrine. In fact, there "is no holiness teaching in the New Testament apart from this direct association with doctrine; it is a deduction from the doctrine."[87]

Therefore, we must hold these doctrinal details "in our minds at all times" and "meditate along these lines."[88] The glory of Christ is at stake in our Christlikeness because the Father's purpose in salvation is that we would be "conformed to the image of his Son" (Rom. 8:29). Lloyd-Jones calls this conformity to Christ the "acme of all teaching concerning salvation."[89] Indeed, he even asserts that the "ultimate object of salvation is to bring us to this height."[90] The Father has predestined that the family of God would have a family resemblance to the Son of God. This likeness is not accidental. It is a derived, intentional likeness, just as the head of a monarch on the coin is not supposed to "vaguely resemble" the monarch; it must match the likeness of the monarch because it is "derived from the very likeness of the monarch himself."[91]

Conclusion: The Glory of God in the Face of Christ

Now that the doctrinal details and the application of them are before us, it is time to connect the dots between the doctrine of God the Father and the doctrine of God the Son. How does one see the glory of God when gazing upon the face of Christ? Some of the ways that God's glory is seen in the face of Christ are rooted in the incarnation. The Son is the "radiance of the glory of God and the exact imprint of his nature" (Heb. 1:3). The attributes of God all shine forth in the flesh because Jesus is the "invisible God" made visible

---

[86] D. Martyn Lloyd-Jones, *The Gospel of God: An Exposition of Romans 1* (Carlisle, PA: Banner of Truth, 1985), 219–20.
[87] Lloyd-Jones, *The New Man*, 271.
[88] D. Martyn Lloyd-Jones, *The Final Perseverance of the Saints: An Exposition of Romans 8:17–39* (Carlisle, PA: Banner of Truth, 1975), 228.
[89] Ibid., 222.
[90] Ibid.
[91] Ibid., 223.

(Col. 1:15). But Paul goes further in saying that the glory of God in the face of Christ is seen in the preaching of the gospel in particular (2 Cor. 4:5–6). Lloyd-Jones unpacks the way that the cross demonstrates the holiness of God and the love of God.

First, many people fail to see the sheer majesty of God's character reflected like a mirror in the cross of Christ. Lloyd-Jones says that there is only one answer as to why Christ had to die: "the holiness of God!"[92] God cannot "deal savingly with a sinner unless sin has been dealt with," and "nothing less than the death of His Son can satisfy the holy demands of this righteous God."[93] The holiness of God made it necessary for God to put Christ "forward as a propitiation . . . to show God's righteousness" (Rom. 3:25).[94]

Rightly knowing God's absolute love for holiness and hatred for sin will deepen and sweeten our assessment of the atonement.[95] Those who try to save the love of God by denying the wrath of God end up destroying both.[96] It is "only as you have some conception of the depth of His wrath that you will understand the depth of His love."[97]

No one can even begin "to understand the love of God and the love of the Lord Jesus Christ who does not believe the substitutionary and penal doctrine of the Atonement."[98] In fact, the Doctor takes this point even further. How do the eternal decrees of God relate to humanity's fall into sin and salvation in Christ? No one can ultimately give all the reasons why God allowed the fall, but one thing we know for sure is that without the fall, we would not have seen certain aspects of his character and being, like the richness of his mercy and the greatness of his love (Eph. 2:4).[99]

The Doctor urges us to get the order right when it comes to the love of God and the cross of Christ:

> The cross is not something that influences the love of God; no, the love
> of God produced it. That is the order. Were it not for His love, God would

---

[92] D. Martyn Lloyd-Jones, *God's Ultimate Purpose: An Exposition of Ephesians 1* (Grand Rapids: Baker, 1978), 134.
[93] Ibid.
[94] Ibid.
[95] Ibid., 72.
[96] Lloyd-Jones, *The Gospel of God*, 349.
[97] Ibid.
[98] D. Martyn Lloyd-Jones, *Darkness and Light: An Exposition of Ephesians 4:17–5:17* (Grand Rapids: Baker, 1982), 310.
[99] D. Martyn Lloyd-Jones, *God's Way of Reconciliation: An Exposition of Ephesians 2* (Grand Rapids: Baker, 1972), 111.

have punished sin in us, and we should all suffer eternal death. Indeed, I do not hesitate to go so far as to say this: nothing anywhere in the Scripture in any way approaches the substitutionary and penal doctrine of the atonement as an exposition and an explanation of the love of God. Is there anything greater than this, that God should take your sins and mine and put them on His own Son and punish His own Son, not sparing Him anything, causing Him to suffer all that, that you and I might be forgiven? Can you tell me any greater exhibition of the love of God than that?[100]

The church loses her way to the degree that she neglects her Bridegroom. She must fan into flame a passion for Christ as her first love. Fanning the fires of love into flame will require meditating upon the mystery of Christ until we can boast in Christ and savor the character of God supremely on display at the cross.

This chapter could give the impression that this stretching work of meditation is something the church does in an unaided way. The next chapter corrects any such false impression with a focus on the role of the Holy Spirit in glorifying the Son.

---

100 Lloyd-Jones, *God the Father, God the Son*, 335.

CHAPTER 4

POWER FROM ON HIGH

The Person and Work of the Holy Spirit

It is a miracle that there is a single Christian in the world or ever has been.

D. MARTYN LLOYD-JONES [1]

Introducing the Doctrine

Lloyd-Jones organized his doctrinal lectures to "follow the order and the plan of salvation."[2] Just as one studies the *Bible* in an orderly way (chapter by chapter), one should study the great *doctrines* in an orderly manner (following the plan of salvation).[3] Those who neglect the plan of salvation are "robbing themselves" of the opportunity to be "impressed by its glory, its greatness, its perfection in every part."[4] Within the plan of salvation, the Spirit functions as the "applier" or "executor" of the plan. The Spirit brings this salvation to us and makes it a reality in us.[5]

The Doctor opens his treatment of the Holy Spirit by lamenting how frequently the doctrine of the Spirit has been neglected in the church.[6] Neglecting the doctrine of God the Holy Spirit would be as sinful as

---

[1] *God's Ultimate Purpose: An Exposition of Ephesians 1* (Grand Rapids: Baker, 1978), 414.
[2] D. Martyn Lloyd-Jones, *Great Doctrines of the Bible: God the Holy Spirit* (Wheaton, IL: Crossway, 1997), 3.
[3] Ibid., 3–4.
[4] Ibid., 3.
[5] Ibid., 4.
[6] Ibid., 4–5.

neglecting the doctrine of God the Father or God the Son. The Spirit is coequal with the Father and the Son. Yet it is tragically true that many Christians do ignore this doctrine partly out of fear of "excesses and freak manifestations."[7]

Ignoring this doctrine is not only sinful but also foolish, because so much practical application flows from it. Lloyd-Jones blames the low level of spiritual life in the church on the widespread failure to learn the truth concerning the person and work of the Holy Spirit.[8] The Doctor addresses this neglect by devoting more lectures to the person and work of the Spirit than to any other topic (twenty-five lectures and 275 pages). For that reason, this chapter will be the longest and densest, most detailed chapter in the book. I have attempted to preserve some of the most weighty discussions in the footnotes. A reader who loves details is free to go deeper with the footnotes, but a reader who wants the basic picture of the Spirit's work can ignore the notes without losing the flow of the discussion. I do not apologize for the depth of discussion in this chapter; a robust doctrine of the Christian life requires a robust doctrine of the work of the Holy Spirit.

Defining the Doctrine

Once again, dividing the doctrine into person and work is the most natural approach.

The Person of the Holy Spirit

The Doctor looks at three dimensions of the Spirit's personhood: (1) his titles, (2) his personality, and (3) his deity. First, the Spirit has many titles that connect him to the Father[9] and the Son.[10] He also has titles that are personal and direct.[11] He is called the "Holy" Spirit because his special work

---

[7] Ibid., 5–6.

[8] Ibid., 6.

[9] Many titles connect the Spirit to the Father: "the Spirit of God" (Gen. 1:2); "my Spirit" (Gen. 6:3); "his Spirit" (Num. 11:29); "the Spirit of the Lord GOD" (Isa. 61:1); "the Spirit of your Father" (Matt. 10:20); "the Spirit of the Lord" (Luke 4:18); "the Spirit of him [God the Father] who raised Jesus from the dead" (Rom. 8:11); "the Spirit of our God" (1 Cor. 6:11); "the Spirit of the living God" (2 Cor. 3:3) (ibid., 7).

[10] Other titles connect the Spirit to the Son: "the Spirit of the Lord" (Acts 5:9); "the Spirit of Christ" (Rom. 8:9); "the Spirit of his Son" (Gal. 4:6); "the Spirit of Jesus Christ" (Phil. 1:19) (ibid.).

[11] He is called "the Holy Spirit" (Matt. 1:18); "the Spirit of truth" (John 14:17); "the Helper" (John 14–16); "the Spirit of holiness" (Rom. 1:4); "the Spirit of life" (Rom. 8:2); "the eternal Spirit" (Heb. 9:14); "the Holy One" (1 John 2:20).

is to "produce holiness."[12] Second, the Spirit has personhood and personality. This teaching must be emphasized because some deny his personality theologically, while others mute his personality in practice by referring to the Spirit as "it." The Doctor cites many reasons for the tendency to minimize the Spirit's personality[13] but offers far better reasons to affirm his personhood.[14] Third, the Doctor uses four proofs to demonstrate the deity of the Spirit.[15]

It is also important to define the relationship of the Spirit to the Father and the Son in some detail. The Doctor highlights that the Spirit "proceeds" from the Father (John 15:26).[16] One should not draw the deduction, however, that only the Father sends the Spirit, because the very same verse affirms that the Son also sends the Spirit. Jesus also says that he is involved with the Father in the sending of the Comforter (John 14). One must stress that the "three are always working together."[17]

The Scriptures reveal that the Spirit is subordinate to both the Father and the Son. Jesus affirmed that the words and the works he did were not his own (John 14:10). The Scriptures add that the Spirit does not speak of himself (John 16:13). He is given words to speak, and his words aim to glorify the Son (John 16:14).[18] The Holy Spirit works in us so that we can see the Son, who in turn shows us the Father.[19]

---

[12] The Spirit produces holiness in nature and creation, but "His ultimate work is to make us a holy people, holy as children of God." The Doctor also proposes that the description "*Holy* Spirit" differentiates him from other spirits and the evil spirits (1 John 4:1). See Lloyd-Jones, *God the Holy Spirit*, 6–8.

[13] The Doctor gives five specific reasons: (1) his *work* seems impersonal or mystical, (2) his *title* seems impersonal (spirit as breath or power), (3) the many *symbols* seem impersonal (dove, oil, fire, and water), (4) *New Testament salutations* mention the Father and the Son, but not the Spirit, (5) the word for "Spirit" is *neuter*, not masculine, and thus some translations wrongly say "the Spirit itself" instead of "the Spirit Himself" (ibid., 8–9).

[14] The Doctor gives six specific reasons. His first argument is that John uses the masculine pronoun for the Spirit, but it is not convincing to use this rationale. His other five reasons are solid: (1) the Holy Spirit is mentioned with the Father and the Son (Matt. 28:19; 2 Cor. 13:14); (2) the Holy Spirit possesses personal qualities like knowledge (1 Cor. 2:11), will (1 Cor. 12:11), and mind (Rom. 8:27); (3) the Spirit performs personal actions like searching (1 Cor. 2:10), speaking (Rev. 2:7), interceding (Rom. 8:26), testifying (John 15:26), and forbidding (Acts 16:6–7); (4) the Spirit has a personal office as Comforter (John 14:16), and (5) the Spirit is susceptible to personal offenses like being lied to (Acts 5:3), blasphemed against (Matt. 12:31), insulted (Heb. 10:29), and grieved (Eph. 4:30). See ibid., 10–15.

[15] First, the Bible specifically refers to the Spirit as God. When Ananias lied to the Spirit, Peter said he lied "to God" (Acts 5:3–4). Second, the Spirit's name appears with the other persons of the Trinity in the baptismal formula (Matt. 28:19) and the apostolic benediction (2 Cor. 13:14). Third, the Bible affirms that the Spirit has divine attributes like eternality (Heb. 9:14), omnipresence (Ps. 139:7), omnipotence (Luke 1:35), and omniscience (1 Cor. 2:10). Fourth, the Bible testifies to the Spirit's divine actions like creation (Gen. 1:2; Job 33:4), regeneration (John 3:5; 6:63), inspiration (2 Pet. 1:20–21), resurrection (Rom. 1:4; 8:11). See ibid., 15–17.

[16] Ibid., 17–18.

[17] Ibid., 19.

[18] Ibid., 19–20.

[19] Ibid., 20.

The Work of the Holy Spirit

Lloyd-Jones proposes that the best way to classify the work of the Holy Spirit is to distinguish between the Spirit's general work and the Spirit's main work in the application of redemption.[20] Our survey of this doctrine will offer a more simplified summary of the Spirit's general work so we can look at the Spirit's main work in a little more detail.

The Doctor listed several things that constitute the Spirit's general work. The Spirit's activity includes (1) creating, (2) sustaining, (3) imparting common grace, (4) giving gifts, (5) enabling prophecy and producing Scripture, (6) baptizing believers into the body at Pentecost, and (7) attending the life and ministry of Jesus.[21]

The general work of the Spirit is important, but the Doctor calls the application of redemption "the main work and function of the Holy Spirit."[22] The work of redemption is thoroughly Trinitarian: the Father planned the work, the Son achieved the work, and the Spirit applies the work.[23] The Doctor divides the Spirit's application of redemption into two sections: (1) the Spirit's general witness and (2) the Spirit's specific work of salvation.[24]

1. *The Spirit's general witness.* The first division deals with the witness of the Spirit in the church in a general sense. The Spirit comes to point to Christ and glorify Christ.

> He [the Spirit] does not teach about Himself or call attention to Himself or glorify Himself. He is all along calling attention to the Lord, and that is the characteristic of the whole of the work of the Holy Spirit. His one function and business, as our Lord Himself teaches here so clearly, is to glorify the Lord Jesus Christ. The whole of our redemption comes out of Christ, every blessing, every experience—*everything.*[25]

The Spirit's work is Christ-exalting in that he validates and verifies that the Son of God is the true Prophet, Priest, and King.[26] The Holy Spirit also points to Christ through the preaching of the Word of God. The Spirit calls

---

[20] Ibid., 22.
[21] Ibid., 22–43.
[22] Ibid., 43.
[23] Ibid.
[24] Ibid.
[25] Ibid., 45.
[26] Ibid., 53–54.

people to come to the love of God (in general) and to salvation (in particular) through repentance of sins and faith in Christ.[27]

2. *The Spirit's specific work of salvation.* The second division deals with "the special work in those who are going to be saved which He does not do in those who will remain lost."[28] Lloyd-Jones surveys the Pelagian, semi-Pelagian, Arminian, Lutheran, and Reformed views. He then sides with the Reformed view, but adds the qualification that one need not understand the mechanics of salvation to have salvation.[29]

The Doctor spends considerable time explaining his approach to the order of salvation in this section of his lectures. His overall perspective is worth quoting in full:

> "So how do you arrive at your order?" asks someone. My answer is that I mainly try to conceive of this work going on within us from the standpoint of God in eternity looking down upon men and women in sin. That is the way that appeals to me most of all; it is the way that I find most helpful. That is not to detract in any way from experience or the experiential standpoint. Some would emphasize that and would have their order according to experience, but I happen to be one of those people who is not content merely with experience. I want to know something about that experience; I want to know what I am experiencing and I want to know why I am experiencing it and how it has come about. It is the child who is content merely with enjoying the experience. If we are to grow in grace and to go forward and exercise our senses, as the author of the epistle to the Hebrews puts it (Heb. 5:14), then we must of necessity ask certain questions and be anxious to know how the things that have happened to us really have come to take place.[30]

The Doctor's passion for the Spirit's role in the application of redemption is evident from the fact that he devotes nine lectures to this topic. He identifies seven ways the Spirit applies redemption, but for purposes of this summary I will describe just four: (1) effectual calling, (2) regeneration, (3) union with Christ, and (4) conversion.[31]

First, *effectual calling* distinguishes between a general, external call

---

[27] Ibid., 51–52.
[28] Ibid., 58.
[29] Ibid., 57–58.
[30] Ibid., 64.
[31] Ibid. The other three he discusses are the Spirit's work in repentance, saving faith, and assurance.

given to everyone and a special, internal call given to some. The general call is an appeal by the preacher for all to repent and come to Christ in order to be saved. Some reject this external human summons, while others respond and receive it. Why? The Doctor argues that those who respond to the gospel with repentance and faith received an internal, effectual summons from the Spirit that enables them to receive the gospel.

This effectual summons is given only to those whom God has predestined. The Doctor points to Paul's clear statement in Romans 8:30: "And those whom he predestined he also called." Many other Scriptures testify to the inseparable connection between the called and the saved (e.g., 1 Cor. 1:2, 23–24; 1 Pet. 1:9–10). The Doctor also expounds Jesus's words in John 6. Those who are saved are not just taught externally *by a preacher*; they are taught internally and effectually *by God* through the Spirit so that they come to Christ (John 6:45, 63–65).[32]

After a survey of many texts, Lloyd-Jones turns to defining the effectual calling of the Spirit. Effectual calling is the "exercise of the power of the Holy Spirit in the soul." This "direct operation" of the Spirit makes a "new mode of spiritual activity possible within us."[33] Spiritual activity is impossible without this miraculous, immediate work. The Doctor also adds that God's effectual operation of the Spirit creates a love for and rejoicing in the things of Christ. The effectual call is not cruel or coercive or unwelcome.

> He does not strike me; He does not beat me; He does not coerce me. No, thank God, what He does is operate upon my will so that I desire these things and rejoice in them and love them. He leads, He persuades, He acts upon my will in such a way that when He does, the call of the gospel is effectual, and it is certain, and it is sure. God's work never fails, and when God works in a man or woman, the work is effective.[34]

Second, the Spirit does a special work of *regeneration* in applying redemption to us. Lloyd-Jones defines regeneration as the "implanting of new life in the soul."[35] Regeneration results in a new "governing disposition of the soul" toward holiness. The new birth is the "first exercise of this new

---

32 Ibid., 67.

33 Ibid., 70. The Doctor also points to the experience of Lydia to illustrate effectual calling. The Lord opened her heart to receive the things Paul was preaching (Acts 16:14). The Lord put something in her heart, this internal work, and the result was that she paid attention, saw the gospel, and received it. The external call became the internal call; the general became effectual (ibid., 72).

34 Ibid., 73.

35 Ibid., 77–78.

disposition."[36] The Doctor ranks this doctrine alongside the atonement as "incomparably the most important doctrine of all."[37] The reason is that we simply "cannot understand Christian doctrine and Christian truth without being clear about the doctrine of regeneration."[38]

How does the effectual call of the Spirit relate to regeneration? Regeneration is what the Spirit does to make the external call effectual. In other words, the call of the gospel to repent and believe becomes effectual "because in these people there is now a principle which was not there before which enables them to respond to this spiritual truth, this divine truth, that comes to them."[39]

The Doctor argues that regeneration precedes the effectual call. He began with the general call in order to note the distinction of two groups (those who reject and those who receive). Those who reject the gospel are "unregenerate," meaning that they have "the natural mind" and are not spiritual. The things of Christ mean nothing to them. "But they mean everything to the others and that is because they are now spiritual, and they are spiritual as the result of regeneration."[40]

The Bible uses many terms to describe this regeneration by the Spirit. The Doctor points to terms involving *regeneration* (Titus 3:5), *begetting* or *begetting again* (John 1:13; 3:3, 4, 5, 6, 7, 8; 1 John 2:29; 3:9; 4:7; 5:1), *bringing forth* (James 1:18); *creating* (2 Cor. 5:17; Gal. 6:15: Eph. 2:10), and *quickening* (Eph. 2:5).

The Doctor then surgically employs negations and affirmations to arrive at a proper understanding of regeneration. Regeneration is not (1) a physical change of substance in human nature through the addition of some physical seed,[41] (2) a complete change in human nature,[42] (3) the production of additional faculties,[43] or (4) a moral reformation.[44] Rather, regeneration is (1) a radical change in the disposition of the soul,[45] (2) a change that

---

[36] Ibid.
[37] Ibid., 75.
[38] Ibid. "I have always been convinced, and I am now more convinced than ever, that people who are in trouble about these great doctrines of grace are generally so because they have never clearly grasped the significance and meaning of the doctrine of regeneration."
[39] Ibid., 84.
[40] Ibid.
[41] It is a spiritual change, not physical (ibid., 78).
[42] We do not become entirely different. We are partakers of the divine nature, but we do not suddenly become divine. We are not like the Lord Jesus, with two natures: truly God and truly human (ibid.).
[43] The five faculties of the soul are "mind, memory, affection, will, and conscience." The Doctor says some have wrongly deduced that regeneration gives an additional faculty or changes existing ones (ibid.).
[44] It is not just a change of will that leads to personal moral reform (ibid.).
[45] It is new spiritual life, not a mere psychological change. The governing disposition of the soul has changed. A disposition is something behind all of the faculties of the soul which governs them all. Two

impacts the whole person,[46] (3) instantaneous,[47] (4) unconscious,[48] and (5) done by God.[49]

Lloyd-Jones also attempts to define the relationship between regeneration and the preached Word. This definition requires that one distinguish between the act of regeneration and the birth itself. There can be a long interval between the two. Therefore, the Bible can say that we are born again "by the word of truth" (James 1:18) or "through . . . the word of God" (1 Pet. 1:23). Those two texts refer to the birth itself. The Word is not involved in "the act of generating," but "in the bringing out into life of that which has already been implanted within."[50]

The Doctor uses the parable of the sower and the soils as an illustration for this principle. The "whole point of the parable" hinges on "the character of the ground" into which the seed is sown. Is the soil stony or surrounded by thorns? Or is it good soil? The parable stresses the governing disposition of the heart. If "that has been changed and put right, then, when the word comes, it will be effectual; it will lead to the result; it will yield the fruit."[51]

The natural mind "set on the flesh is hostile to God" and will not and cannot submit to him (Rom. 8:7). Unregenerate humanity will not accept the gospel of God. "The natural person does not accept the things of the Spirit of God, for they are folly to him, and he is not able to understand them because they are spiritually discerned" (1 Cor. 2:14). Therefore, regen-

---

people can have the same faculties and make completely different decisions because they have two completely different dispositions. The Doctor uses the apostle Paul as an example. He had the same faculties before and after becoming a Christian, but his life was radically reoriented because of a new disposition (ibid., 79–80). Regeneration is a complete change of disposition. It is the new covenant promise of a new heart and a new spirit (Ezek. 36:26). This text refers to an entirely "new disposition that controls and determines everything else" (ibid., 84).

46 Ibid., 80–81. It is not that the whole person is changed, but a change in disposition will impact the whole person. "The way I use my mind will be affected, the operation of my emotions will be affected, and so will my will, because, by definition, the disposition is at the back of all those and gives direction to them. So when this disposition of mine is changed, then I am like a person with a new mind. Before, I was not interested in the gospel; now I am very interested in it. Before, I could not understand it; now I do."

47 There are no stages; life is implanted or it is not. One cannot be almost pregnant or partially implanted. The germination is immediate (ibid., 81).

48 This germination or implantation happens in the subconscious or the unconscious. It is a "secret" operation that "cannot be directly perceived by us." The Doctor appeals to Jesus's explanation to Nicodemus about the wind blowing where it wills (John 3:8). One cannot see the wind and know where it started or where it is going. One sees only the results (ibid., 81–82).

49 "It is a creative act of God in which men and women are entirely passive and contribute nothing, nothing whatsoever." The Doctor points to John 1:13 (born by the will of God) and John 3:5–6 (born of the Spirit, not the flesh) (ibid., 82).

50 Ibid., 91. That distinction is also important when considering the salvation of infants. The Doctor said infants can be saved apart from responding to the preaching of the Word. "He can implant the seed of spiritual life in an unconscious infant with the same ease as He can do it in an adult person. Therefore you see why it is important for us to consider whether regeneration is something that happens indirectly through the word or whether it is indeed the direct operation of God upon us" (ibid., 93).

51 Ibid., 90–91.

eration is essential because "it is impossible for anything to happen in us which can make us Christians until regeneration has taken place."[52]

Third, the Spirit applies redemption in *uniting* us to Christ. The Doctor addresses three issues here: (1) what type of union it is, (2) how the union happens, and (3) what the consequences of the union are. The union does not confuse or mix the persons involved.[53] It is not a loose union of sympathy or interest.[54] Union with Christ is (1) spiritual, (2) mystical, (3) vital, (4) organic, (5) personal, and (6) indissoluble.

First, the union is spiritual. Paul testifies that someone joined to a prostitute is one flesh with her (a sinful union). But then he shares the glorious, spiritual union of the believer with Christ: "But he who is joined to the Lord becomes one spirit with him" (1 Cor. 6:17).[55] Second, the union is mystical in the sense that there is an intimate union of the two becoming one that is difficult to put into language (Eph. 5:32). Third, the union is vital or living in the sense that "our spiritual life is drawn directly from the Lord Jesus Christ." Galatians 2:20 testifies to this vital union because "it is no longer I who live, but Christ who lives in me."[56] Fourth, the union is organic. The difference between *vital* and *organic* is that *organic* involves twofold growth in that we both give and receive. The body grows up "into Christ" (the head of the body), but the body also grows and builds itself up in love "when each part is working properly" (Eph. 4:15–16). The parts of the body receive and contribute.[57] Fifth, the union is personal in the sense that every person has a direct and personal union with Christ.[58] Sixth, the union is indissoluble in the sense that we don't go in and back out again. It is "once and forever," as Romans 8:38–39 so wondrously celebrates.[59]

With the nature of the union clearly defined, the Doctor moves to consider how the union happens. He stresses, above all, that union is the work of the Holy Spirit. In fact, he believes that *the* special and particular work of the Holy Spirit is to produce this union.[60] The Spirit has made us

---

[52] Ibid., 89.
[53] Ibid., 107. "The Bible teaches very clearly that you and I will exist as individuals throughout the countless ages of eternity. We do not become lost or merged and absorbed into God."
[54] "It is not merely a loose, general, external association of separate persons who happen to have the same interest, or the same enthusiasm" (ibid., 107).
[55] Ibid., 108.
[56] Ibid., 108–9.
[57] Ibid., 110.
[58] This teaching guards against the Roman Catholic error that says we do not have a direct connection to Christ; we only have a connection to him through the church (ibid., 110).
[59] Ibid., 111.
[60] Ibid., 102.

alive "together with Christ" (Eph. 2:5).[61] The result of the Spirit's work is that faith comes into being, which is an indispensable part of this union.[62] Here the Doctor makes a key distinction between the Spirit's work and our faith:

> [Faith] is not the first thing, it is the second, and quite inevitably this leads us on to the consideration of the biblical doctrine of faith. Our faith helps to sustain the union, to develop it and to strengthen it—this union that is primarily established as the result of the work of the Holy Spirit. It is only as faith becomes active that we become aware of this union and of our regeneration and all the other things that we have been considering.[63]

Three glorious consequences come from this union. (1) We are united to Christ as our federal head. Romans 5 forces us to see the federal parallels between the head of fallen humanity (Adam) and the Head of the new humanity (Christ). Our federal union with Adam as the head of the human family means that what he did applies to us. Now that we are joined to Christ as our federal head or representative, all that he did applies to us.[64] Therefore, through our union with Christ, he became "wisdom from God, righteousness and sanctification and redemption" (1 Cor. 1:30). This federal union is forensic. All these things are true legally and positionally, and now they must be worked out "actually and experientially" in our sanctification.[65] (2) We are adopted as sons and daughters of God and become "heirs of God" and "fellow heirs with Christ" (Rom. 8:17). (3) We have fellowship with God in Christ and rich spiritual transformation follows as we are conformed to his image from one degree of glory to the next (Rom. 8:29; 2 Cor. 3:18).

The Doctor has dissected how regeneration relates to effectual calling and preaching. Now he brings greater clarity to how regeneration relates to union with Christ. Chronologically, they happen at the same time. Logically, you almost have to put the union before the regeneration, but they are still inseparable. The Doctor has dealt with regeneration first because of his decision to start with the concepts of the general and the effectual calling. But he strongly stresses the inseparable nature of regeneration and union:

---

[61] Ibid., 111.
[62] Ibid.
[63] Ibid., 111–12.
[64] Ibid., 113.
[65] Ibid., 114.

Regeneration and union must never be separated. You cannot be born again without being in Christ; you are born again because you are in Christ. The moment you are in Him you are born again and you cannot regard your regeneration as something separate and think that union is something you will eventually arrive at. Not at all! Regeneration and union must always be considered together and at the same time because the one depends upon the other and leads to the other; they are mutually self-supporting.[66]

Fourth, the Spirit applies redemption in his work of *conversion*. Conversion is "the first exercise of the new nature in ceasing from old forms of life and starting a new life." This turning from something to something is the heart of conversion: a turning from the old ways of life to the new life.[67]

It is important to distinguish regeneration and conversion. Regeneration is "the planting of the seed," and conversion is "the result of planting the seed."[68] Conversion is something we do through the Spirit, whereas regeneration is something that is done to us by God alone. Conversion is a turning away from one thing to another in practice, but that is not the meaning of regeneration. "We can put it like this: when people convert themselves or turn, they are giving proof of the fact that they are regenerate. Conversion is something that follows upon regeneration."[69]

One of the biggest differences between regeneration and conversion is the presence of human activity. In regeneration and union with Christ by the Spirit, "we are absolutely passive; we play no part at all; it is entirely the work of the Spirit of God in the heart." Conversion is different. In "conversion we act, we move, we are called and we do it."[70] In other words, the life of regeneration must show itself in the movement or turning of conversion. Lloyd-Jones uses the analogy of the life of a newborn baby and the signs of life: "A baby gives proof of the fact that it is born alive and not still born, by screaming or moving. You cannot have life without some kind of manifestation of that life and that is as true of spiritual life as it is of any other form of life."[71]

---

66 Ibid., 105.
67 Ibid., 117–18.
68 Ibid., 77.
69 Ibid. The Doctor stressed that these doctrines can be kept separate as ideas, but not so clearly in terms of timing. "So many of these things really cannot be divided up in terms of time like this. We must keep them clear in our minds, we must keep them clear as ideas, but so many seem to happen at almost exactly the same moment" (ibid., 117).
70 Ibid., 119.
71 Ibid., 96.

The Doctor distinguishes true, Spirit-wrought conversion from temporary or counterfeit conversions. Jesus constantly addressed temporary conversions (e.g., Matt. 13:20–21). One sees temporary conversions in the narrative of Acts (8:13–23) and in the epistles of Paul (1 Tim. 1:19–20; 2 Tim. 4:10). Temporary conversions take place outwardly in response to truth, while counterfeit conversions take place by some other agency (e.g., psychological change).

But true conversion consists of two essential elements: repentance and faith. Acts 20:21 mentions both: "repentance toward God and . . . faith in our Lord Jesus Christ." The Doctor expounds upon their inseparability: "Those are the essential and the only essential elements in conversion. Repentance and faith. Sudden or gradual, it does not matter. Repentance must be there; faith must be there. If one is missing it is not conversion. Both are essential."[72] The Doctor recommends starting with repentance. The Gospels and Acts begin the message of salvation with repentance (Mark 1:15; Acts 2:37–38). What is repentance? It is "a gift of grace, leading to action on our part."[73] What faculties actively engage in repentance? If you have tracked with the Doctor's approach to the Christian life at all up to this point, the answer comes as no surprise. The answer is "the whole person." If it does not include the whole person (mind, heart, and will—Rom. 6:17), then "it is not really repentance."[74]

The Doctor climaxes his discussion of the Spirit's work with a definition of faith "Faith is the instrument or the channel by which all salvation that is in Christ Jesus enters into us and is appropriated."[75] Faith "links us to the fullness that dwells in our Lord and Savior Jesus Christ."[76] Saving faith is not a natural faculty that all fallen sinners have. Where does it originate? Faith is "the gift of God" (Eph. 2:8),[77] and it consists of firm conviction, confidence, and commitment.[78]

Applying the Doctrine

Applying the doctrine of the Spirit will involve at least three aspects. We must (1) savor the Spirit specifically, (2) see the miracle of salvation, and (3) seek the Spirit.

---

[72] Ibid., 125.
[73] Ibid., 130.
[74] Ibid., 131.
[75] Ibid., 139.
[76] Ibid.
[77] Ibid., 142.
[78] Ibid., 143–44.

Savor the Spirit Specifically

Lloyd-Jones warns us not to view the Spirit impersonally as a force or energy. He is a person. We can know and worship him, or we can neglect, quench, or grieve him. When we review the overwhelming amount of doctrinal information the Doctor shares about the Holy Spirit, we should have one goal in mind: to make it personal and specific. The Spirit does specific works in the application of redemption. He should get distinct praise for each distinct action or application. This is a lifelong work of worship on our part, and it is worth it. One can feel the wonder of meeting the Holy Spirit in personal ways. Often these personal encounters lead to greater Trinitarian communion with God because the Spirit reveals the Son, who in turn takes us to the Father.

Furthermore, as you ponder the breadth and depth of the Spirit's work in your salvation, you will also begin to view your Christian life in a different light. You will view it less as a decision and more as a miracle.

See the Miracle of Salvation

The Doctor exclaims that it "is a miracle that there is a single Christian in the world or ever has been."[79] He says again, "If you are not amazed at yourself you are not a Christian, my friend! All Christians are miracles and they should be amazed at themselves."[80] He reminds us that "there is no such thing as an 'ordinary Christian.'"[81]

As we saw earlier, the Doctor's wife, Bethan Lloyd-Jones, had to come to grips with true Christianity and the miracle of regeneration.

> I tried to do all a "Christian" should do in such duties as church attendance and I accepted the Bible as the Word of God. But I had no inner peace or joy and I knew nothing of the glorious release of the gospel.
>
> I rejoiced to see men and women converted . . . and I envied them and sometimes wished, when I saw their radiant faces and changed lives, that I had been a drunkard or worse, so that I could be converted! I never imagined that I needed to be converted, having always been a "Christian" or that I could get any more than I had already![82]

---

[79] Lloyd-Jones, *God's Ultimate Purpose*, 414.
[80] D. Martyn Lloyd-Jones, *God's Sovereign Purpose: An Exposition of Romans 9* (Carlisle, PA: Banner of Truth, 1991), 241.
[81] D. Martyn Lloyd-Jones, *Life in God: Studies in 1 John* (Wheaton, IL: Crossway, 1995), 94.
[82] Lynette G. Clark, *Far above Rubies: The Life of Bethan Lloyd-Jones* (Fearn, Ross-shire, UK: Christian Focus, 2015), 55. As I noted in chap. 1, Iain Murray believes that Mrs. Lloyd-Jones was already converted but lacked assurance (personal correspondence with the author, August 4, 2017).

Bethan wished she could have been a "drunkard or worse" so that she could become converted and have a sensational testimony. But she realized how wrong she was only after she became a Christian. She witnessed the miracle of regeneration and the new birth.

Some people have the wrong idea that being saved from a religious, self-righteous life is a boring testimony. They almost wish that they had been addicted to drugs or sex or some other red-letter, scandalous sin in order to have a sensational testimony. The Doctor's exposition of regeneration reminds all believers that we were dead in transgressions and sins, and God by the power of the Spirit made us alive together with Christ. The doctrine of regeneration proves that you do not have a boring testimony, because being raised from the dead is *not* boring.

Seek the Spirit

The first two applications cultivate a settled sense of awe and appreciation for what the Spirit has done to create new life within us. The third application now focuses on how to seek the Spirit for continued growth in the Christian life. The search for more of the Spirit's power must first reckon with the fact that the Spirit hides himself to put all our attention on the Son. Therefore, we should not seek the power of the Spirit directly. We seek Christ directly. This intentional pursuit of Christ is an invitation for the Spirit to glorify Christ by revealing him to us in greater measure. The Spirit shows us the Son, who takes us to the Father.

> This is, to me, one of the most amazing and remarkable things about the biblical doctrine of the Holy Spirit. The Holy Spirit seems to hide Himself and to conceal Himself. He is always, as it were, putting the focus on the Son, and that is why I believe, and I believe profoundly, that the best test of all as to whether we have received the Spirit is to ask ourselves, what do we think of, and what do we know about, the Son. Is the Son real to us? That is the work of the Spirit. He is glorified indirectly; He is always pointing us to the Son.[83]

John Piper expresses the same approach to the empowering of the Spirit:

> In seeking to be filled and empowered by the Spirit we must pursue him indirectly—we must look to the wonder of Christ. If we look away from

---

[83] Lloyd-Jones, *God the Holy Spirit*, 20.

Jesus and seek the Spirit and his power directly, we will end up in the mire of our own subjective emotions. The Spirit does not reveal himself. The Spirit reveals Christ. The fullness of the Spirit is the fullness that he gives as we gaze on Christ. The power of the Spirit is the power we feel in the presence of Christ. The joy of the Spirit is the joy we feel from the promises of Christ. Many of us know what it is to crouch on the floor and cry out to the Holy Spirit for joy and power, and experience nothing; but the next day devote ourselves to earnest meditation on the glory of Jesus Christ and be filled with the Spirit.[84]

Conclusion: The Spirit and the Christian Life

This application section could easily fill many more pages. The work of the Spirit is absolutely indispensable for our daily Christian walk. We are called to "walk by the Spirit" (Gal. 5:16), "keep in step with the Spirit" (Gal. 5:25), and be "praying in the Holy Spirit" (Jude 20). It would be counterproductive to make a long chapter even longer by diving deep into a more detailed discussion. Part 3 is really the place where this deeper look at the Spirit's work will show up. Part 3 takes up different aspects of the Christian life, like Bible reading, prayer, walking by faith, and living out our faith in the spheres of marriage, family, and work. Lloyd-Jones will define each one and then diagnose what makes them so difficult. He then will put forth a prescription for overcoming the difficulty. Without fail, these prescriptions will involve the power of the Spirit. Chapter 9 is a good case in point. The Doctor diagnoses different difficulties in prayer and his solution is learning to pray in the Holy Spirit.

---

[84] John Piper, "Christ Conceived by the Holy Spirit" (sermon preached on March 11, 1984), http://www.desiringgod.org/messages/christ-conceived-by-the-holy-spirit.

CHAPTER 5

REDEMPTION APPLIED

Justification and Sanctification

Indeed, we could say that the theme of Romans 6, 7 and 8 is to de-
nounce, with horror, the tendency of people to separate justification
from sanctification; to say that if you think you can stop at justification,
you are doing something which the Apostle believes is so terrible that he
can say nothing about it but, "God forbid" that anybody should think
such a thing or ever draw such a deduction.

D. MARTYN LLOYD-JONES [1]

Introducing the Doctrines

Lloyd-Jones had a passionate desire that his people would have a personal
understanding of justification and sanctification. This personal knowledge
needed to go beyond a generic knowledge. He did not pull any punches
while addressing Christians who lacked an interest in doctrine.

> If God has chosen to use such terms as righteousness, justification, sanc-
> tification, redemption, atonement, reconciliation, propitiation, then it
> is our duty to face those terms and to consider their meaning; it is dis-
> honoring to God not to do so. Someone may say, for instance, "I am not
> interested in all those terms; I believe in God, and I believe in living as
> good a life as I can in order to please Him." But how can you please God if

---

[1] *Great Doctrines of the Bible: God the Holy Spirit* (Wheaton, IL: Crossway, 1997), 223.

you refuse to consider the very terms that He Himself has revealed to the men who wrote the record?[2]

This chapter will thus "face" the doctrines of justification and sanctification. The previous chapter spoke of regeneration as a new-creation work of the Holy Spirit. The Doctor has stressed that regeneration and justification must be kept distinct in terms of logical sequence, even if they are simultaneous in terms of temporal sequence. Logical sequence places stress on the proper grounds of salvation (why), not on the timing (when).

> It is not our regeneration that saves us. It is not the fact that we are born again that saves us. It is the righteousness of Christ that saves us. God justifies the ungodly, and the ungodly are not regenerate. It is while we are ungodly that we are declared righteous. Regeneration comes practically at the same time, but it is something different.[3]

Therefore, the Doctor emphasizes that we are not justified "because we are regenerate" or "have a new nature" or "have become sanctified."[4] The Doctor describes that teaching as "the Roman Catholic error and heresy."[5] Paul makes it crystal clear that we were justified while we were "ungodly" and "sinful," "without any change in our nature." It must be clear in our minds that our justification is not based on our regeneration.[6]

So, on the one hand, justification and sanctification must be distinguished, but, on the other hand, they must not be separated.[7] Lloyd-Jones asserts that the doctrines of justification and sanctification are directly dependent upon the person of Christ. One cannot "take justification only" or "sanctification only." Christ is "indivisible," and thus we "have all these in Christ."[8] The Doctor regards union with Christ as the key to both justification and sanctification, which is why he lectured on union with Christ first. He declares in no uncertain terms that dividing these doctrines is unthinkable because Christ is indivisible. Paul denounces "with horror" that "anybody should think such a thing or ever draw such a deduction."[9]

---

[2] D. Martyn Lloyd-Jones, *Walking with God: Studies in 1 John* (Wheaton, IL: Crossway, 1993), 23.
[3] D. Martyn Lloyd-Jones, *Assurance: An Exposition of Romans 5* (Carlisle, PA: Banner of Truth, 1998), 134.
[4] Lloyd-Jones, *God the Holy Spirit*, 206.
[5] Ibid.
[6] Ibid.
[7] Ibid., 201.
[8] Lloyd-Jones, *Assurance*, 54.
[9] Lloyd-Jones, *God the Holy Spirit*, 223.

In the next section, on defining the doctrines, I have chosen to honor the Doctor's emphasis even in the way the doctrines are presented. I discuss the doctrines and distinguish them, but I do not place them in segregated places within the chapter. I pray that even the method of presentation will highlight the important fact that while they are two distinct works, they belong together in one glorious God-centered package.

Defining the Doctrines (Five Distinctions)

Lloyd-Jones makes five distinctions between justification and sanctification, which can be illustrated in table 1.

Table 1

Justification	Sanctification
involves a declared righteous	involves being made righteous
yields an imputed righteousness	yields an imparted righteousness
is an instantaneous act	is a continuous process
addresses the condemning power of sin	addresses the corrupting power of sin
involves no works on our part	involves works on our part

Justification—God Declares Us Righteous; Sanctification—God Makes Us Righteous

First, the Doctor distinguishes these two doctrines on the basis of the types of action involved: to *declare* us righteous versus to *make* us righteous. The doctrine of justification draws its language from the legal sphere of the courtroom. It is "a judicial act of God in which He declares that He regards those of us who believe in the Lord Jesus Christ, as righteous on the grounds of the work and merit of Christ. God imputes and ascribes Christ's righteousness to us, and we rest on that by faith."[10]

The biblical witness consistently testifies to the legal and declarative aspect of justification. The Bible calls a judge to *justify* the righteous and condemn the wicked. A judge does not change the nature of the people in the courtroom. He makes a *legal* declaration that one is in the right and the other is in the wrong. Luke 7:29 also speaks of people justifying God. It is obvious that the people do not alter the "nature or being of God." They simply make a declaration about him. They declare that God is right

---

[10] Ibid., 169.

and true.[11] The biblical texts that testify directly to our justification have exactly the same sense (Acts 13:39; Rom. 3:20–28; 4:5–7; 5:1).

Justification takes place outside us (in a tribunal), while sanctification takes place inside us. Justification is declarative, but sanctification is transformative. This statement about sanctification requires a key qualification. Sanctification has two senses: a positional aspect (we are regarded as holy) and an inward aspect (we are made holy). The positional aspect is something that happens outside us: God regards us as holy in the sense that we are set apart positionally from sin for God's service (Acts 26:18; 1 Cor. 6:11; Heb. 10:10). The second aspect refers to something that happens inside us. There is an inner cleansing by the Holy Spirit and a process that transforms us from glory to glory (2 Cor. 3:18) so that we progressively become conformed to the image of Christ (Rom. 8:29). This chapter will follow the Doctor's lead in speaking of sanctification in that second sense.

Lloyd-Jones defines this second aspect of sanctification as "that gracious and continuous operation of the Holy Spirit by which He delivers the justified sinner from the pollution of sin, renews his whole nature in the image of God and enables him to perform good works."[12]

The difference between justification and the process of sanctification must be kept clear in our minds. Justification is a declaration that does not do anything *to us*; it says something *about us*. It says nothing about our internal condition; it refers to our external standing before God.[13] Sanctification is an internal condition in which we are changed into the image of Christ from glory to glory.[14] The Doctor keeps them distinct in this way: "In justification we are not *made* righteous, we are *declared* to be righteous— the thing is quite different. To say that in justification you are made righteous is to confuse it with sanctification."[15]

Justification—We Have an Imputed Righteousness;
Sanctification—We Have an Imparted Righteousness

Second, the Doctor also differentiates justification and sanctification based on how righteousness is received:

---

11 Ibid., 171.
12 Ibid., 195.
13 Ibid., 169.
14 Ibid., 218.
15 Ibid., 169.

In justification righteousness is imputed to us, put to our account. God, you remember, justifies the ungodly. He does not wait until people are fully sanctified before He justifies them. . . . No, God looks at men and women in their sins, and, applying to them the righteousness of Christ, declares them to be just. That is *imputed* righteousness. But in sanctification, we are discussing *imparted* righteousness. Not the righteousness that is put to my account, but the righteousness that is created within me and produced within me.[16]

Justification Is an Instantaneous, Once-and-for-All Act; Sanctification Is a Continuous Process

Third, the Doctor also notes that the two doctrines are different in terms of the timing of the actions: immediate versus continuous.

By definition justification is a once-and-for-all act. It is never to be repeated because it cannot be repeated and never needs to be repeated. It is not a process but a declaration that we are declared just once and for ever, by God. Sanctification, on the other hand, is a continuous process. We continue to grow in grace and in the knowledge of the Lord until beyond the veil we are perfect.[17]

The declaration of justification is made immediately and completely when faith, the instrument of justification, receives the passive and active work of Christ.[18] Sanctification is a process that "begins the moment we are justified. You cannot be justified without the process of sanctification having already started."[19] The Bible's terms for sanctification stress progressive growth—the move from "babes in Christ" to maturity in Christ. One does not "suddenly jump from birth to adulthood."[20]

Justification Addresses the Penalty and Condemning Power of Sin; Sanctification Addresses the Corrupting Power and Pollution of Sin

Fourth, the Doctor distinguishes between the different ways in which the doctrines address the problem of sin. Justification "removes the

---

[16] Ibid., 195.
[17] Ibid., 175.
[18] The Doctor discusses these two aspects of justification as the negative and the positive. In the negative work, our sins are blotted out and forgiven through the death of Christ. In the positive work, the positive righteousness of the Lord Jesus is imputed or reckoned to my account. See ibid., 172.
[19] Ibid., 247.
[20] Ibid., 220.

guilt of sin," while sanctification "removes the pollution of sin and renews us in the image of God."[21] In this sense, justification is primarily an action of the Father based on the work of the Son, while sanctification happens primarily through the cleansing and empowering work of the Holy Spirit.[22]

Justification Involves No Works on Our Part; Sanctification Involves Continuous Work on Our Part

The fifth distinction involves the absence or presence of our work or activity. "Now here, once more, we come to a vital point of difference between justification and sanctification. In justification, as I have reminded you, we do nothing because we cannot. It is the declaratory act of God. But here [in sanctification], we are called to activity."[23]

The apostle Paul constantly declares that justification is by faith apart from our activity and works (Rom. 3:20; 4:5; Gal. 2:16; 3:11). Here it is vitally important to declare that faith is not a work, and Christians are not saved because of faith. Paul makes it clear that "faith is not the grounds of our justification."[24] The righteousness of Christ, imputed to us, is the sole ground of justification. Faith is not the ground; it is the *instrument* of our justification. Faith is not the righteousness that saves me; faith *receives* the righteousness that saves me. Therefore, "Christ, and not my faith, is my righteousness. It is not my believing in Him that saves me. It is He who saves me."[25] Furthermore, not only does faith receive the free gift of salvation, but the faith that receives the free gift is itself part of the free gift. "If we had not been given the gift of faith, we could not receive the righteousness of Christ."[26]

Justification does not involve our works, but sanctification does. There is nothing passive about progressive sanctification. We are active in the sense that we "work out" (Phil. 2:12) what God works in us (Phil. 2:13). The Doctor regarded the "let go and let God" view of sanctification as a major error. If that teaching were true, then none of the New Testament

---

[21] Ibid., 175.
[22] "Justification is an act of God the Father, as we have seen; sanctification is essentially the work of God the Holy Spirit" (ibid.).
[23] Ibid., 207.
[24] Ibid., 176.
[25] Ibid. See also D. Martyn Lloyd-Jones, *God's Way of Reconciliation: An Exposition of Ephesians 2* (Grand Rapids: Baker, 1972), 135.
[26] Lloyd-Jones, *God the Holy Spirit*, 176–77.

epistles "need ever have been written."[27] This perspective takes the reader right to the core of the Doctor's approach to doctrine and life once again. If sanctification is "letting go and letting God," then the apostles wasted vast amounts of time, ink, and energy engaging in doctrinal discussions. Here is the Doctor's summary of the apostles' approach: "Therefore, in the light of that, now then, apply it; do this, don't do that, cleanse yourselves."[28] One never finds the apostles simplistically boiling down sanctification to a call to "surrender, wait, look, and abide."[29]

People often mistake these two principles at work in justification and sanctification and thus they wrongly reverse the biblical order. Ephesians 2:8–9 declares that we are not saved by works but are saved by grace through faith. Ephesians 2:10 adds that we are saved not *by* good works but *for* good works, which God prepared in advance for us to walk in.[30]

The order of the doctrines becomes important at this point once again. The human activity involved in sanctification is directly due to regeneration and union with Christ. Paul declares that sin shall not have dominion, because believers are under grace, not law (Rom. 6:14). This principle comes from union with Christ, which is why the Doctor lectured on union with Christ before sanctification.[31]

Human activity is also directly dependent upon the empowerment of the Spirit. The Doctor says that the Spirit "works upon our wills; He creates desires after holiness; He reveals sin to us in all its foulness and ugliness and creates aspirations after purity and the life of God."[32] The Spirit creates (1) a love for holiness, (2) a hatred for sin, and (3) power for obedience.[33]

Furthermore, the Spirit, "as the author of the truth," takes us "to the truth and gives us an understanding of it."[34] The Spirit leads us to put to death the sinful deeds of the body that seek to kill us (Rom. 8:13). In summary, the Doctor stresses that "we can never emphasize too strongly that sanctification is first of all, and primarily, the work of God in us, through and by the Holy Spirit."[35]

---

27 Ibid., 209.
28 Ibid.
29 Ibid.
30 Lloyd-Jones, *God's Way of Reconciliation*, 134–35.
31 Lloyd-Jones, *God the Holy Spirit*, 225–26.
32 Ibid., 231–32.
33 Ibid. The Spirit "gives us strength and power, enabling us to do what we now want to do."
34 Ibid.
35 Ibid., 206–7.

Applying the Doctrines

Applying the doctrines of justification and sanctification means addressing three areas of our lives: (1) the mind, (2) the heart, and (3) the will.

The Mind: Reckoning Ourselves Rightly

We have seen that *justification* refers to the glorious reality of God reckoning us righteous on the basis of what Christ has done in our behalf. Sanctification includes a reckoning as well. We must reckon ourselves dead to sin and alive to God (Rom. 6:11). We must come to grips with the decisive change that has already taken place. "As a believer in Christ I can never again go back into the bondage and the captivity of the realm and the rule and the reign of sin—never!"[36]

Right reckoning is a form of doctrinal deduction at the heart of holiness. Holiness "is not something we are called upon to do in order that we may become something; it is something we are to do because of what we already are."[37] Sanctification itself is always a "great doctrinal matter," and thus we must never fail to see it "in terms of our whole relationship to God." The New Testament Epistles "always put the teaching about holiness in terms of ultimate doctrine."[38] There cannot be any "holiness teaching" apart from doctrine, because holiness "is a deduction from the doctrine."[39]

One such deduction regarding holiness comes from the doctrine of union with Christ. We were united to him in his death and resurrection. We died to sin decisively with him. Therefore, we reckon ourselves dead to sin. We "cease to live as if we were still in Adam."[40] The "old man" is no longer there. "The only way to stop living as if he were still there is to realize that he is not there."[41] Lloyd-Jones labels this "the New Testament method of teaching sanctification."[42] If we are to *act* in accord with who we are, we have to *know* who we are.

A practical example of this reckoning may help. If a person acts in an immature way, someone might respond with the challenge "Why don't you act your age?" The questioner is not assuming that the immature person

---

[36] D. Martyn Lloyd-Jones, *The New Man: An Exposition of Romans 6* (Carlisle, PA: Banner of Truth, 1972), 122.
[37] D. Martyn Lloyd-Jones, *Life in Christ: Studies in 1 John* (Wheaton, IL: Crossway, 2002), 41.
[38] Ibid., 42.
[39] Lloyd-Jones, *The New Man*, 271.
[40] Ibid., 65.
[41] Ibid.
[42] Ibid.

has physically gone back and become a child. One cannot go back, but an adult can think and act in childish ways. Likewise, a Christian cannot go back to the position of being an unbeliever (in the realm and rule of sin), but he or she can think or act like it.

Therefore, we must fight the doctrinal amnesia we face daily. We are all too prone to forget who we are and what is true of us in Christ. We must reckon ourselves rightly. If we are in Christ, then "as it is true to say of Him that He died unto sin once and for ever, so we also have finished with the realm and the rule and the reign of sin."[43] The Doctor calls the New Testament summons to holiness the "most reasonable and common sense thing imaginable."[44] Those who are not concerned about holiness "are utterly unreasonable and self-contradictory."[45] They think and act in a manner that is contradictory to the core.

The Heart: Savoring Grace

The Doctor orders a test of the connection between the head and the heart when it comes to the doctrine of justification: "There is no better test that we who are Christians can apply to ourselves to know the quality of life that we really have in Christ, than this one: What is our reaction to the mere mention of the word 'justification'?"[46] The word "justification" should make a distinct impression on our spiritual taste buds. Doctrinal understanding should leave a sweet taste in our mouths that shouts of God's goodness toward us in Christ.

But the sheer wonder the heart has for justification should also extend to sanctification. Think for a moment about the miracle of positional sanctification. To help us picture the miracle, the Doctor asks us to imagine a picturesque British countryside with a road passing between two fields. Each field has a high rock wall. A person begins in one field by virtue of physical birth. The field is under the dominion of Satan as a realm of sin and death. The person is a slave there, with no hope for escape, because he cannot scale the wall in his own strength. But God, by the power of the Holy Spirit, is able to do what the person cannot. He reaches down and plucks the person from the first field, lifts him up and over the wall, and transfers him to the new field. Now the person is under the gracious

---

43 Ibid., 121.
44 D. Martyn Lloyd-Jones, *Expository Sermons on 2 Peter* (Carlisle, PA: Banner of Truth, 1983), 42.
45 Ibid.
46 Ibid., 167.

dominion and protection of Christ Jesus as the Ruler of the new field.[47] This picture of positional change mirrors that of Colossians 1:13: "He has delivered us from the domain of darkness and transferred us to the kingdom of his beloved Son."

The doctrines of justification and positional sanctification are great works of God, but one must not miss the holistic greatness of Christ's work by ignoring or minimizing the profound miracle of progressive sanctification. The Father's glorious purpose is to conform us to the image of Christ. This purpose cannot fail because union with Christ means we are "in Christ" and Christ is "in us." What a wonder that Christ himself comes to live and rule and reign inside us.

> What is a Christian? Just a good man? Somebody who is just a little bit better than somebody else? Not at all! He is like Christ! Conformed to the image of God's Son! How can a man who is dead in trespasses and sins raise himself to that? It is impossible. "By grace ye are saved"; "not of yourselves," "no boasting." No man can attain to this, no man can raise himself to this. It is God's work, and God's work alone. The Christian is one who is meant to be like Christ. He has the life of Christ within him. "I live, yet not I, but Christ liveth in me." What is Christianity? It is "Christ in you, the hope of glory"; "Made after the image of God's own Son." Thank God it is of grace![48]

The Will: Becoming What We Are

The positional change in sanctification can now be lived out in progressive change. The deduction that we should continue in sin because we are justified by grace is a "monstrous" suggestion. The inevitable practical deduction is quite the opposite: "we are delivered from sin and the practice of sin."[49]

The Doctor reminds us that believers experience a change with respect to the Devil. The world lies in his grip, but not believers. Positional sanctification means we have been lifted over the high rock wall of the Devil's field and have been transferred into Christ's field. The Devil now can only "shout across the road at us."[50] Therefore, every Christian who listens to him is a fool, because the Bible clearly proclaims our freedom. We don't have to go

---

47 Lloyd-Jones, *The New Man*, 26–27.
48 Lloyd-Jones, *God's Way of Reconciliation*, 139.
49 Lloyd-Jones, *The New Man*, 163.
50 Ibid., 27.

back to the old ways, but "like the slaves that had been set free, we tend to forget it, and when he speaks to us we listen to him and fall under his spell." Rather, we should resist him, and he will flee (James 4:7).[51]

The believer also has a fundamentally different relationship with sin. He is no longer a slave to sin but a slave to righteousness. Sin is now a departure from our true identity in Christ. It is choosing to align with a contradictory identity. Lloyd-Jones declares that a Christian "does not sin as a slave, but as a free man who is choosing to do that which is wrong."[52]

Sin must not be coddled, but killed. The believer must put sin to death and make no provision for it to reign. Progressive sanctification means becoming an active participant in the process of pruning. In a vivid illustration of the relationship between regeneration and mortification, the Doctor asks the reader to imagine a pear tree:

> You may be anxious, for instance, to grow a certain type of pear. Now a way in which it is often done is this: you are given just a graft, a portion, a shoot, of the variety you like. Then you take a common wild pear tree and hack into it and into that wound which you have made in the tree, you put this shoot, this sprout. Then you bind them together. And eventually you will have a wonderful pear tree, producing nothing but your chosen variety of pear.
>
> But in the meantime you have many things to do. You do not merely leave it at that. What happens is that the strength and the power, as it were, the life and the sap that comes up through that wild pear tree, will enter into this shoot and it will produce fruit. Yes, but below the level of the grafting, the wild pear tree will still tend to throw out its own wild shoots and branches and want to produce its own fruit. So you have to lop off these natural branches. You have to cut them, prune them right down and, if you do that, a time will arrive when the tree will produce only this wonderful type of pear that you are anxious to grow.
>
> You see, at first you seem to have two natures in the one tree, but if you prune off the old the new will gradually master the whole and you will eventually have a pear tree which is producing the type of fruit that you want. Now that seems to me to be incomparably the best illustration that has ever been used with regard to this matter. You are putting new life in so that at one stage you have got one tree but with two natures—the cultured, cultivated nature, and the wild nature. Yes, but if, by pruning off

---

[51] Ibid.
[52] Ibid., 128–29.

these wild branches, you see to it that the strength of that tree is only allowed to go into the grafted-in branch, not only will that be strengthened and bear its fruit, it will gradually conquer and master the other. It seems to have a power to send its life down into the old until eventually you have the excellent pear tree that you desired at the beginning.[53]

The grafting is regeneration, and the pruning is mortification (putting to death the deeds of the body). This new disposition we receive in regeneration will direct the process of sanctification toward pruning the wild shoots of sin in our lives. Regeneration and the ongoing power of the Spirit produce a love for holiness, a hatred for sin, and a power for obedience. The implanting of the new life and the indwelling of the Spirit give obedience an organic quality. This organic dimension of sanctification means one can view true Christianity as a living tree and false Christianity as a Christmas tree.

The difference between the non-Christian and the Christian is the difference between a Christmas tree on which people hang presents, and a living tree that bears fruit. They have to put them on the Christmas tree; it does not and cannot produce anything. But in the case of the growing tree it produces fruit. The fruit is no longer imposed from outside; it is something produced from the life, the sap and the power that are in the living tree.[54]

Conclusion: What God Has Joined Together

If dividing justification and sanctification is unthinkable because Christ is indivisible, then the church in every generation must examine where it is in danger of dividing these doctrines. Sanctification divorced from justification will inevitably degenerate into a deadly form of legalism. Justification divorced from sanctification will invariably drift into a deadly antinomianism that downplays obedience to Christ. An ugly irony of the unbiblical divorce of justification from sanctification is that stressing only one part of Christ's work eventually diminishes the fullness of Christ's work and the unity of his person.[55]

---

[53] Lloyd-Jones, *God the Holy Spirit*, 84–86.

[54] D. Martyn Lloyd-Jones, *The Sons of God: An Exposition of Romans 8:5–17* (Carlisle, PA: Banner of Truth, 1974), 36.

[55] Sinclair Ferguson reached very similar conclusions in his book on the topic of the Marrow controversy. See Ferguson, *The Whole Christ: Legalism, Antinomianism, and Gospel Assurance—Why the Marrow Controversy Still Matters* (Wheaton, IL: Crossway, 2016). Mark Jones makes a similar point in his critique of antinomianism. See Jones, *Antinomianism: Reformed Theology's Unwelcome Guest* (Phillipsburg, NJ: P&R, 2013).

CHAPTER 6

THE CHURCH

The Body of Christ and the Bride of Christ

If the Church had been left to us, and to people like us, the story would have ended long ago.

D. MARTYN LLOYD-JONES [1]

Introducing the Doctrine

There is a logical inevitability once again with the doctrines. The Church could never exist as the bride of Christ without the saving work of Christ. No one would ever see Christ and believe in him without the Spirit, who is given to glorify Christ. Individual believers would never have come together in the body of Christ without the work of the Spirit baptizing them into the body. Lloyd-Jones's lecture on the church was immediately preceded by the discussion of spiritual gifts to build up the church. The Spirit gave these gifts as he willed *for the church*, and now the inevitable next step is to explore the doctrine *of the church*. [2]

Defining the Doctrine

The Doctor unpacks the doctrine of the church by making four key distinctions, between (1) the kingdom of God and the church of Christ, (2) the invisible church and the visible church, (3) biblical unity and ecumenical

---

[1] *Assurance: An Exposition of Romans 5* (Carlisle, PA: Banner of Truth, 1998), 333.
[2] D. Martyn Lloyd-Jones, *Great Doctrines of the Bible: The Church and the Last Things* (Wheaton, IL: Crossway, 1998), 1–2.

unity, and (4) right and wrong understandings of the marks of the church. Each of these doctrinal distinctions must be firmly grasped before they can be applied in the next section.

The Distinction between the Kingdom of God and the Church of Christ

The essential difference between the church and the kingdom is that the church is an "expression" of the kingdom, but cannot be "equated" with it.[3] The kingdom of God is "wider and bigger than the Church," because it is the "rule and reign of God" over everything. The church is an expression of the kingdom "wherever the Lord Jesus Christ is acknowledged as Lord."[4] If the church is a manifestation and materialization of the kingdom, then one must look in more detail at how the church manifests God's rule and Christ's lordship.

The Distinction between the Spiritual, Invisible Church and the Local, Visible Church

One must distinguish between the church as a general idea and the church as a local or particular idea. A few biblical instances of the word translated "church" have the wider sense (Acts 9:31; 1 Cor. 12:28; Eph. 1:22–23; 3:10; 5:23–32).[5] But the majority of instances have a local, not universal sense. When applied to Christians in the New Testament, the word most often refers to a local assembly of Christians (e.g., the church at Rome or the churches of Galatia).

The Doctor looks at the phrase "churches of Galatia" (Gal. 1:2) and discerns an important distinction over against the ecumenical movement. He declares that Paul speaks not of "one unit divided in local branches" but of individual churches or a plurality of units in Galatia.[6] When Paul refers to a group of Christians meeting in the home of Aquila and Priscilla, he does not hesitate to call the gathering a "church" ("the church in their house"— Rom. 16:5). Paul is not thinking in terms of "the great ecumenical ideal, according to which *the Church* is the great thing."[7]

The New Testament also uses many pictures or analogies for the church: (1) body, (2) temple, (3) bride, and (4) empire/citizens. Lloyd-Jones's

---

[3] Ibid., 4.
[4] Ibid.
[5] Ibid., 6.
[6] Ibid., 5.
[7] Ibid.

survey shows that the church is a spiritual and invisible reality, but it has visible or local manifestations in specific places like Corinth or Rome. This distinction between the invisible and the visible, or the spiritual and the local, is vitally important. One cannot be a Christian without being a member of the spiritual and invisible church. Christians are members of Christ's body. However, one can be a Christian without being a member of the visible and local church (though one *should* be a member). One can also be a member of the visible and local church and not be a member of the spiritual and invisible church.[8]

This distinction was personal to Lloyd-Jones because of something that happened to him at age fourteen.

> When I was personally received as a full member of the Christian church in which I was brought up, I was asked one question only. I was asked to name the brook which our Lord and the disciples had to cross while going from the Upper Room to the place of trial. I could not remember the answer to that question; nevertheless I was received into the full membership of the church. That literally is what happened to me at the age of fourteen.[9]

The Doctor lays great stress on regenerate church membership because he believes he was not regenerate when he became a member at his local church. The membership roll of a local church should align—as far as we can tell—with the Lamb's book of life. The names on the local church membership roll should be names that are already written in heaven.

The Distinction between Biblical Unity and Ecumenical Unity

This discussion of the importance of the local church raises questions about how local churches ought to relate to one another. Should churches automatically regard other assemblies as true churches and have unity on that basis?

As Lloyd-Jones's childhood experience illustrates, the ecumenical movement has tended to minimize doctrinal definitions of what makes someone a Christian. Rather, people should be accepted as Christians if they claim to be Christians. In the same way, churches that claim to be

---

8 Ibid., 7. When he surveys church government in the next lecture, Lloyd-Jones argues that the independent conception of the church (e.g., Congregationalist) has the most scriptural support (ibid., 23).

9 D. Martyn Lloyd-Jones, *Christian Unity: An Exposition of Ephesians 4:1–16* (Grand Rapids: Baker, 1981), 61.

Christian should be regarded as true Christian churches and should join together in unity, according to this view.

The Doctor firmly believes that such ecumenical unity is a far cry from biblical unity. Unity in the pages of the New Testament is something spiritual and doctrinal at its core. When Jesus speaks of unity in John 17, he asks that believers be one as he and the Father are one (17:21–22). These believers are defined as those who acknowledge that the Father sent Jesus (17:8).

> So our Lord's words about unity are only applicable to people who believe that particular doctrine, and if people tell me that they are Christians but say that Jesus was only a man, then I have no unity with them. I do not belong to them. They may call themselves Christians, but if they have not believed and accepted this, there is no basis for unity.[10]

Lloyd-Jones surveys text after text to show that believers cannot have church unity without unity around the apostle's teaching (Acts 2:42; 1 John 2:19; 2 John 10–11).[11] John the elder is crystal clear in his insistence upon unity of doctrine in 2 John 10–11, the Doctor explains: "The significance he attaches to doctrine and to truth is so great that he says, in effect, 'You mustn't receive the man into your house because if you do you're encouraging him. If you give him a meal and send him on his journey you are encouraging his false doctrine. Don't do it.'"[12] If there are spiritual and doctrinal marks that make one church true and another church false, then those marks must be clearly stated and explained.

The Distinction between Right and Wrong
Understandings of the Marks of the Church

Lloyd-Jones teaches that there are three marks of a true church: (1) the Word is truly preached, (2) the sacraments are truly administered, and (3) discipline is truly exercised. Preaching is the primary business of the church, and preaching should have two main objects in view: upbuilding the saints and evangelizing the lost. The church is "essential to believers," because conversion means they are "born as babes in Christ" and desperately need to be "instructed" and "warned against error and safeguarded against heresy."[13] Preaching must also focus on proclaiming the good

---

10 Lloyd-Jones, *The Church and the Last Things*, 8.
11 Ibid., 9–10.
12 Ibid., 10.
13 Ibid., 13.

news of salvation to the lost. This task is a vital concern of Jesus's prayer in John 17. Jesus makes it clear that he is sending the disciples so that others would believe in him through them.[14]

The sacraments must be rightly understood in order to be rightly administered. Sacraments are means of grace that build up, encourage, and strengthen the church.[15] The Doctor affirms the traditional Protestant understanding of the sacraments. Grace comes "through the word of God and the application of the word of God by the Holy Spirit and through the sacraments."[16] That understanding stresses that the sacraments must never be "separated from the word."[17] A sacrament is also "an outward, visible sign of an inward, spiritual grace."[18]

The Doctor stresses that the sacraments were not invented by man but instituted by Christ in order to aid the church:

> It is our Lord Himself who commanded His people to do these things. And there can be very little doubt but that His reason was to call in the aid of something which can be seen, to help that which has been heard. Now most people are undoubtedly helped by seeing things. That is why when we teach children the alphabet, we generally do it in the form of pictures. We say, "A for Apple," and show a picture of an apple, and the child remembers the picture. Children are always helped by pictures; it is easier to learn things by having a visual representation than by just listening.[19]

The Doctor then asks what the relationship is between the physical symbol and the spiritual grace. He parts ways both with the Roman Catholic view (grace is contained in the symbol itself, so it is received mechanically by eating the bread or being sprinkled with the water) and with the Zwinglian view (there is no grace in the symbol; the grace comes only as one remembers or commemorates what it means). Lloyd-Jones takes the more traditional Reformed view, in which the symbol is both a sign and a seal of grace. A seal on a document does not add to a document; it authenticates the contents of the document. A wedding ring does not add to the content of the promises; wearing the wedding ring authenticates and seals the promises already made.

---

[14] Ibid., 13–14.
[15] Ibid., 25.
[16] Ibid., 26.
[17] Ibid.
[18] Ibid., 27. Lloyd-Jones is here following the language of Augustine.
[19] Ibid.

Lloyd-Jones goes one step further as he follows the teaching of the Westminster Confession. The sacraments are not just signs and seals of grace but also displays through which grace is conveyed. One may object that this teaching is inconsistent in that now it sounds like something is being added, in that it is conveyed. The Doctor argues that this teaching is not the same as Roman Catholic theology (in which the symbol actually contains the grace). He goes back to the wedding ring analogy. The woman has already received the man's love and promises, but she *feels* as though she now has received something extra in that she is receiving his love in a special way that she had not before. The ring is a sign and seal and a display of what she really has, and it gives her an extra sense of "assurance to confirm what she already knows and believes."[20]

Therefore, baptism and the Lord's Supper signify, seal, and convey a special sense of grace in a direct, personal way. Jesus commanded these things in order to say essentially, "Now this is the way that I have chosen to tell you that my grace is given to *you* in particular."[21] The sacraments also function as a "visible badge or sign of our membership of the Church."[22]

What do the sacraments specifically signify and seal? Baptism "is a sign and seal of (1) our remission of sins and our justification," (2) "our regeneration, . . . our union with Christ, and . . . our receiving of the Holy Spirit," and (3) our "membership of the Church, which is His body."[23] The Lord's Supper is a sign and seal of (1) Christ's "broken body and shed blood," (2) "a believer's participation in the crucified Christ," and (3) a believer's participation "in all the benefits of the new covenant."[24]

The Doctor diagnoses that the doctrine of church discipline is sorely neglected:

> Indeed, if I were asked to explain why it is that things are as they are in the Church; if I were asked to explain why statistics show the dwindling numbers, the lack of power and the lack of influence upon men and women; if I were asked to explain why it is that so many churches seem

---

[20] Ibid., 30. The reader could find a more detailed discussion of this point in Keith A. Mathison, "The Lord's Supper," in *Reformation Theology: A Systematic Summary*, ed. Matthew Barrett (Wheaton, IL: Crossway, 2017).

[21] Lloyd-Jones, *The Church and the Last Things*, 31.

[22] Ibid.

[23] Ibid., 38–39. Lloyd-Jones argues that only adult believers should be baptized because it is not just a sign but also a seal of what has taken place. He also argues that one should allow for either sprinkling or immersion as the mode of baptism (ibid., 45).

[24] Ibid., 50–51.

to be incapable of sustaining the cause without resorting to whist drives and dances and things like that; if I were asked to explain why it is that the Church is in such a parlous condition, I should have to say that the ultimate cause is the failure to exercise discipline.[25]

Some try to justify a neglect of discipline by appealing to the parable of the wheat and the tares (Matt. 13:38). Some say that exercising discipline would be like uprooting the tares, which the Lord said not to do until the final harvest. The Doctor says that this view fails to understand the distinction made earlier between the church and the kingdom. Matthew 13 is a parable of the kingdom, and the field in which the wheat and tares are sown is the world, not the church (13:38). Within the world, there are two groups: those who belong to Christ and those who belong to the Devil. The church is an expression of the kingdom, but the two are not synonymous.

Churches must exercise church discipline in two areas: doctrine and life.

> We must, therefore, exercise discipline with regard to doctrine and equally we must exercise it with regard to life and living because if the members of the Christian Church are deniers of her doctrine in their lives and in their practice, who is going to believe it? It is the negation of our Lord's words: "Let your light so shine before men, that they may see your good works, and glorify your Father which is in heaven" (Matt. 5:16).[26]

If people do not start with doctrine, they will drift into seeker-driven pragmatism that does whatever it takes to draw people. The church must recover the doctrine of what it is called to be. It must be doctrinally driven, not seeker driven. "The greatest need of all today is a true and an adequate conception of the nature of the Christian Church. It is because we who belong to her lack this that we fail to attract those who are outside."[27]

---

25 Ibid., 14. The Doctor also observes that times of revival bring with them a revival of church discipline. He relays a story from John Wesley's journal in which Wesley visited a church in Dublin that had six hundred members. A few days later after Wesley had examined them all, there were only three hundred. The Doctor asks, "What would John Wesley do today if he returned?" (ibid., 17–18).
26 Ibid., 17.
27 D. Martyn Lloyd-Jones, *God's Way of Reconciliation: An Exposition of Ephesians 2* (Grand Rapids: Baker, 1972), 394.

Applying the Doctrine

The doctrine of the church gives guidance in four areas for the Christian life: (1) impressions of the church, (2) expectations of the church, (3) experiences in the church, and (4) praying for the church.

Impressions of the Church

Think through the impressions we get from others and the impression we give to others about church attendance.

> Do we give the impression when we come to our places of worship that we are doing the most wonderful and thrilling thing in the world? Are we alive, are we rejoicing? How do we compare with these other people? A staid, lifeless Christian is a denial, in many respects, of the gospel at its most glorious point. To be heavy-footed, slow-moving, lethargic, having to be whipped up and roused constantly, and urged to do this and that instead of running to it, and rejoicing in it, is a sad misrepresentation of Christianity.[28]

Church attendance as a lifeless routine lies about the gospel. Why? Lifeless church attendance says that happiness is found somewhere else, outside the church of Jesus Christ. Is our real happiness to be found outside the church in what the world has to offer? The idea that our real happiness is found on the television or on the golf course or on the beach is an "utter denial" of the "whole of the New Testament."[29]

Expectations of the Church

Lloyd-Jones says that "a dead church is a contradiction in terms."[30] How can a church avoid being a contradiction in terms? This is where expectations matter. A nonbiblical conception of the church will lead to nonbiblical expectations of the church. "The church is not a place where people are to be entertained, or where people come to sit and listen either to singing or to the accounts of other people's experiences, coupled with a brief, light, comfortable message."[31] If the church is a place of entertainment and de-

---

[28] D. Martyn Lloyd-Jones, *The Christian Soldier: An Exposition of Ephesians 6:10–20* (Grand Rapids: Baker, 1977), 285.

[29] D. Martyn Lloyd-Jones, *Joy Unspeakable: Power and Renewal in the Holy Spirit* (Wheaton, IL: Shaw, 1984), 110.

[30] D. Martyn Lloyd-Jones, *Christian Conduct: An Exposition of Romans 12:1–12* (Carlisle, PA: Banner of Truth, 2000), 199.

[31] D. Martyn Lloyd-Jones, *God's Ultimate Purpose: An Exposition of Ephesians 1* (Grand Rapids: Baker, 1978), 424.

corum, the church is defined apart from the breath of the Spirit. The Doctor regarded the church of his day as "dying of decorum." Church services can be beautiful and well planned, but without the breath of the Spirit, the church will be a valley of dry bones.[32]

A biblical *conception* of the church should create biblical *expectations* of the church. What should we expect? "Paul's whole conception of the Church is that it is a place where God is working in the hearts of men and women."[33] The church building is a place where people of God gather to meet with the living God.

> [Some] go to God's house, not with the idea of meeting with God, not with the idea of waiting upon him, it never crosses their minds, or enters into their hearts that something may happen in a service. No, we always do this on Sunday morning. It is our custom. It is our habit. It is a right thing to do. But the idea that God may suddenly visit his people, and descend upon them, the whole thrill of being in the presence of God, and sensing his nearness, and his power, never even enters their imaginations. The whole thing is formal, it is this smug contentment.[34]

The Doctor reminds his own church members of the historical rationale for calling the church building a "meeting house." Even though the church building is a place where people meet with one another, the "essential meaning" is that the church is the place where, Sunday by Sunday, we say to ourselves, "We are going to meet with God."[35]

Experiences in the Church

A nonbiblical conception of the church will lead to nonbiblical expectations of the church and nonbiblical experiences in the church. But a biblical conception of the church will lead to biblical expectations and biblical experiences.

What happens when God meets with his people? His presence is healing for the soul. The "house of God has delivered me from the 'mumps and measles of the soul' a thousand times and more—merely to enter its doors."[36]

32 D. Martyn Lloyd-Jones, *The Christian Warfare: An Exposition of Ephesians 6:10–13* (Grand Rapids: Baker, 1976), 284.
33 D. Martyn Lloyd-Jones, *The Life of Joy: An Exposition of Philippians 1 and 2* (Grand Rapids: Baker, 1989), 38.
34 D. Martyn Lloyd-Jones, *Revival* (Wheaton, IL: Crossway, 1987), 72.
35 Ibid., 162–63.
36 D. Martyn Lloyd-Jones, *Faith on Trial: Studies on Psalm 73* (Grand Rapids: Baker, 1965), 39.

If healing and encouragement come in the midst of the gathered assembly, then those who forsake assembling together are forsaking that grace. Lloyd-Jones states that his experience has taught him that "those who are least regular in their attendance are the ones who are most troubled by problems and perplexities."[37]

The ministry of the Word will also have an effect upon the people. The sermon will not be a performance that people judge. They will not sit back "in a detached manner" and rate the speaker according to what quotation or illustration they liked. True preaching transforms the whole dynamic of the "audience." One moment the listener acts as the judge, but suddenly the same listener realizes that he or she is under the Word and thus under judgment, because God is the audience. When this happens, the listener no longer asks, "How did the preacher do?" The listener now evaluates how his or her own soul has fared under the ministry of the Word.[38]

True preaching is God acting upon the people through the Spirit. The Doctor diagnoses what happens to people when the Spirit makes his presence felt:

> What about the people? They sense it at once; they can tell the difference immediately. They are gripped, they become serious, they are convicted, they are moved, they are humbled. Some are convicted of sin, others are lifted up to the heavens, anything may happen to any one of them. They know at once that something quite unusual and exceptional is happening. As a result they begin to delight in the things of God and they want more and more teaching.[39]

These biblical expectations of the church begin to expand our desires so that we earnestly long for an alignment of expectation and reality. This dynamic will enlarge our practice of prayer.

Praying for the Church

When experience and reality do not match, the Doctor says you should fall on your knees, remember what the church is, and look away from your own ability and to God for his power.

> Until the church is crushed to her knees, and has come to the end of her own power and ability, and looks to God for his power and the might of

---

[37] Ibid., 40.
[38] D. Martyn Lloyd-Jones, *Preaching and Preachers* (Grand Rapids: Zondervan, 1971), 56.
[39] Ibid., 325.

the Holy Spirit—until then I am certain that the declension will continue and even increase. When the church of God is in a state of eclipse and of apparent defeat, it is always because she has forgotten who she is, has forgotten her reliance upon God and has been trusting, in her folly, to her own ability and her own prowess.[40]

Lloyd-Jones would ask you a point-blank question: When did you last pray before attending a worship service that "the Spirit of God might come upon the preacher and use him and his message?"[41] If you are not praying that way, then you are merely looking to a man and trusting in him, not God.

Lloyd-Jones says that the "church should be the most exciting and thrilling place in the world." If it is not, then "we are somehow or other 'quenching the Spirit.'"[42] This statement calls for some serious soul-searching and prayer.

Conclusion: The Doctrine of the Church and Prayer

If we are going to pray rightly *for* the church, we must think rightly *about* the church. A true conception of the church is essential for brokenhearted praying.

> If only we had a true conception of the Christian Church! If we only re-ally saw her as she is in the New Testament, if we had but some dim and vague notion of what she was in the early years, and indeed in the early centuries, if we but really understood what she was like in every period of revival and re-awakening, then we would be heart-broken at the pres-ent condition. We would be grieved and filled with a sense of sorrow. Are we all troubled when we see something that once was great and famous going down or ceasing to be? The decline and fall of an Empire is a sad spectacle. It is a sad thing to see a great business going down. It is sad to see a great professional man losing his grip. It is sad to see a man who is great at sport suddenly, because of age, beginning to fail. It is something that always fills us with a sense of sorrow and of sadness. Well, multiply all that by infinity, and then try to conceive of the Church of God as she is in the mind of God, and as she was formed and founded, and contrast that with what she is today.[43]

---

[40] D. Martyn Lloyd-Jones, *Old Testament Evangelistic Sermons* (Carlisle, PA: Banner of Truth, 1996), 64–65.
[41] Lloyd-Jones, *Revival*, 124.
[42] Lloyd-Jones, *The Christian Warfare*, 280.
[43] Lloyd-Jones, *Revival*, 252–53.

The church of Jesus Christ urgently needs to recover the doctrine of the church. The question in every age is whether the church will be doctrinally defined or seeker driven. The impressions we receive, the expectations we have, the experiences we enjoy, and the petitions we pray will all flow in part from a right understanding of the church. May we heed the Doctor's call for the church of Christ to shine as the bride of Christ.

CHAPTER 7

THE LAST THINGS

Death and "the Glory"

[A Christian] is a man who can be certain about the ultimate even when he is most uncertain about the immediate.

D. MARTYN LLOYD-JONES[1]

Introducing the Doctrine

The doctrine of the last things is a culminating doctrine. It testifies to the final redemption and consummation in the future (the blessed hope). This doctrine also speaks comfort into the storm of present suffering while providing a powerful catalyst for obedience. "It is the blessed hope, it is that to which the Church is looking forward and at the same time, of course, it is the greatest incentive to holy living."[2]

This doctrine needs to be carefully defined. Lloyd-Jones stresses that the term "last times" covers the entire period from the first coming of Christ to his second coming.[3] The first and second comings have a surprising statistical relationship. The Doctor tabulates that "for every one reference to the first coming of Christ as the baby of Bethlehem, there are eight references to His final, His second, coming.[4]

---

[1] *The Final Perseverance of the Saints: An Exposition of Romans 8:17–39* (Carlisle, PA: Banner of Truth, 1975), 177.
[2] D. Martyn Lloyd-Jones, *Great Doctrines of the Bible: The Church and the Last Things* (Wheaton, IL: Crossway, 1998), 85.
[3] Ibid. 98.
[4] Ibid., 82–83.

If the doctrine of the last things is so important and essential in Scripture, then one has to wonder why it has been so neglected. The Doctor gives three reasons: (1) spiritual lethargy, (2) false teaching, and (3) caution from careful Christians in response to the extravagant teachings and obsessive tendencies of some.[5] The only way to overcome this neglect is to spend time carefully defining and unpacking the doctrine.

Defining the Doctrine

The doctrine of the last things generally divides into two categories: (1) our individual destiny and (2) the destiny of the whole world. They can be distinguished but not separated, because our personal destiny is bound up with something that will impact the entire cosmos.[6]

The doctrine of the second coming has a more specific focus within the larger doctrine of the last things. Two things are absolutely certain from Scripture: there is a wide array of terms for (1) Christ's return and its importance (*apocalypse, epiphany, parousia, day of God, day of the Lord*), as well as for (2) the manner of his coming (*personal, physical, visible, sudden, glorious*).[7]

The Doctor admits that the timing of Christ's coming is a complete mystery, because no one (not even the Son of Man) knows the day or hour (Mark 13:32): "Obviously, therefore, I shall not give you any help or indication whatsoever in a precise form as to when this second coming will take place."[8] He admits that his "whole endeavor was simply to concentrate on those things about which we can be absolutely certain and," he says, "I have already mentioned them."[9]

His aim in the rest of the lectures is to put the various viewpoints in front of the people for their consideration without any dogmatism. In fact, one of his aims for the lectures is a little counterintuitive when one first hears it.

> As for the rest, all I shall endeavor to do is put various views before you and ask you to weigh them in the light of the scriptural evidence, asking God to guide you. Indeed, I shall be very pleased if, by the end of this

---

[5] Ibid., 85–87.
[6] Ibid., 82.
[7] Ibid., 89–93.
[8] Ibid., 97.
[9] Ibid.

series of discourses, you feel less certain than you were at the beginning! I shall feel that I have achieved my object because if there is one subject about which dogmatism should be entirely excluded it is this.[10]

A proper approach to this doctrine will root out dogmatism on the things in Scripture that are not clear, but it will also cultivate a sense of confidence in the things that are clear. One of the clearest points in Scripture is that the ultimate purpose for everything is the glory of God. The Doctor comments on how to connect the last judgment to God's fame:

> What is the purpose of the last judgment? There is only one answer: it is for the glory of God. It is the final assertion of the glory of God in the presence of those who have not given Him the glory. The Bible says this, and for this reason: the essence of sin is that it refuses to give glory to God. When Satan stood up against God, he was attempting to detract from His glory. But the glory of God is supreme, it is over all, and redemption, salvation, will not be complete until the glory of God is again finally and completely established. And the glory of God is manifested not only in the salvation of those who belong to Him, but also in the punishment of those who have persisted in rejecting Him.[11]

Understanding that we will bask in the glory of God is much more important than knowing all the details of what heaven will be like. The blessed hope is that we shall be with the Lord forever (1 Thess. 4:17). Our "final destiny" will be one in which we are "ever enjoying the glory of God, basking in it, reflecting it, growing in it."[12]

The second coming and the last things also have an important part to play in daily life. The last judgment helps believers see the balance between justification by faith and the judgment according to works.

> There is a danger, I sometimes think, that in our emphasis upon justification by faith only, we fall into the error of forgetting this further differentiation on the basis of our works, of our faithfulness as Christian people. We have to fight for the great doctrine of justification by faith, it is constantly being attacked, but it would be a very grievous thing if, in

---

10 Ibid. The Doctor was an amillennialist (Christ rules today in his millennial reign in heaven, and so there is no need for a future thousand-year reign of Christ on earth), but he was not dogmatic on his position (ibid., 225).
11 Ibid., 241.
12 Ibid., 248.

asserting that, we in any way detracted from this other teaching which reminds Christian people that all their works are observed by the Lord, the righteous judge, and that what you and I do as Christians in this world will have an effect upon our life in glory in the next world.[13]

It is unthinkable that the doctrine of the last things should lead us to become lax about holy living. Scripture tells a very different story.

> Our concern about the second coming of the Lord should always be in terms of our relationship to Him, and unless it has the effect upon us of making us strive to be holy and to be ready for that great day, then there has been something wrong in the way we have been approaching it: "Every man that hath this hope in him purifieth himself, even as he is pure" (1 John 3:3). Unless you are filled with a desire to be purified, and are determined to purify yourself, then either I shall have failed very badly in what I have been saying, or else you will not have been listening to what I am saying! That is the context and we must never forget it. So we must examine our motives.[14]

Applying the Doctrine

There are at least three ways to apply this doctrine of the second coming and the last times: (1) examine yourself now; (2) don't fear death; and (3) live in light of the future now.

Examine Yourself

The Doctor says that the "ultimate test" of self-examination is whether we are "living for this world" or "for the one to come."[15] Part of self-examination should be dying to ourselves and surrendering all worldly claims upon our lives. We must die to ourselves *before* we die physically. Life and freedom are found on the other side of that first death. Lloyd-Jones gives the example of George Müller of Bristol, the founder and establisher of Müller's Homes. He was able to live so fully for the Lord because he died so completely to himself long before his physical death.[16]

---

13 Ibid., 246.
14 Ibid., 96.
15 D. Martyn Lloyd-Jones, *Authentic Christianity: Studies in the Book of Acts* (Wheaton, IL: Crossway, 2000), 125.
16 D. Martyn Lloyd-Jones, *The Christian Warfare: An Exposition of Ephesians 6:10–13* (Grand Rapids: Baker, 1976), 343.

One should not wait for old age to start the process of self-examination. Old age, however, offers a unique test that may surprise us with the realization that we have been living for something other than what we have thought. Many find their joy and meaning in their activities. And when these activities cease, they have nothing left to live for. So they give up completely and pass suddenly. Their activities prove to be all they have lived for. Old age can quickly reveal whether our hope is in this world or in the world to come.[17]

Have No Fear of Death

Our views of the last things will diagnose not only what we *live for* but also what we are *afraid of*. Some people say they believe that Christ defeated death, but they live as those defeated by the fear of death. Christ delivered believers not only from death but also from the paralyzing fear of it.[18] All the doctrines come into play as we face death. If we truly believe them, we will not fear death. "When a man has a true grasp of the doctrine of justification by faith he no longer has a fear of death, no longer a fear of the judgment."[19] The justified person already knows the final judgment because the verdict has been rendered: Not guilty!

One also need not fear death because of what death brings: translation into the presence of Christ.

> Let the bombs fall, let war come, let disease and pestilence ravage the lands, let me die—what is it? Translation! To be with him! This old body of mine, the body of my humiliation, the body of infirmity, the body of disease, the body of death, transfigured, changed, glorified, made like the body of Christ's resurrection, and I, in this new, glorified body, ushered into his blessed presence to spend my eternity with him. It is because they knew things like that that these people were filled with gladness.[20]

The Lord Jesus delivered believers from the fear of death through a greater sense of glorious anticipation. Death is gain (Phil. 1:21) because the Christian "knows where he is going." The Christian "is not only not afraid; there is a sense of anticipation."[21]

---

[17] D. Martyn Lloyd-Jones, *Expository Sermons on 2 Peter* (Carlisle, PA: Banner of Truth, 1983), 49–50.
[18] D. Martyn Lloyd-Jones, *Liberty and Conscience: An Exposition of Romans 14:1–17* (Carlisle, PA: Banner of Truth, 2003), 123.
[19] D. Martyn Lloyd-Jones, *Assurance: An Exposition of Romans 5* (Carlisle, PA: Banner of Truth, 1998), 21.
[20] Lloyd-Jones, *Authentic Christianity*, 198.
[21] D. Martyn Lloyd-Jones, *Studies in the Sermon on the Mount*, 2 vols. in 1 (Grand Rapids: Eerdmans, 1974), 318.

Don't Just Die Well—Live Well

The Doctor sums up the practical implications of the doctrine of the second coming in a compelling way: "If a philosophy of life cannot help me to die, then in a sense it cannot help me to live."[22] The Christian view of death is a homegoing. Our whole lives have been pointing in that direction (to know Christ!), and the believer arrives at that very place through the open door of death.

> That is the Christian view of death. It is going home, it is entering into harbor, "An entrance will be ministered unto you." Not a setting out on to an uncharted ocean, not going vaguely into some dim, uncharted world. Not at all, but an entrance into the haven, going home. What does it all mean? It means that the Christian dies like that because he knows God. He has striven diligently to know Him better and better. He knows Christ. He knows where he is going. He does not feel lonely as he is dying because Christ is with him. . . . So the fear of death is gone—he does not object to going because he knows exactly where he is going, and to whom he is going. He thinks also of the "abundant" entrance.[23]

Conclusion: The Eternal Optimist

The doctrine of the second coming helps a believer not just die well but also live well, because the believer knows for certain where he or she is going. Hardship and suffering have a disorienting effect, but the second coming enables believers to find their bearings. Lloyd-Jones celebrates that a Christian is someone "who can be certain about the ultimate, even when he is most uncertain about the immediate."[24] Therefore, the Christian is an eternal optimist. The hope of what life will look like in ten thousand years has a powerful impact on what life can look like today.

> The Christian knows that that Christ who is now in the heavenly places will come again to this world in a visible form, riding upon the clouds of heaven, surrounded by the holy angels and the saints who are already with Him; and those who remain on earth when He comes will be changed and will rise into the air to meet Him, and all will be "for ever with the Lord." He will rout His enemies, and banish sin and evil. His kingdom

---

22 D. Martyn Lloyd-Jones, quoted in Dick Alderson, compiler, "The Wisdom of Martyn Lloyd-Jones: Selections of Sayings," *Banner of Truth*, no. 275 (August-September, 1986): 7–12.
23 Lloyd-Jones, *Expository Sermons on 2 Peter*, 50–51.
24 Lloyd-Jones, *The Final Perseverance of the Saints*, 177.

shall "stretch from shore to shore" and He shall be acclaimed as Lord by "things that are in heaven and on the earth and things that are under the earth" (Philippians 2:10). That is Christian optimism, and it means that we know that it is Christ alone who can and will conquer.[25]

That vision of glory has a decisive impact on how we live today. The Doctor points out that 1 John 3:3 ("Everyone who thus hopes in him purifies himself as he is pure") immediately follows 1 John 3:2 ("Beloved, we are God's children now, and what we will be has not yet appeared; but we know that when he appears we shall be like him, because we shall see him as he is"). The order matters because it shows how a vision of future glory gets translated into everyday life.

> There is a sense in which we can say that the whole object of verse 2 is to lead to verse 3, and if we fail to regard the second verse in that light, if we fail to see that its real object and purpose is to prepare the way for this third verse, then we have abused the second verse entirely, and we have failed to appreciate its true message to us. . . . You and I, having had a vision of glory, have to come down and translate it into practice and put it into daily operation, and if it does not lead to that, then we are abusing the Scripture.[26]

We will see how the Doctor himself preached that the hope of glory is the essential acid test of one's Christian profession when we come to chapter 13.

25 D. Martyn Lloyd-Jones, *God's Ultimate Purpose: An Exposition of Ephesians 1* (Grand Rapids: Baker, 1978), 80.
26 D. Martyn Lloyd-Jones, *Life in Christ* (Wheaton, IL: Crossway, 2002), 296.

PART 3

THE CHRISTIAN LIFE

Lloyd-Jones believes that doctrine must always precede life. Therefore, the Christian life is the consistent outworking of biblical doctrines in the power of the Holy Spirit. Part 2 attempted to define those doctrines and then highlight the organic connection between each doctrine and its application. Part 3 goes further as it considers some of the complexities of living the Christian life. We have the opportunity to hear the Doctor's counsel about Christian disciplines like Bible reading (chap. 8) and prayer (chap. 9). We also receive more instruction on what faith working through love looks like in the life of a believer (chap. 10), especially in the spheres of the home and work (chap. 11). The Doctor also provides a prescription for how to face difficulties like spiritual depression (chap. 12) and death (chap. 13). Each chapter will feature the same structure in order to clarify the flow of discussion. In recognition of the Doctor's medical cast of mind, I will utilize the deductive structure of (1) definition, (2) diagnosis, and (3) prescription. I will also include a generous number of block quotations to preserve some of the heraldic quality of the Doctor's writings.

CHAPTER 8

THE WORD

If you really believe that just to read a few verses and a short comment on them in a matter of five minutes, and to have a brief word of prayer, is adequate for your day, then I say that you do not know anything about the wiles of the devil.

D. MARTYN LLOYD-JONES[1]

Introduction

This section of the book takes the doctrines of the Christian life and applies them in ways that push past the resistance that comes from the world, the flesh, and the Devil. We begin with a definition of the Word and then move to consider what makes Bible reading so difficult. We close with the Doctor's prescription for facing these difficulties.

The Doctor's Definition—What the Word Is

Lloyd-Jones has a robust belief that the Bible is the divine Word of God. It is perfectly inspired without any mixture of error. The Doctor approaches the Word of God with the same sense of reverence one must have when approaching God himself. How could the Doctor maintain this belief that the Bible is God's Word if it is also the word of man? A doctrine of Scripture must stress at least three interrelated realities. The Bible is both (1) the

---

[1] *The Christian Warfare: An Exposition of Ephesians 6:10–13* (Grand Rapids: Baker, 1976), 153.

125

Word of God and (2) the word of man, because of (3) the superintending work of the Holy Spirit.

First, Scripture is *the inspired Word of God*. The fact that the Bible is God's Word means that it is both the revelation of God (personal revelation) and revelation from God (propositional revelation). It is *personal* revelation because God personally reveals himself in his Word. "I have no knowledge of God apart from what the Bible tells me."[2]

It is *propositional* revelation because the propositional content of all of it is revelation from God. The conviction that the very words are breathed out by God is often known as the doctrine of verbal plenary inspiration. The Doctor affirms that when the Bible speaks, God speaks. He claims that the Bible is the book of God in an exclusive sense: "There is no other book which is the voice of God."[3] Lloyd-Jones glories in the interchangeable use of the terms "God said," "the Spirit said," and "the Scripture said."[4]

The doctrine of inspiration upholds a key distinction between the original manuscripts and translations based upon them. "We believe that the Word of God is definitely inspired, but that does not mean that every translation is definitely inspired."[5] The Doctor accepts textual criticism and rejects higher criticism.[6]

Second, the Doctor also affirms that Scripture is *the word of man*. Each human author retained his own unique style and personality, and thus inspiration does not mean a "mere mechanical dictation."[7]

Third, the Doctor affirms that the Scriptures can be both the Word of God and the word of man only because of *the superintending work of the Spirit*. Lloyd-Jones holds that Scripture is the word of man, but not in a way

---

2 D. Martyn Lloyd-Jones, *Great Doctrines of the Bible: God the Father, God the Son* (Wheaton, IL: Crossway, 1996), 36.

3 D. Martyn Lloyd-Jones, *Evangelistic Sermons at Aberavon* (Carlisle, PA: Banner of Truth, 1983), 25.

4 D. Martyn Lloyd-Jones, *God's Sovereign Purpose: An Exposition of Romans 9* (Carlisle, PA: Banner of Truth, 1991), 166.

5 D. Martyn Lloyd-Jones, *Children of God: Studies in 1 John* (Wheaton, IL: Crossway, 1994), 74. The Doctor criticizes a narrow view of the Bible that ignores this distinction. He says that someone who boasts that he accepts the Authorized Version (KJV) "from cover to cover including all the commas as well" is a person who is "unaware of the problems of a translator and is probably equally oblivious of the nature of the writings in the earliest manuscripts and their lack of punctuation marks" (D. Martyn Lloyd-Jones, *Knowing the Times: Addresses Delivered on Various Occasions* [Carlisle, PA: Banner of Truth, 1989], 40).

6 "'Are you not suddenly becoming a higher critic?' No, I am not! I am a textual critic, and there is all the difference in the world between these two things. It is right that you should know the relevant texts and their relative value" (D. Martyn Lloyd-Jones, *Saving Faith: An Exposition of Romans 10* [Carlisle, PA: Banner of Truth, 1998], 292). He rejects higher criticism because it decides what should or should not be in a text based on "man's mind and opinion and philosophy" (Lloyd-Jones, *Liberty and Conscience: An Exposition of Romans 14:1–17* [Carlisle, PA: Banner of Truth, 2003], 95). Higher criticism as a whole reads the Bible like any other book and thus "denies a unique inspiration" and "certainly denies infallibility" (Lloyd-Jones, *God's Sovereign Purposes*, 80).

7 D. Martyn Lloyd-Jones, *Life in God: Studies in 1 John* (Wheaton, IL: Crossway, 1995), 130.

that detracts from its status as the Word of God. How could he maintain a "both–and" and not an "either–or" when it comes to the dual nature of Scripture? The Doctor affirms the doctrine of concursus: the Spirit controls the process of writing in a way that keeps the human authors from error without erasing their human personalities and styles.[8] Therefore, the Spirit's superintending work ensures that the word of man is the Word of God. The Bible makes this claim for itself: "Men spoke from God as they were carried along by the Holy Spirit" (2 Pet. 1:21). It is the word of man because *"men spoke,"* but it is also the Word of God because "men spoke *from God.*" The reason they spoke from God is that they were "carried along *by the Holy Spirit.*" The Spirit's superintending work ensured that there is a profound unity and wholeness to the Scriptures.[9] The Bible has "no contradictions."[10]

Lloyd-Jones also points to the promise of Jesus that the Spirit would guide his disciples into all truth. This promise was fulfilled in the writing of the New Testament.[11] God also guided the church in its confirmation of the canonical writings. The church did not make them the Word of God; the church recognized the writings that already were the Word of God.[12]

The Doctor frequently stresses that the Bible is one book with one theme and one message of salvation.[13] Rather than seeing a division between the Old and New Testaments, he sees the real division as "everything you get from Genesis 1:1 to Genesis 3:14; then everything from Genesis 3:15 to the very end of the Bible."[14]

At the beginning of this chapter, we saw the Doctor's glorious claim that the Bible is God's own personal revelation to us. It is a staggering thought, which ought to have a direct bearing upon how we approach the Word. We should approach God's Word the way we approach God himself: with reverence and awe.

> But, you see, already we are beginning to find that the Bible is nothing but a great book in which God has been pleased to reveal Himself. You

---

8 "We believe in the absolute control of the Spirit over the minds and thinking and style and everything else of the writers. He so controlled them that they were kept from error, but the Holy Spirit did not dictate to them mechanically, otherwise there would be no variation in the style" (D. Martyn Lloyd-Jones, *The Final Perseverance of the Saints: An Exposition of Romans 8:17–39* [Carlisle, PA: Banner of Truth, 1975], 159).
9 D. Martyn Lloyd-Jones, *Fellowship with God: Studies in 1 John* (Wheaton, IL: Crossway, 1992), 10.
10 Lloyd-Jones, *The Final Perseverance of the Saints*, 362.
11 D. Martyn Lloyd-Jones, *The Love of God: Studies in 1 John* (Wheaton, IL: Crossway, 1994), 123.
12 Ibid.
13 D. Martyn Lloyd-Jones, *Old Testament Evangelistic Sermons* (Carlisle, PA: Banner of Truth, 1996), 33, 128.
14 D. Martyn Lloyd-Jones, *Great Doctrines of the Bible: God the Father, God the Son* (Wheaton, IL: Crossway, 1996), 228.

cannot get away from revelation. It is God showing Himself, manifesting Himself, in order that we may know Him, in order that we may worship Him, in order that we may have fellowship with Him. So, then, once more we bear in mind the injunction to take our shoes from off our feet because the ground whereon we are standing is holy ground; once more we remind ourselves that God is not a phenomenon which we are to investigate, and that when we approach the attributes of God's great and eternal personality we are as far removed as can be imagined from the scientific procedure of dissection. No, no; we simply take what God has been pleased to tell us about Himself. We note it. We try to bear it in mind. And humbly, and full of worship and praise, we thank Him for His condescension.[15]

This last point poses a serious problem. If the Bible is as glorious as our doctrine about it affirms, then why does the Bible sometimes seem so dry and difficult to read? The Doctor says that the temptation is "to rush into action and apply various treatments." But "intelligent treatment must always be preceded by diagnosis."[16]

The Doctor's Diagnosis: The Difficulty of Bible Reading

The fact that a professing Christian finds Bible reading difficult cannot automatically cancel his or her claim to be a child of God. Several factors contribute to the difficulty, but I will limit myself to three main areas: (1) the Devil's attacks, (2) personal difficulties, and (3) biblical difficulties.

Difficulty 1: The Devil's Attacks

The apostle John says that young men who know God have the Word of God abiding in them and have overcome the Evil One (1 John 2:13–14). The logic seems to be that people were able to overcome a supernatural enemy only because they had a supernatural weapon: the Word of God. Lloyd-Jones believes that the Devil is always tempting us to ignore or downplay the Bible because it is such an effective weapon against him. The Doctor identifies a defect in the way C. S. Lewis portrays spiritual warfare in *The Screwtape Letters*:

It is a very interesting point to notice about *The Screwtape Letters* that C.S. Lewis does not deal with this question of not reading the Word. That is a

---

[15] Ibid., 59.
[16] D. Martyn Lloyd-Jones, *Truth Unchanged, Unchanging* (Wheaton, IL: Crossway, 1950), 37.

significant point which reveals a real defect in his teaching. The chief of the evil spirits of whom Lewis writes does not give any instruction to his underlings to prevent the believers from reading the Bible. But this is one of our main weapons.[17]

The Devil has many ways to tempt us to neglect the Bible. He can assault us with accusations designed to bury us under an avalanche of guilt and shame. Another favorite way is to convince us that the Bible is over our heads. "The devil is ever at hand to say to us, 'This or that is of no use to you, you cannot follow it, leave it to the theologians.'"[18]

Difficulty 2: Personal Challenges

Second, many personal challenges plague us when we read the Bible. We can feel weighed down by both physical factors (overwork, sleepiness, depression) and spiritual factors (paralyzing guilt, anxiety about the future, temptations and trials). These difficulties can come together in an oppressive way that causes us to feel far from God in a dry and weary land where we wander from the Word. Personal difficulties often open the door to a thousand other distractions that seem more appealing or less demanding. As a result, the Bible is not so much rejected as neglected.

We can also struggle to read the Bible because we are just plain lazy. We fall into the trap of breezy Bible reading that never lingers long enough to see the glory and beauty that are there.

I regard the Scripture and these great statements in it as being comparable to a great art gallery where there are famous paintings hanging on the walls. Certain people, when they visit such a place, buy a catalogue from the guide at the door, and then holding it in their hands walk round the gallery. They notice that Item number 1 is a painting by Van Dyck, let us say; and they say "Ah, that is a Van Dyck." Then they pass on hurriedly to Item number 2, which is perhaps a portrait by Rembrandt. "Ah," they say, "that's a Rembrandt, a famous picture." Then they move on to further Items in the same way. I grant that that is a possible way of viewing the treasures of an art gallery; and yet I have a feeling that when such a person has gone through every room of the gallery and has said, "Well,

---

17 D. Martyn Lloyd-Jones, *The Christian Warfare: An Exposition of Ephesians 6:10–13* (Grand Rapids: Baker, 1976), 152.
18 D. Martyn Lloyd-Jones, *The Law: Its Function and Limits. An Exposition of Romans 7:1–8:4* (Carlisle, PA: Banner of Truth, 1973), 189.

we have 'done' the National Gallery, let us now go to the Tate Gallery," the truth is that they have never really seen either of the galleries or their treasures. It is the same in regard to the Scriptures. There are people who walk through this first chapter of this Epistle to the Ephesians in some such manner as I have described, and they feel that they have "done" it. It is surely better to stand, if necessary, for hours before this chapter which has been given to us by God Himself through His Spirit, and to gaze upon it, and to try to discover its riches both in general and in detail.[19]

Sometimes it is difficult to read the Bible because it is hard to accept what it says about us. The Bible is "the only book in the world that tells me the truth about myself."[20] The Doctor notes that perhaps the "most difficult thing in the world is to read the Bible with an open mind."[21] In fact, we ought to read the Bible with "a shudder" and an "awful fright," because the Bible displays "man as he is and at his worst."[22] It contains a "terrible exposition" about our fallen condition.

> The Bible in the first instance is a terrible exposition and a graphic delineation of the effects of sin. That is why it gives all that history in the Old Testament; why, for instance, it shows a man like David, one of its greatest heroes, falling into gross sin, committing adultery and murder. Why does it do that? It is to impress upon us the effects of sin, to teach us that there is something in all of us that can drag us down to that, that we are all by nature false and foul and vile.[23]

Sometimes it is difficult to *swallow* what the Bible says, but at other times it is difficult to *understand* what the Bible says. The latter speaks to the Bible's interpretive challenges.

Difficulty 3: Interpretive Challenges

During my first pastorate, I convinced some members to read through the Bible systematically. They began in Genesis and never made it out. It did not feel like a well-watered oasis; it felt like a sweltering swamp of confusion and frustration. They did not feel spiritually fed and full; they felt baffled.

---

[19] D. Martyn Lloyd-Jones, *God's Ultimate Purpose: An Exposition of Ephesians 1* (Grand Rapids: Baker, 1978), 171.

[20] D. Martyn Lloyd-Jones, *Love So Amazing: An Exposition of Colossians 1* (Grand Rapids: Baker, 1995), 129.

[21] D. Martyn Lloyd-Jones, *The Heart of the Gospel* (Wheaton, IL: Crossway, 1991), 86.

[22] Lloyd-Jones, *Old Testament Evangelistic Sermons*, 236.

[23] D. Martyn Lloyd-Jones, *Studies in the Sermon on the Mount*, 2 vols. in 1 (Grand Rapids: Eerdmans, 1974), 307–8.

Lloyd-Jones believes that this type of experience is to be expected. Even Peter declared that some things in Paul's writings were difficult to understand (2 Pet. 3:16). Some passages and doctrines will cause difficulty until they are resolved in glory. Says the Doctor, "Eventually, I believe, in glory we shall be given an understanding of some of these things that baffle us now."[24]

As noted above, it is at this point that the Devil will sow sinister seeds of doubt in terms of our ability to read the Word. He whispers that perhaps we should just walk away and "leave it to the theologians."[25]

Now that the Doctor has diagnosed why Bible reading is often difficult, let us turn to consider his prescription for reading the Bible in the power of the Spirit.

The Doctor's Prescription: The Word and the Spirit

Lloyd-Jones has a three-part prescription for a Spirit-filled pursuit of Scripture. We must engage with Scripture (1) prayerfully, (2) wisely, and (3) corporately.

Prescription 1: Read the Bible Prayerfully

A posture of prayer is an open-ended invitation for the Spirit to take our Bible reading far beyond our fallen limitations. How does the Spirit empower our Bible reading through prayer? One could highlight several areas, but I will limit myself to two: the informational (head) and the attitudinal (heart).

First is *the Spirit's impact on our understanding of the information in the Bible.* Prayer cries out for the empowering illumination of the Spirit, which causes the light of what is really there in Scripture to shine forth with a greater force. We pray,

> Open my eyes, that I may behold
> wondrous things out of your law. (Ps. 119:18)

This illumination is essential because Bible reading is more than a physical act; it is a spiritual activity. We need to bring our intelligence to bear in this work, but our intelligence is not enough. "Every bit of intelligence

---

24 D. Martyn Lloyd-Jones, *Assurance: An Exposition of Romans 5* (Carlisle, PA: Banner of Truth, 1998), 251.
25 Lloyd-Jones, *The Law*, 189.

we possess is needed as we read the Scriptures; all our faculties and propensities must be employed. Even that is not enough; we must pray for the illumination and inspiration of the Holy Spirit."[26]

Second, *the Spirit's work also has an attitudinal dimension.* The Spirit works in the heart so that it is open and humbly ready to receive from God, not closed and arrogantly ready to question God. Prayerful Bible reading invites the Spirit to create a right attitude or disposition in the heart.

> Instead of rejecting it because you cannot understand it, get your spirit right, come back to the Word, try to consider it again, pray God to give you understanding and enlightenment. Nothing is more important, as you come to Scripture, than your spirit; it is much more important than your intelligence, or your training.[27]

Why is this work of the Spirit so necessary? Apart from the grace of God, fallen humanity has a disposition of presumption. Prayerful Bible reading is a seek-and-destroy mission against this fallen disposition of pride. Prayer is a full frontal assault on our natural tendency to lean on our own understanding or depend upon our own abilities. This work of the Spirit in the heart puts us in a posture of submission that overcomes our native rebellion. Pride would put us in opposition to God, contending for supremacy; humility puts us under God and his Word, ready to receive grace.

Prayer is not only a *request for* an attitude of humility; prayer is also an *act of* humility. Instead of opposing God in our pride, we humble ourselves under the mighty hand of God to receive grace. How do we humble ourselves? Peter says it is by "casting all [our] anxieties on him" (1 Pet. 5:7). Pride tells us to arrogantly carry our own anxieties instead of humbly casting them upon the Lord. The same principle is at work when we put ourselves under the Word. A submissive posture says that we trust in the Lord instead of leaning on our own understanding. We either humbly submit to the authority of Scripture or arrogantly make ourselves the authority. But, says Lloyd-Jones, "I am not big enough to be an authority; I am too fallible to be an authority. No man is capable of being such an authority. I either submit to the authority of the Scriptures or else I am in a morass where there is no standing."[28]

---

26 D. Martyn Lloyd-Jones, *The Unsearchable Riches of Christ: An Exposition of Ephesians 3* (Grand Rapids: Baker, 1979), 266.

27 Lloyd-Jones, *God's Sovereign Purpose*, 147.

28 Lloyd-Jones, *Assurance*, 222.

This humble attitude toward Scripture is a work of the Spirit in producing the fruit of faith. The posture of leaning on our own understanding reflects a demand to grasp everything before submitting and resting. Faith is a restful repose under the Word of God. Faith means that the mind and heart are at rest and, in a word, content. "I am content not to understand certain things in this life and in this world."[29] In the final analysis, contentment is found in God himself. The Doctor says that we must be "content to 'believe where we cannot prove,' to accept where we cannot understand, and to realize that the final synthesis is to be found in God's holy Being and character."[30]

Lloyd-Jones again places great stress on the proper order. Faith precedes knowledge because faith defines our approach to biblical knowledge.

> I think the New Testament does teach very clearly that our knowledge always follows our belief. It is like a horse drawing a carriage; they are bound together, and they are never separated, but the horse is always in front, and the carriage is being drawn by him. Belief, then knowledge— that is the position.[31]

Faith in the Word of an infinite God is the opposite of faith in our finite intellectual ability. God's infinity means that our puny intellects will sometimes feel defeated. We recognize that we are out of our depth whenever we approach the Word of God. We must humbly accept that God is God and we will not grasp all revelation with equal clarity. "There are certain final antinomies in the Bible, and as people of faith we must be ready to accept that. When somebody says, 'Oh, but you cannot reconcile those two,' you must be ready to say, 'I cannot. I do not pretend to be able to. I do not know. I believe what I am told in the Scriptures.'"[32]

Prescription 2: Read the Bible Wisely

Wise Bible reading has three main features: it is (1) systematic, (2) serious, and (3) careful.

First, wise Bible reading engages the Word systematically, not selectively or randomly. "My main advice here is: read your Bible systematically. The danger is to read at random, and that means that one tends to be

---

29 Ibid., 250.
30 Ibid., 252.
31 Lloyd-Jones, *The Love of God*, 147.
32 Lloyd-Jones, *God the Father, God the Son*, 95.

reading only one's favorite passages. In other words one fails to read the whole Bible."[33] A systematic approach to Scripture is the opposite of a pick-and-choose attitude toward the Bible.

> We are entirely confined to the Scriptures, and we can add nothing to them. Neither must we take anything from them. We are in no position to pick and choose from them. We cannot say, I believe this and I reject that, I rather like the teaching of Jesus, but I do not believe in miracles; I admire the way in which He died, but I do not believe that He was born of a virgin or that He rose in the body from the grave. The moment you begin to do that you are denying revelation. You are saying that your unaided human intellect is capable of judging revelation, and sifting it and finding what is true and what is false. That is to deny the whole principle of revelation, of the apostolate, and of this unique work of the Holy Spirit.[34]

Why are people tempted to take the pick-and-choose approach? The Doctor sees the problem as pursuing comfort first, not the revelation of God himself first. But those who take the former approach miss out on passages that should disturb us. "They only read certain parts of the Bible, and they say they find it very comforting, very nice. It never disturbs them, of course, because they want only comfort, that is what they go for, and they get nothing else. They take parts of the Scripture and leave the rest."[35] Believers should read systematically because the Bible speaks to every problem we face. "Here in this Book is a message that would solve every single problem of the human race."[36]

If the first feature of wise Bible reading focuses on breadth, the second emphasizes depth. One must approach the Scriptures in a serious and rigorous way, not a shallow and subjective way. The Doctor believes that too many people read the Bible superficially.[37] He says that the "first thing the Bible does is make a man take a serious view of life."[38] That serious view of life *from the Bible* requires a serious approach *to the Bible*, one that is rigorous and deep, not subjective and shallow. In fact, Lloyd-Jones is prepared to call a subjective, shallow reading of the Bible the "main

---

[33] D. Martyn Lloyd-Jones, *Preaching and Preachers* (Grand Rapids: Zondervan, 1971), 171.

[34] Lloyd-Jones, *The Unsearchable Riches of Christ*, 37.

[35] D. Martyn Lloyd-Jones, *The Righteous Judgment of God: An Exposition of Romans 2:1–3:20* (Carlisle, PA: Banner of Truth, 1985), 8–9.

[36] Lloyd-Jones, *Old Testament Evangelistic Sermons*, 130.

[37] "Our reading of the Scriptures is often far too superficial" (Lloyd-Jones, *Assurance*, 160).

[38] D. Martyn Lloyd-Jones, quoted in Dick Alderson, compiler, "The Wisdom of Martyn Lloyd-Jones: Selections of Sayings," *Banner of Truth*, no. 275 (August/September 1986): 7–12.

trouble" today: "I verily believe that the main trouble of most evangelical people today is that they read their Bibles too devotionally, which means, I say, subjectively."[39]

The Doctor fiercely objects to sentimental readings of Scripture that despise the depth of rigorous reading and doctrinal investigation:

> The Word of God does not merely give us general comfort, what it gives us always is an argument. There is nothing that I so dislike and abominate as a sentimental way of reading the Scriptures. . . . There are many people who read the Scriptures in a purely sentimental manner. They are in trouble and they do not know what to do. They say, "I will read a Psalm—it is so soothing . . ." That is not the way to read the Scriptures. . . . We can never bring too much of our intelligence to our reading of them, they are not merely meant to give general comfort and soothing—follow the argument; let them reason it out with you.[40]

Deep reading is like total immersion—a Bible bath. The benefits are incalculable. "Think of its ennobling and elevating character, of how you feel when you read it—truly as if you had a spiritual bath—how you are searched and examined and made to feel ashamed; and how good and noble desires are stimulated within you, and a longing after a better life."[41]

The third feature of wise Bible reading is a careful and skillful reading that rightly handles the Word. This type of reading requires careful interpretive principles that take into account the context and genre of a passage, but also the whole canon of Scripture.

The Doctor stresses the need to go back and examine the context of a passage. The more difficult the passage, the more one may need to back up to get a running start.

> In athletics, if you come up against a particularly high hurdle that you have to jump, you take a longer run! If you want to vault over it, you go further back. You do not try to lift yourself up over this very high hurdle from where you are on the ground. The further back you go, the longer your run, and the momentum will carry you over. That is a very valuable principle in the exposition of Scripture and the elucidation of some [of these] problems with which it present us.[42]

---

39 D. Martyn Lloyd-Jones, *Revival* (Wheaton, IL: Crossway, 1987), 96.
40 D. Martyn Lloyd-Jones, *Spiritual Depression: Its Causes and Its Cure* (Grand Rapids: Eerdmans, 1965), 253.
41 D. Martyn Lloyd-Jones, *I Am Not Ashamed: Advice to Timothy* (Grand Rapids: Baker, 1986), 47.
42 Lloyd-Jones, *Saving Faith*, 253.

Stepping back enables us to consider the context of a passage. We must sometimes see the forest to understand an individual tree.

> When a difficult section of Scripture like this confronts us, it is always good to stand back, as it were, and look at it as a whole first. Do not get immersed in the details immediately or you will be confused. Stand back; get hold of the main principle, and having seen that, it will be easier for you to master the various particular statements.[43]

Sometimes one must step back beyond the literary context, all the way to the canonical context of a passage. This principle is often described as reading Scripture in the light of Scripture. The Doctor states the principle succinctly: "If ever you come across a difficult passage, then try to find something similar that will help to cast light upon it."[44] In fact, he suggests that "it is a good and wise thing to gather together everything that Scripture has to tell us about the subject."[45] This approach refuses to develop a doctrine that stands in conflict with other clear statements of Scripture.[46]

This type of careful reading requires the patience of multiple readings, not the laziness and indifference of single readings.

> Do not be impatient with yourself when you are studying a difficult passage in Scripture; keep on, hold on, reading or listening; and suddenly you will find that not only do you know much more than you thought you knew, but you will be able to follow and to understand. It is necessary that one should say things like that from time to time, because the devil is ever at hand to say to us, "This or that is of no use to you, you cannot follow it, leave it to the theologians." Do not listen to him, but say, "I belong to the Christian family and I intend to listen and to read until I do understand it." Do that, and you will not only defeat the enemy, but you will soon find that you have an understanding.[47]

It is at this point that a believer must know the doctrine of Scripture and work out its application. What we believe about the Bible should lead to careful and constant readings of the Bible. This manner of reading flows

---

[43] Lloyd-Jones, *Assurance*, 189.
[44] D. Martyn Lloyd-Jones, *Great Doctrines of the Bible: The Church and the Last Things* (Wheaton, IL: Crossway, 1998), 220.
[45] Lloyd-Jones, *Life in God*, 116.
[46] Ibid. See also Lloyd-Jones, *The Law*, 148.
[47] Lloyd-Jones, *The Law*, 189.

downstream from the belief that every word of Scripture is precious and true and treasured because every word is breathed out by God. "Every term is important, every word counts, and therefore we must look at them and examine them carefully."[48]

Careful readings will be active readings in which we are alert and alive.

> Let us remind ourselves that when we are reading the Scriptures we must never take anything for granted; we must always be alert and alive, and always ready to ask questions. How easily one can miss the great blessings found in the very introduction to an Epistle . . . by simply sliding over the terms as if they did not matter![49]

As noted above, one obvious sign that our Bible reading is alert and alive is that we are peppering the Bible with questions. "If you really want to enjoy your reading and studying of the Bible, always ask it questions. So, when Paul says 'Wherefore,' you ask, 'Why did he say "wherefore"? What was his purpose and object in doing so here?' You then try to work out the answer."[50]

Prescription 3: Receive the Bible Corporately

The Doctor believed that God would often bless his Word with a special anointing when the church gathered to hear the Word preached. In these moments, the people of God would have the unique sense that they had met with the living God. The Doctor describes the impact of the Spirit upon the people in Spirit-filled preaching:

> What about the people? They sense it at once; they can tell the difference immediately. They are gripped, they become serious, they are convicted, they are moved, they are humbled. Some are convicted of sin, others are lifted up to the heavens, anything may happen to any one of them. They know at once that something quite unusual and exceptional is happening. As a result they begin to delight in the things of God and they want more and more teaching.[51]

When the people of God assemble as the church of Jesus Christ, Word and Spirit should come together with life-transforming power. Wherever our

---

[48] Lloyd-Jones, *Assurance*, 230.
[49] Lloyd-Jones, *God's Ultimate Purpose*, 138.
[50] Lloyd-Jones, *Assurance*, 171.
[51] Lloyd-Jones, *Preaching and Preachers*, 325.

experience falls short of this reality, the church must plead with God for power from on high.

Conclusion: A Living and Active Word

Lloyd-Jones would ask us if our approach *to* the Bible really matches our beliefs *about* the Bible. Do we really believe that the Bible is living and active (Heb. 4:12)? We open the Bible not just because we are pursuing God but also because we believe an open Bible is the way God pursues us. If the Bible is alive, then the Word becomes like the feet of God in active pursuit of us. If the Bible is alive, then the Word becomes like arms of God that grab hold of us. His voice speaks directly, not just to our minds but also straight to the heart.

> If you would know the love of Jesus "what it is," give Him opportunities of telling you. He will meet you in the Scriptures, and He will tell you. Give time, give place, give opportunity. Set other things aside, and say to other people, "I cannot do what you ask me to do; I have another appointment, I know He is coming and I am waiting for Him." Do you look for Him, are you expecting Him, do you allow Him, do you give Him opportunities to speak to you, and to let you know His love to you?[52]

The Doctor would counsel us to surround ourselves with Christian friends who will speak the Word to us. Don't forsake the assembly of believers. Go hear the Bible sung and heralded at a Bible-believing, Bible-singing, Bible-preaching church. The Doctor's prescription is to open the Word with a sense of expectation. It is a book like no other. Not only do we read it; it reads us. It discerns the thoughts and intentions of the heart (Heb. 4:12).

---

[52] Lloyd-Jones, *The Law*, 62.

CHAPTER 9

PRAYER

If your knowledge of doctrine does not make you a great man of prayer,
you had better examine yourself again.

D. MARTYN LLOYD-JONES [1]

Introduction

Sinclair Ferguson captures the essence of Lloyd-Jones's approach to prayer in an interview found in the documentary *Logic on Fire*: "He did not believe in prayer. He believed in God and therefore he prayed." [2] Prayer ceases to be prayer when it is divorced from the doctrine of God. Lloyd-Jones defines prayer, first and foremost, as communion with God.

The Doctor's Definition: Prayer and Doctrine

Private prayer takes place when a person gets on his or her knees in a worshipful act of communion with God. [3] The Doctor calls this "the noblest activity," because "the highest picture you can ever have of man is to look at him on his knees waiting upon God." [4]

Notice the Doctor's prescribed posture for prayer: kneeling. This

---

[1] Quoted in Dick Alderson, compiler, "The Wisdom of Martyn Lloyd-Jones: Selections of Sayings," *Banner of Truth*, no. 275 (August/September, 1986): 7–12.
[2] Sinclair B. Ferguson, in *Logic on Fire* (documentary), directed by Matthew Robinson (New Albany, MS: Media Gratiae, 2015), DVD.
[3] D. Martyn Lloyd-Jones, *Studies in the Sermon on the Mount*, 2 vols. in 1 (Grand Rapids: Eerdmans, 1974), 301.
[4] Ibid.

posture guards against presumption in prayer because it encourages submission.

> Now while I am talking, I am in control, and while I am discussing I am in control. Someone may be examining me, but I am still able to defend myself. When I am engaged in thought and meditation, I am still in control. But when I get on my knees in prayer, then, in a sense, I am doing nothing, I am submitting myself, I am abandoning myself before Him. It is He who is in control, it is He who is doing everything, and that is why prayer tests us in a way which nothing else can possibly do.[5]

Much more could be said about prayer beyond this basic definition, but not less. One's understanding of doctrine will shape prayer in absolutely indelible ways. Unpacking all the various ways that doctrine impacts prayer would fill up many books. We have space here for only five brief examples.

First, real prayer arises from a right assessment and adoration of God's greatness. We must be mindful of the fact that the God to whom we pray is infinite. He is free from all restrictions, all limitations, all boundaries. He is exalted as the cause of everything because the existence of everything depends upon him and derives from him. He is supreme over and above everything. We should never pray without reminding ourselves of God's infinity.[6] Small views of God lead to puny prayers.[7] Lloyd-Jones stresses that "great prayer is always the outcome of great understanding."[8] As our vision of God expands, the scope of our prayers will expand. "There is no limit, we are praying to the eternal and the illimitable God."[9]

Second, perhaps the greatest example of how doctrine and prayer belong together is the doctrine of the atonement. This doctrine doesn't just make prayer *understandable*; it makes prayer *possible*. No one could come into God's presence in prayer without the atonement. People "cannot pray without doctrine; they cannot go into the presence of God except 'by the blood of Jesus.'"[10]

---

[5] D. Martyn Lloyd-Jones, *The Children of God: Studies in 1 John* (Wheaton, IL: Crossway, 1994), 124.

[6] D. Martyn Lloyd-Jones, *Great Doctrines of the Bible: God the Father, God the Son* (Wheaton, IL: Crossway, 1996), 53. When it comes to reconciling God's sovereignty and prayer, Lloyd-Jones says that we should not try to plumb the depths of the interrelationship. The Bible teaches both, and so we hold on to both. We hold on to the doctrine of God's sovereignty, and we pray. "I am not concerned about reconciling them. I cannot. Nobody else can. I imagine that in the glory we shall be given an explanation" (D. Martyn Lloyd-Jones, *Saving Faith: An Exposition of Romans 10* [Carlisle, PA: Banner of Truth, 1998], 9–10).

[7] "Shame on us for our puny prayers" (D. Martyn Lloyd-Jones, *Revival* [Wheaton, IL: Crossway, 1987], 61).

[8] Ibid., 293.

[9] Ibid., 314. He says, "There is no limit to what you should pray for, no limit at all" (ibid., 313).

[10] D. Martyn Lloyd-Jones, *The Final Perseverance of the Saints: An Exposition of Romans 8:17–39* (Carlisle, PA: Banner of Truth, 1975), 148. He makes this same point on multiple occasions. See D. Martyn Lloyd-Jones, *Assurance: An Exposition of Romans 5* (Carlisle, PA: Banner of Truth, 1998), 262.

Third, our prayers should faithfully reflect the doctrine of the Trinity in that each member of the blessed holy Trinity does a distinct work. This knowledge should shape, for example, the opening and closing of our prayers. Biblical prayers are most often addressed to God the Father and offered to him through Christ the Mediator.

> Many Christians seem to think that the hallmark of spirituality is to pray to the Lord Jesus Christ. But when we turn to the Scriptures we discover that that is not really so, and that, as here, prayers are normally offered to the Father. The Lord Jesus Christ is the Mediator, not the end; He is the One who brings us to the Father.[11]

The doctrine of the triune God is essential for prayer because all the members of the Trinity are actively involved in our very access to God. Paul gives profound testimony to this truth in the compact space of one verse: "*Through* him [Christ] we both have access *in* one Spirit *to* the Father" (Eph. 2:18). The prepositions here are profound. If prayer is addressed *to* God the Father and offered to him *through* Christ the Mediator, then prayer is carried *in* the Holy Spirit. This third reality (praying in the Holy Spirit) is a special emphasis for Lloyd-Jones. In fact, it is probably the area of his teaching on prayer that has profoundly challenged and shaped my prayer life more than any other. I will expound more on that theme near the end of this chapter.

Fourth, the doctrine of adoption is an essential element for confidence in prayer. "If we have eternal life, if we are His children, we, I say it with reverence, have the ear of God—we can be confident that He is always waiting to listen to us."[12]

Fifth, prayer cannot be divorced from the doctrine of God because prayer *is* communion with God. Lloyd-Jones says, "The thing that keeps one going in the Christian life is prayer—communion and fellowship with God; it is something which is absolutely essential. I would go further and say that the Christian life is really impossible without it."[13] Prayer does not *add* communion with God, to make it more meaningful; prayer *is* communion with God. Think through the implications of that. Because prayer is communion with God, our prayer life reflects the quality of our communion

11 D. Martyn Lloyd-Jones, *God's Ultimate Purpose: An Exposition of Ephesians 1* (Grand Rapids: Baker, 1978), 328.
12 D. Martyn Lloyd-Jones, *Life in God: Studies in 1 John* (Wheaton, IL: Crossway, 1995), 119.
13 D. Martyn Lloyd-Jones, *Children of God: Studies in 1 John* (Wheaton, IL: Crossway, 1994), 120.

with him. Lloyd-Jones sees prayer as "the greatest indicator of one's spiritual health" and "the ultimate test of a man's true spiritual condition."[14]

Therefore, a thriving prayer life reveals the vibrancy of our relationship with God, but a poor prayer life exposes the poverty of our relationship with God. These considerations cause us to ask the Doctor why we sometimes find prayer so difficult.

The Doctor's Diagnosis: The Difficulty of Prayer

Prayer as communion with God is a profound activity, but it can quickly prove profoundly difficult. "If you have never had difficulty in prayer, it is absolutely certain that you have never prayed."[15] Lloyd-Jones even goes so far as to say, "Everything we do in the Christian life is easier than prayer."[16]

Why is prayer so difficult? There are several factors. First, difficulty in prayer, as argued above, could point to the deeper problem of the poverty of our relationship with God. Do we talk to God far less than we talk to others? In fact, do we talk to God less when we are alone with him than when we are in the presence of others (e.g., small group prayer gatherings)? "Have we not all known what it is to find that, somehow, we have less to say to God when we are alone than when we are in the presence of others?"[17]

Second, the doctrine of sin explains the difficulty of prayer because sin so often pollutes prayer. Sin presents problems not merely when we are wandering far from God. The sinfulness of sin has its most chilling and horrid manifestation in prayer, in that it will "follow us to the gates of heaven, [and]—if it were possible—into heaven itself."[18] Lloyd-Jones explains:

> This thing that has entered into our very nature and constitution as
> human beings, is something that is so polluting our whole being that
> when man is engaged in his highest form of activity he still has a battle
> to wage with it. It has always been agreed, I think, that the highest picture

---

14 Lloyd-Jones, *Sermon on the Mount*, 46. See also D. Martyn Lloyd-Jones, *Authentic Christianity: Studies in the Book of Acts* (Wheaton, IL: Crossway, 2000), 173.
15 Lloyd-Jones, quoted in Alderson, "The Wisdom of Martyn Lloyd-Jones," 7–12. The Doctor says elsewhere that the person he worries about is the one who does not find prayer difficult: "there is certainly something wrong about him" (Lloyd-Jones, *The Assurance of Our Salvation: Studies in John 17* [Wheaton, IL: Crossway, 2000], 16).
16 Lloyd-Jones, quoted in Alderson, "The Wisdom of Martyn Lloyd-Jones," 7–12. The Doctor says similar things in many places. "I think a case should be made for saying the most difficult thing of all is to pray." See Lloyd-Jones, *Children of God*, 121.
17 Lloyd-Jones, *Sermon on the Mount*, 46.
18 Ibid., 300–301.

that you can ever have of man is to look at him on his knees waiting upon God. That is the highest achievement of man, it is his noblest activity. Man is never greater than when he is there in communion and contact with God. Now, according to our Lord, sin is something which affects us so profoundly that even at that point it is with us and assailing us. Indeed, we must surely agree on the basis of New Testament teaching that it is only there we really begin to understand sin.[19]

Sin pollutes our prayers through the intrusion of self. In prayer, a person comes face-to-face with the temptation "to think about himself," and in this self-focus and fixation a person finds himself "really to be worshipping himself rather than God."[20]

Third, some attempts at prayer fall far short of communion with God because they take place in the power of the flesh. Fleshly prayers fall into the ditch of either formalism or escapism. It is formalism when we simply say words and go through the motions and perform the mechanical ritual. It is escapism when we pray in order to avoid thinking through our problems. We all know what it means to go through the motions in prayer, but what about this notion of escapism? Listen to how the Doctor addresses this problem:

> Prayer is not a simple thing in one sense; it may be very difficult. Prayer is sometimes an excuse for not thinking, an excuse for avoiding a problem or a situation. Have we not all known something of this in our personal experience? We have often been in difficulty and we have prayed to God to deliver us, but in the meantime we have not put something right in our lives as we should have done. Instead of facing the trouble and doing what we knew we should be doing, we have prayed. I suggest that at a point like that, our duty is not to pray but to face the truth, to face the doctrine and to apply it. Then we are entitled to pray, and not until then.[21]

He repeats the same advice in his sermons on spiritual depression:

> There are particular problems in the Christian life concerning which I say that if you do nothing but pray about them you will never solve them. You must stop praying at times because your prayer may just be reminding

19 Ibid., 301.
20 Ibid.
21 D. Martyn Lloyd-Jones, *Fellowship with God: Studies in 1 John* (Wheaton, IL: Crossway, 1992), 13.

you of the problem and keeping your mind fixed upon it. So you must stop praying and think and work out your doctrine.[22]

Now that the Doctor has shown us why prayer is often difficult, let us turn to his prescription for praying in the Spirit.

The Doctor's Prescription: Praying in the Spirit

Lloyd-Jones prescribes praying in the Holy Spirit as the cure for the disease of our difficulty in prayer. He regards the inability to pray in the Spirit as the greatest hindrance to prayer.[23] Praying in the Spirit has four main steps: (1) admitting our inability; (2) enjoying a living communion with God; (3) pleading the promises of God with boldness, liberty, and assurance; and (4) obeying the Spirit's prompts to pray.

Step 1: Admitting Our Inability to Pray

Lloyd-Jones believes that it is "impossible" to engage in real prayer without the Spirit.[24] The doctrine of the fall becomes a felt doctrine in prayer. The Spirit brings us face-to-face with a startling sense of our "inability and our need of the Spirit."[25] Our attempts to pray leave us feeling dead and dull, and thus we find prayer to be a difficult task. "We must start praying by asking God to help us pray, acknowledging our lifelessness and our dullness and our slowness."[26] This step is not passive; it is the act of yielding ourselves to the Spirit. We wait for him expectantly and desperately because we know viscerally that only he can change the deadness and dullness of prayer and make it living and vibrant. This step of expectation leads to the second step of realization.

Step 2: Enjoying a Living Communion with God

Praying in the Spirit is the blessed union between the doctrine of the person and work of the Spirit and the practice of prayer. The Spirit gives life, and thus the Spirit makes prayer a "living act."

> We all know what it is to feel deadness in prayer, difficulty in prayer, to be tongue-tied, with nothing to say, as it were, having to force ourselves to

---

[22] D. Martyn Lloyd-Jones, *Spiritual Depression: Its Causes and Its Cure* (Grand Rapids: Eerdmans, 1965), 69.
[23] D. Martyn Lloyd-Jones, *Living Water: Studies in John 4* (Wheaton, IL: Crossway, 2009), 88.
[24] Ibid. "We could not pray at all were it not for the Holy Spirit" (D. Martyn Lloyd-Jones, *The Final Perseverance of the Saints: An Exposition of Romans 8:17–39* [Carlisle, PA: Banner of Truth, 1975], 138).
[25] Lloyd-Jones, *Living Water*, 86.
[26] Ibid., 93.

try. Well, to the extent that is true of us, we are not praying in the Spirit. The Spirit is a Spirit of life as well as truth, and the first thing that he always does is to make everything living and vital. And, of course, there is all the difference in the world between the life and the liveliness produced by the Spirit and the kind of artifact, the bright and breezy imitation, produced by people.[27]

Lloyd-Jones gives examples of counterfeit and artificial attempts at adding life to prayer meetings. Excessive structuring of prayer meetings can be an attempt to work up some artificial life through singing hymns and choruses or other methods, but if our confidence is in our planning, "it is all mechanical, it is all human and carnal."[28] By contrast, the Spirit makes prayer real so that it becomes a living communion with God.

> You are aware of a communion, a sharing, a give-and-take, if I may use such an expression. You are not dragging yourself along; you are not forcing the situation; you are not trying to make conversation with somebody whom you do not know. No, no! The Spirit of adoption in you brings you right into the presence of God, and it is a living act of fellowship and communion, vibrant with life.[29]

The life that the Spirit produces in prayer starts with this awareness of the presence of God, and thus it is the first evidence that one is praying in the Spirit. Lloyd-Jones states this in no uncertain terms: "To realize the presence of God is an absolute proof that you are praying in the Spirit because it is the Spirit who gives us this blessed assurance."[30] The Doctor notes that there are degrees of awareness of God's presence, but not degrees of certainty.

> It can be vivid, dramatic, as it were, absolutely certain, and there are lesser degrees, but they are equally certain. . . . Now only the Holy Spirit can do that. This is something that cannot be counterfeited. This is the particular operation of the Spirit upon us, and the moment you ever have any realization of the presence of God, you can be certain that you are praying in the Spirit.[31]

---

27 Ibid., 99.
28 Ibid.
29 Ibid., 100.
30 Ibid., 97.
31 Ibid.

This realization of God's presence means that one cannot equate praying with talking. Prayer is communing with God, which is much more comprehensive than talking to God. Therefore, Lloyd-Jones is resolute that one must not start speaking immediately. Again, he cites the example of George Müller:

> One of the greatest men of prayer of the last century was the saintly George Müller of Bristol. He was an expert in prayer; and he always taught that the first thing to do in prayer is to realize the presence of God. You do not start speaking immediately. . . . There must be this fellowship, this communion, this conversation. And the realization that you are in His presence is infinitely more important than anything you may say.[32]

An awareness of God's presence invariably brings a sense of awe and worship to prayer. The Spirit enlightens our hearts and cleanses our consciences with the truth of atonement by the blood of Christ, justification by faith, and adoption as sons. When we feel cold as strangers or condemned as lawbreakers, and we know deep down that we have forfeited every right to come into God's presence, the Spirit comes and proclaims: "You are justified by faith. You have peace with God. Your sins have been dealt with."[33] We move from an accusing conscience to an overwhelming "assurance that we can approach God."[34] The Spirit of adoption swiftly testifies that we are children of God.

The result of the Spirit's work is that we bow before God as his humbled children in awe of him. We don't bow before an unknown or far-away god, and we don't skip into God's presence with breezy familiarity. We come with an awakened sense of intimacy and awe. We realize that we are "in the holiest of all," and we are gripped with the sense that "to be admitted there, to have an audience, to have access, is the greatest privilege that can ever fall to the lot of a human being."[35] Therefore, the Spirit's work creates an inevitable humility and a deep and reverent fear of the Lord.

The next step of praying in the Spirit may seem to introduce a paradox, but there is no contradiction between steps 2 and 3, because the Spirit produces both effects. In the second step, the Spirit creates a sense of over-

---

[32] D. Martyn Lloyd-Jones, *The Christian Soldier: An Exposition of Ephesians 6:10–20* (Grand Rapids: Baker, 1977), 82.
[33] Lloyd-Jones, *Living Water*, 95.
[34] Ibid.
[35] Ibid., 98.

whelming awe in the presence of God, who is a "consuming fire" (Heb. 12:28–29); and as we are about to see in the third step, the Spirit creates a boldness that takes hold of God and his promises and does not let go.[36] Because these two attitudes are both Spirit-wrought, the boldness of step 3 is not a "carnal confidence," but a holy confidence.[37]

Step 3: Pleading the Promises of God with Boldness and Assurance

Hebrews chapters 4 and 10 both exhort the believer to come boldly to the throne of grace based on confidence in Christ and his atoning work. Lloyd-Jones stresses that the exhortations to boldness are "always the result of this argument" of the atonement. Therefore, one does not try to whip oneself into a state of boldness or carnal confidence. Rather, "you take the doctrine, you accept it and work it out, and then you find that it leads to this confidence."[38] This bold confidence is "always a manifestation of a true enlightenment of the Spirit."[39] Boldness thus becomes an "infallible test" of praying in the Spirit. "There is no hesitation, no uncertainty, but with 'full assurance of faith' you go right into the presence of God; it is purely spiritual," not carnal or fleshly.[40]

Spirit-wrought prayers urgently plead the promises of God with God in the very presence of God. Pleading the promises *with God* also means that we are preaching the promises *to ourselves* in prayer. "I am more than ever convinced that the trouble with many Christian people is that they do not preach to themselves. We should spend time every day preaching to ourselves, and never more so than when we get on our knees in prayer."[41] In fact, Lloyd-Jones calls this kind of bold praying "the great characteristic of all prayers that have ever prevailed."[42] This stress on urgency in prayer is a theme that the Doctor comes back to again and again. "Without an element of importunity and persistence, or urgency and almost a holy violence with God, we have little right to expect that God will hear our prayer and answer it."[43] Lloyd-Jones labels this boldness "holy" or "spiritual" to distinguish it from a presumptuous, carnal

---

36 Lloyd-Jones, *Revival*, 305.
37 Lloyd-Jones, *Living Water*, 103.
38 Ibid.
39 Ibid.
40 Ibid.
41 D. Martyn Lloyd-Jones, *The Unsearchable Riches of Christ: An Exposition of Ephesians 3* (Grand Rapids: Baker, 1979), 102.
42 Lloyd-Jones, *Revival*, 195.
43 Lloyd-Jones, *Joy Unspeakable: Power and Renewal in the Holy Spirit* (Wheaton, IL: Shaw, 1984), 382.

kind of boldness.[44] How does one know if he or she has crossed the line into presumption? Holy boldness ends and sinful boldness starts when the element of demand enters the prayer. Claiming or demanding is presumptuous and dangerous; it has no place in prayer.

> Do not claim, do not demand, let your requests be made known, let them come from your heart. God will understand. We have no right to demand even revival. Some Christians are tending to do so at the present time. Pray urgently, plead, use all the arguments, use all the promises; but do not demand, do not claim. Never put yourself into the position of saying, "If we but do this, then that must happen." God is a sovereign Lord, and these things are beyond our understanding. Never let the terminology of claiming or of demanding be used.[45]

Bold pleading will bring to bear the fervency of the whole person into prayer. The Holy Spirit deals with us not in a divided way—through the mind or the heart or the will—but as whole persons.[46] Praying in the Spirit will bring the fervency of fire to our prayer vocabulary. Bold prayer on fire will witness the persistent appearance of little exclamatory words, like "Oh!"

> Is there an "Oh" in your praying? That is another very good test of prayer, that this "Oh" comes in. "Oh, Lord." . . . That is how the prophet prayed. That is how the men of God have always prayed: this, "Oh." Somebody once said that a sign, the best sign, of a coming revival is that the word, "Oh" begins to enter into the prayers of the people. "Oh, Lord!"[47]

Bold praying in the Spirit will also be marked by liberty and freedom, which Lloyd-Jones calls the "most thorough test." He compares this freedom to the experience of preaching in the liberty of the Spirit. It is an experience almost impossible to describe—"just one of those things that you know."[48] He does try to put the experience into words: "Do you know the difference between forcing yourself to pray, struggling to find words and thoughts, desires, and expressions, and, on the other hand, being carried along, as it were, on the crest of a wave while you are more or less a spectator?"[49]

---

44 Lloyd-Jones, *The Unsearchable Riches of Christ*, 113.
45 Lloyd-Jones, *The Final Perseverance of the Saints*, 155.
46 Lloyd-Jones, *Living Water*, 105.
47 Lloyd-Jones, *Revival*, 301.
48 Lloyd-Jones, *Living Water*, 106.
49 Ibid.

Finally, boldly pleading the promises of God will sometimes have an immediate and full assurance. This assurance that our prayer will be answered sets apart what Paul calls the "prayer of faith."

> There is a prayer given sometimes by the Spirit concerning which He tells you that it is going to be answered. That is "the prayer of faith." It is not an experiment, it is not a trying to persuade yourself, or to "work yourself up." It is an absolute certainty that is given by the Spirit, and you know, therefore, when you are praying and making your requests, that your prayer is answered. And it happens because the prayer was given, and the assurance of it was given, by the blessed Holy Spirit Himself.[50]

Lloyd-Jones asserts that we are given this gift on occasion, but our Lord Jesus always had it.[51] This observation fills me with fresh adoration for our incomparable Lord Jesus as I witness his prayer life in the Gospels.

Step 4: Obeying the Prompts of the Spirit

Praying in the Spirit will also, on occasion, include immediate prompts from the Spirit to pray. The quickest way to quench the Spirit is to resist an impulse to pray. "Above all—and this I regard as most important of all—always respond to every impulse to pray."[52] Lloyd-Jones pleads with us to obey these prompts:

> The moment you feel the slightest drawing or indication of His love, act upon it at once, however it may come. You may be reading a book, for instance, and not really thinking very much about this particular matter, when suddenly you become aware of some urge or some call to prayer. The whole essence of wisdom in this matter is to put down your book immediately, no matter how interesting it may be, and begin to pray. . . . The moment you feel the slightest movement or indication of His love, respond, act, yield to Him immediately. Whatever He calls you to do, do it at once. And as you do so, you will find that He will come more frequently, and the manifestations will be plainer and clearer.[53]

This last point is very personal to me because of something that happened during my doctoral studies. I worked the night shift and never

---

[50] Lloyd-Jones, *The Final Perseverance of the Saints*, 157.

[51] Lloyd-Jones, *The Christian Soldier*, 328.

[52] D. Martyn Lloyd-Jones, *Preaching and Preachers* (Grand Rapids: Zondervan, 1971), 170–71.

[53] Lloyd-Jones, *The Unsearchable Riches of Christ*, 274–75.

seemed to get sufficient sleep. One particular morning, I drove home at about 4:30 a.m. and started falling asleep at the wheel. I tried everything to stay awake. I turned up the radio and tried to sing along. I even slapped myself. The next thing I knew, I woke up in my driveway. I was more than a little shaken. I didn't know how I got there. I walked inside the house now eerily wide awake, and I noticed the strangest thing: my wife was wide awake too. She would normally be asleep, but instead she was sitting up in bed waiting for me. She said, "Hi, honey, how was your drive?" I said, "It's funny you should ask. I really struggled to stay awake on the drive home. In fact, I don't know how I got here." She said, "Yeah I figured." "Okay," I said, "please continue!" "Well," she said, "I woke up at about 4:30 very suddenly and felt this intense prompting to pray. I figured you must be struggling on the road since that is around the time you normally come home. So I prayed for you." I think I am still alive and typing these words because my wife did not quench the Spirit. She obeyed the Spirit's prompting to pray.

Conclusion: The Overflow of Childlike Communion

This chapter began with the quote: "If your knowledge of doctrine does not make you a great man of prayer, you had better examine yourself again."[54] The Doctor would ask us what our prayer life reveals about the quality of our relationship with God. He says, "Show me a man who does not pray very much and I will tell you the real problem of that man."[55] What is the problem? "It is that he does not know God, he does not know God as his Father." Prayer is an overflow of a childlike communion between Father and child. "Those who know God best are the ones who speak to him most of all."[56]

This work of prayer is not a work of the flesh but a work of the Spirit. The Doctor would ask another probing question about the Spirit's place in our prayers: "How often do I pray; do I find freedom in prayer, do I delight in prayer, or is prayer a wearisome task; do I never know enlargement and liberty in it?"[57]

It is impossible to love God and not prize prayer. Let us follow the Doctor's admonition to look for the Spirit's empowerment in prayer and yield to the Spirit in obeying every impulse to pray.

---

[54] Lloyd-Jones, in Alderson, "The Wisdom of Martyn Lloyd-Jones, 7–12.
[55] Lloyd-Jones, *Assurance of Our Salvation*, 33.
[56] Ibid.
[57] Lloyd-Jones, *Fellowship with God*, 84.

CHAPTER 10

FAITH WORKING THROUGH LOVE

The first Christians conquered the ancient world just by being Christian. It was their love for one another and their type of life that made such an impact upon that pagan world, and there is no question but that this is the greatest need of the hour—the Christian quality of life being demonstrated among men and women. That is something to which we are all called and something which we can all do.

D. MARTYN LLOYD-JONES[1]

Introduction

It is easy to assume that we truly grasp what a word means simply because it is familiar. *Faith* and *love* are two of the most familiar terms in the lingo of the Christian life. The problem is that these words are deceptively deep, and thus one must not be content with a shallow understanding of them. In what follows, we will allow the Doctor to define these two great terms and then to diagnose why faith working through love can be so difficult to live out. He will then prescribe the solution to the difficulties.

---

[1] *The Life of Joy: An Exposition of Philippians 1 and 2* (Grand Rapids: Baker, 1989), 22.

The Doctor's Definition: Faith and Love

Faith

Lloyd-Jones is quick to confess that faith "is a very big term" that "embraces a number of concepts."[2] He avers that there is "no better definition of faith" than the one found in Hebrews 11.[3] The author of Hebrews stresses three essential qualities:[4] "There are these three essential elements in faith—believing, being persuaded, and acting. To put it another way, the mind is involved, the heart is involved, and the will is involved."[5] Faith is a vital activity; there can be no passivity because faith involves the whole person. When the truth of God comes to a person, the dawning of faith causes three realities to rise: the truth of God is (1) believed with the mind, (2) grasped with the heart, and (3) acted upon by the will.

Love

What is love? Lloyd-Jones distinguishes loving from liking. Liking is something natural and instinctual; it is "not the result of effort."[6] Love is the opposite in many respects. Love goes beyond the natural and the instinctual, looking past what it does not like in order to act kindly toward the person who stands behind the flaws. Loving those "we do not like means that we treat them as if we did like them."[7]

This approach is firmly rooted and grounded in the gospel because this is the same type of love we received in the gospel. God loved us when we were enemies, not friends. This type of love goes above neighbor love, which has self as the defining element ("love your neighbor as yourself"—Matt. 19:19), and makes Christ's love the defining element ("love one another as I have loved you"—John 15:12). It goes above the golden rule, whereby we do to others as we would have them do to us. Gospel love means "we do to others what He has done for us."[8] Loving this way is possible only for Christians, and thus loving this way "proves" that we are Christians and have passed from darkness and death to light and life (Eph. 5:8; 1 John 3:14).[9]

---

[2] D. Martyn Lloyd-Jones, *The Gospel of God: An Exposition of Romans 1* (Carlisle, PA: Banner of Truth, 1985), 312.
[3] Ibid., 313.
[4] Ibid.
[5] Ibid.
[6] D. Martyn Lloyd-Jones, *Life in Christ: Studies in 1 John* (Wheaton, IL: Crossway, 2002), 358.
[7] Ibid., 359.
[8] D. Martyn Lloyd-Jones, *Darkness and Light: An Exposition of Ephesians 4:17–5:17* (Grand Rapids: Baker, 1982), 311.
[9] Ibid.

The Doctor emphasizes that love has a totalitarian, all-inclusive character: "Love is all-inclusive. When you love, every part of you is involved. You cannot love in sections of your personality; love is always totalitarian in its demands and responses."[10]

Clear definitions of biblical terms can give the impression that the issues are simple and clear cut. But we also need help diagnosing why faith and love can be easy to define but difficult to live and apply.

The Doctor's Diagnosis: The Difficulty of Faith and Love

Difficulty 1: The Devil

The Devil hates Christians, and so he sadistically delights in shooting fiery darts of doubts at them. Does the presence of doubt equal the absence of faith? The Doctor distinguishes between the temptation to doubt and the act of doubting:

> Do not conclude, then, that because you are assailed by doubts you are not a Christian. It is the devil that is at work. He will hurl doubts at you. The Apostle describes them as "the fiery darts of the wicked one." They come at you from every direction. He will suggest all sorts of difficulties and doubts, anything to stop men believing in God. There is nothing more important than that we should differentiate between the temptation to doubt and the act of doubting itself.[11]

Difficulty 2: Sin

Sin will often express itself in ways that are antithetical to love, like selfishness or apathy toward others. How can love win the war against a sinful lack of love? We must have a kind of spiritual honesty that is willing to own up to our specific faults. Acknowledging that we are sinners is a painful process because fighting our sins means knowing them and confessing them in detail, not in general.

> I must confess my particular sins, I must name them one by one; it means that I must not gloss over them, I must not attempt to deny them. I must confess them, I must look at them. There must be no attempt to dismiss

---

10 D. Martyn Lloyd-Jones, *The Final Perseverance of the Saints: An Exposition of Romans 8:17–39* (Carlisle, PA: Banner of Truth, 1975), 185.
11 D. Martyn Lloyd-Jones, *The Christian Warfare: An Exposition of Ephesians 6:10–13* (Grand Rapids: Baker, 1976), 86.

them as quickly as possible. Confession means facing them, not trying to balance up the sins I have committed and the good deeds I have done. No I must let the light so search me that I feel miserable and wretched—this honest facing of the things I have done and of what I am; it means that I must confess it to God in words.[12]

But knowledge and confession are not enough. The Doctor declares that "knowledge of sin has never prevented anybody from sinning. Indeed, the more one knows about it the more one is subject to the temptation to do it."[13] The battle for real faith and love is fought not only in the heart but also with the mind. Faulty definitions can also wreak havoc on faith and love.

Difficulty 3: Counterfeit Versions of Faith and Love

Lloyd-Jones looks at the way the word *faith* is being misused and calls it "one of the real tragedies of the age in which we live."[14] One counterfeit version of faith could be called "bare believism." Lloyd-Jones speaks against this counterfeit by stressing that faith is "never bare." It is not a mere matter of saying, "Yes, I believe, I accept that teaching."[15]

Another counterfeit version of faith conflates faith with feelings so that faith becomes a mindless emotionalism. Emotionalism "is a state and condition in which the emotions run riot" and are "in control."[16] The Doctor clarifies that "emotion is a vital part of Christian faith; but emotionalism is not."[17]

How does one discern the difference? The Doctor says that people cannot manufacture emotion. It is far too deep for artificial production or manipulation. Real emotion is always a response to truth and is characterized by its depth and element of wonder. Emotionalism, however, is shallow and frothy, always remaining on the surface without going down to the depths of true emotion.[18]

Genuine faith contains a real depth of emotion.

Can a man see himself as a damned sinner without emotion? Can a man look into hell without emotion? Can a man listen to the thunderings of

12 D. Martyn Lloyd-Jones, *Fellowship with God: Studies in 1 John* (Wheaton, IL: Crossway, 1992), 32.

13 D. Martyn Lloyd-Jones, *Assurance: An Exposition of Romans 5* (Carlisle, PA: Banner of Truth, 1998), 294.

14 D. Martyn Lloyd-Jones, *Children of God: Studies in 1 John* (Wheaton, IL: Crossway, 1994), 109.

15 D. Martyn Lloyd-Jones, *The Sons of God: An Exposition of Romans 8:5–17* (Carlisle, PA: Banner of Truth, 1974), 270.

16 D. Martyn Lloyd-Jones, *Revival* (Wheaton, IL: Crossway, 1987), 75.

17 Lloyd-Jones, *The Christian Warfare*, 157.

18 Ibid., 204.

the Law and feel nothing? Or conversely, can a man really contemplate the love of God in Christ Jesus and feel no emotion? The whole position is utterly ridiculous.[19]

In the same way, the word *love* has become so twisted and distorted that the resulting counterfeit version is a complete departure from biblical love. Recall the distinction between loving and liking, described at the beginning of this chapter.[20] Lloyd-Jones calls worldly versions of love "sickly and sentimental."[21] God knows that counterfeit versions of love will appear, and so the Bible insists on defining "exactly the use of its own terms."[22]

Even though the Bible insists upon its own definitions, many people still move in the wrong direction. Instead of starting with Scripture, they begin with a distorted definition of love and then attribute it to the God of the Bible.

> The truth is, of course, that we are in sin and all our ideas are wrong; our conception of love is more wrong than anything else and if we begin to think of God's love in terms of what *we* do and what *we* think, then—I say it with reverence—God help us! If we are going to attribute our sentimental, loose, unjust and unrighteous notions of love to the everlasting Godhead, then we place ourselves in the most precarious position.[23]

One must begin with the love of God because "it is love alone that can appreciate love."[24] Biblical love also does not fixate or terminate on love itself. Loving the feeling of love is different from love.[25] Love is defined not by itself but by its object. It is never self-absorbed but is absorbed in its object. Love "manifests itself by loving persons in the concrete," not the abstract.[26] Therefore, "love is not a sentiment, it is the most active, vital thing in the world."[27]

---

19 D. Martyn Lloyd-Jones, *Preaching and Preachers* (Grand Rapids: Zondervan, 1971), 95.

20 Lloyd-Jones, *Life in Christ*, 358.

21 Lloyd-Jones, *Darkness and Light*, 302.

22 Ibid.

23 D. Martyn Lloyd-Jones, *Great Doctrines of the Bible: God the Father, God the Son* (Wheaton, IL: Crossway, 1996), 333.

24 D. Martyn Lloyd-Jones, *The Unsearchable Riches of Christ: An Exposition of Ephesians 3* (Grand Rapids: Baker, 1979), 214.

25 "How easy it is to fall in love with loving instead of actually loving!" (Lloyd-Jones, *Children of God*, 111).

26 D. Martyn Lloyd-Jones, *The Love of God: Studies in 1 John* (Wheaton, IL: Crossway, 1994), 77.

27 D. Martyn Lloyd-Jones, *Life in God: Studies in 1 John* (Wheaton, IL: Crossway, 1995), 30.

Difficulty 4: Counterfeit Versions of Cultivating Faith and Love

It should come as no surprise that if people cling to counterfeit definitions of faith and love, then they will construct counterfeit methods of cultivating faith and love. If faith is confused with emotionalism and love is confused with sentimentalism, then church services will be calculated to produce those things.

> Some people live on emotionalism or on sentimentalism. As they believe that nothing matters except this kind of riot or excitement of the emotions, they will, of course, do everything they can to encourage it; and quite often it is deliberately worked up. There are services in which people clap their hands and shout and sing and repeat certain types of choruses—it is done deliberately to work up excitement. And the more excited they get, and the more emotional they become, the more wonderful, they think, the blessing of the Spirit has been. It is mere emotionalism.[28]

The Doctor declares that if "emotionalism is bad, how much worse is a deliberate attempt to produce it."[29] The New Testament clearly condemns that approach.[30]

Difficulty 5: Lack of Balance

Christian expressions of faith and love must have a "balanced finality."[31] All of the counterfeit versions of faith and love are lopsided and lack this sense of balance. The genuine reality will always include head, heart, and will. Faith that is only intellectual assent (head, but no heart or will) is always a counterfeit.[32] Love that is only a sentiment or an empty word, without will or action or truth, is a counterfeit.[33] Lloyd-Jones stresses the truth of 1 John 3:18: "Little children, let us not love in word or talk but in deed and in truth."

The Doctor's Prescription: Life in the Spirit

In light of all the difficulties discussed above, believers must work out the doctrine. What does faith working through love look like? The Doctor gives

---

28 Lloyd-Jones, *The Christian Warfare*, 198–99.
29 Lloyd-Jones, *Revival*, 75.
30 Ibid.
31 D. Martyn Lloyd-Jones, *Spiritual Depression: Its Causes and Its Cure* (Grand Rapids: Eerdmans, 1965), 60.
32 Lloyd-Jones, *The Sons of God*, 270.
33 Lloyd-Jones, *The Final Perseverance of the Saints*, 185.

a three-part prescription: (1) see the sovereign source, (2) apply faith to the situation, and (3) walk in love.

Prescription 1: See the Sovereign Source

Recall Lloyd-Jones's exposition of God's sovereignty in chapter 2 (see p. 53, "The Eternal Decrees of God"). Faith comes only because God first gives the gift of faith (Eph. 2:8; Phil. 1:29). In the same way, we love only because he first loved us (1 John 4:19). One must begin with the fundamentals. Nothing is more foundational than what God did before the foundation of the world: in love, God chose us in Christ (Eph. 1:4–5). Christian faith and love owe their very existence to God's grace and power.[34] "It is here we see how our ideas of what the Christian is, fall hopelessly short of the biblical teaching. A Christian is *a new creation*. He is not just a good man, or a man who has been improved somewhat; he is a new man, 'created in Christ Jesus.'"[35] In the same way, love is the result of this new creation. Biblical love is not something that comes natural to the natural man. It is supernatural. It takes a new birth.

> It is no use asking the world to "love one another." It is impossible; they are incapable of doing it. We need the divine nature within us before we can truly love one another. If within the church you have failure on the part of men and women to love one another, what hope is there for the world to do this? It is utterly impossible.[36]

Faith and love owe their existence to the power of God, but that does not mean that faith and love are passive realities on our part. We come now to the second part of the Doctor's prescription.

Prescription 2: Apply Faith to the Situation

Lloyd-Jones carefully distinguishes between the gift of faith and the life of faith. He strongly believes that many people have misunderstood the nature of faith. "Faith in conversion is a gift. It is given as a gift but subsequently there is a walk of faith or the life of faith."[37] When faith is not actively applied, it is what Jesus called "little faith." This type of faith leads

---

[34] D. Martyn Lloyd-Jones, *God's Way of Reconciliation: An Exposition of Ephesians 2* (Grand Rapids: Baker, 1972), 137.
[35] Ibid., 138.
[36] Lloyd-Jones, *The Love of God*, 45.
[37] Lloyd-Jones, *Spiritual Depression*, 135.

to an impoverished Christian life. "It is a poor type of Christianity that has this wonderful faith with respect to salvation and then whimpers and cries when confronted by the daily trials of life. We must apply our faith. 'Little faith' does not do this."[38] Faith is "always practical."[39] That means it is never passive. "Faith is an activity, it is something that has to be exercised. It does not come into operation itself, you and I have to put it into operation."[40] Jesus taught this principle with crystal clarity when he questioned the disciples in the story of the stilling of the storm. The Doctor explains:

> You observe our Lord's question. It seems to imply that He knows perfectly well that they have faith. The question He asks them is: "Where is it? You have got faith, but where is it at this moment? It ought to be here, where is it?" Now that gives us the key to the understanding of the nature of faith.[41]

Faith is not a feeling and it is not an automated response. Faith always comes "in response to truth"[42] and must be "applied" in a specific situation.[43] Faith clearly involves the mind, the heart, and the will, but once again the order matters. The mind comes first. The Doctor could even say that faith is "primarily thinking":

> Faith, according to our Lord's teaching . . . is primarily thinking; and the whole trouble with a man of little faith is that he does not think. He allows circumstances to bludgeon him. That is the real difficulty in life. Life comes to us with a club in its hand and strikes us upon the head, and we become incapable of thought, helpless and defeated. The way to avoid that, according to our Lord, is to think.[44]

The failure of the disciples in the storm came because they let the situation control them, rather than taking charge of the situation by applying their faith to it.[45] Taking charge of a situation by faith will involve three

---

38 D. Martyn Lloyd-Jones, *Studies in the Sermon on the Mount*, 2 vols. in 1 (Grand Rapids: Eerdmans, 1974), 403.
39 D. Martyn Lloyd-Jones, *The Christian Soldier: An Exposition of Ephesians 6:10–20* (Grand Rapids: Baker, 1977), 305.
40 Lloyd-Jones, *Spiritual Depression*, 143.
41 Ibid., 142.
42 Ibid.
43 Ibid., 147.
44 Lloyd-Jones, *Sermon on the Mount*, 399.
45 Lloyd-Jones, *Spiritual Depression*, 143.

steps: (1) faith will refuse to panic; (2) then faith will recall the content of what it believes and knows; (3) then faith will apply all of it to the present situation.[46] This process of application must be God-centered, because our faith is in God. We don't put faith in our faith, or faith in ourselves or others, or faith in our circumstances. Faith will face the event at hand and say, "All right, but I know this about God, and because that is true I am going to apply it to this situation."[47]

Lloyd-Jones reminds us also that we don't put faith in how much faith we have. Even "little" faith connects us to the almighty object of faith: the Lord Jesus Christ. The Lord himself pointed out to his disciples that a small amount of faith has great value, as the Doctor explains: "However poor and small and however incomplete the faith of these disciples was on this occasion, they at any rate had a sufficient amount of faith to make them do the right thing in the end. They went to Him."[48] How does Jesus respond to "little faith"? He does not try to conceal his disappointment. He rebukes our tiny trust, but as we are "blessed by His Name, He will nevertheless still receive us. He does not drive us away."[49]

Someone may ask at this point why God even allows trials. The Doctor answers that God ordains our trials in part to test our faith. Trials and tribulations always vex a faith that is nothing more than bare belief,[50] the counterfeit faith of mere "intellectual assent"[51] or "mere believism."[52] The Doctor urges us during these trials to think rightly about the fight of faith and avoid two ditches. Faith is not the *absence* of doubting, but neither is it *chronic* doubting. This distinction matters very much to him. Consider the first ditch, the absence of doubting. Recall how the Doctor called attention to Satan's fiery darts of doubt (see p. 153, "Difficulty 1: The Devil"). Lloyd-Jones wants to distinguish between the temptation to doubt and the act of doubting.

> Do not conclude, then, that because you are assailed by doubts you are
> not a Christian. It is the devil that is at work. He will hurl doubts at you.
> The Apostle describes them as "the fiery darts of the wicked one." They
> come at you from every direction. He will suggest all sorts of difficulties

---

46 Ibid., 144–45.
47 Ibid., 146.
48 Ibid.
49 Ibid.
50 Lloyd-Jones, *Assurance*, 62.
51 Lloyd-Jones, *The Gospel of God*, 312.
52 Lloyd-Jones, *Assurance*, 62.

and doubts, anything to stop men believing in God. There is nothing more important than that we should differentiate between the temptation to doubt and the act of doubting itself.[53]

But consider also the second ditch. Lloyd-Jones says it is part of the very character of faith to be free from constant, chronic doubting:

> It seems to me that to interpret faith as a kind of constant uncertainty is to deny the teaching of the Word of God that we are His children. Indeed, "the Spirit itself beareth witness with our spirit, that we are the children of God" (Romans 8:16). Such knowledge is possible to us. We ought to be in a position of knowing that we have eternal life, that we know God, and that we know Christ.[54]

Therefore, the Doctor believes there will always be a mixture of doubting and assurance within the life of faith. Though faith may have occasional doubts, there will always be an "element" of assurance underneath.[55] One should not expect faith to be completely free from doubts, as if a believer will have the fullest possible assurance of faith at all times.

Faith in the midst of trials will often go through a process of agitated doubting before returning to its resting place. The Doctor offers this illustration:

> Faith in this matter is remarkably like the needle of a compass, always there pointing to the magnetic north. But if you introduce a very powerful magnet at some other point of the compass it will draw the needle over to it and cause it to swing backwards and forwards and be most unstable. But it is certain that the true compass needle will get back to its true centre, it will find its place of rest in the north. It may know agitation, it may know a lot of violence, but it will go back to its centre, it always finds the place of rest, and the same thing is always true of faith. So the mere fact that we may be tempted to doubt, the mere fact that we may have to struggle and bring out all arguments, and go over the whole question again, does not mean that we have not got faith. In a sense it is a proof of faith, as long as we always arrive back at the position of rest.[56]

---

[53] Lloyd-Jones, *The Christian Warfare*, 86.
[54] Lloyd-Jones, *Life in God*, 93.
[55] Lloyd-Jones, *Assurance*, 24.
[56] Ibid.

Prescription 3: Walk in Love

Once again, the Doctor calls us to work out our doctrine[57]—in this case, the doctrines of adoption and the atonement.

First, how do we apply the doctrine of our adoption? The apostles Paul and John both call Christians to show love because we are children of God, who is love (Eph. 5:1; 1 John 4:7–8). We imitate God not in order to become beloved children. We imitate God precisely because we are beloved (Eph. 5:1), born again (1 John 4:7) children of God.[58] Paul stresses that we are children not merely in a legal sense; we are children also in a beloved sense. Lloyd-Jones's exposition of this fact soars with excitement:

> Do you know, that if you are a true Christian you are dear to God? I have the authority of the Lord Jesus Christ for saying this. The very hairs of your head are all numbered [Luke 12:7]! God knows His children one by one, He is interested in us; the analogy is a human one, but we can multiply it by infinity. God's interest in and concern for His children is infinitely greater than the greatest and the noblest natural parent's interest in his or her child. God is lovingly concerned about us. He watches us just as the natural parent watches his little child beginning to walk for the first time, or as the child goes out to school for the first time. He stands at the gate and watches him as he goes round the corner and out of sight; that is an expression of loving interest. It is not a mechanical relationship; children are dear, children are beloved! And, says Paul, that is God's relationship to us; He has looked down upon us, and He loves us; He is interested in us, we are dear to His heart, He is taking an intense personal interest in us.[59]

If it is natural for a parent to love a child, it is also natural for a child to imitate a parent.

> Again, if we realize the truth of this relationship, our greatest desire in life will be to be like God. Look at a little boy who loves his father and knows his father's love to him; his great desire is to be like his father. He likes to sit in his father's chair; likes to take his father's place; tries to walk like his father; tries to speak like his father! He is imitating his father the whole time. He wants to grow up to be a man like his father! That is

---

[57] The Doctor says, "Now we can never be tired of repeating this; the New Testament never calls upon us to do anything without first of all reminding us of who we are. That is its invariable method: doctrine—practice; the whole doctrinal position—the inevitable practical outlook" (Lloyd-Jones, *Life in Christ*, 336).
[58] Ibid.; *Darkness and Light*, 294.
[59] Lloyd-Jones, *Darkness and Light*, 295.

human nature, is it not? That is ordinary human love at its best. Again, I say, cleanse it, multiply it by infinity, and you discover what the Apostle is telling us to do. "Become imitators of God" [Eph. 5:1]—why?—because He is your Father![60]

Our adoption as God's children creates an inevitable sense of desiring to honor our Father.

> If you realize the honor, you will be careful about your behavior. As you walk down the street you will say to yourself, I am a child of God, I belong to the royal family of heaven, and people are looking at me and watching me, and they are perfectly right in doing so; they will be judging God, they will be judging Christ by what they see in me. So, Paul says, "Be imitators of God," walk down the street, if I may so put it, as God's representative. Live in such a way that everybody knowing you will be made to think of God, because you are a child of God.[61]

Second, how do we work out the doctrine of the atonement?[62] We must work out its implications with specificity, because too many people talk about God's love generically. The Bible does not follow that method. Paul unpacks the doctrine of God's love as seen specifically in the death of Christ for sinners.[63]

Working out the doctrine of the atonement means loving others *as* Christ loved us. How did Christ love? In Lloyd-Jones's exposition of both Paul and John, he appeals to the mind of Christ from Philippians 2. Christ did not consider himself (Phil. 2:5–8), but gave himself up for us (Eph. 5:2), laying down his life for us (1 John 3:16). The Son of God did not elevate his feelings, his comforts, or his rights over others. He gave up all of himself. And we must do the same.[64]

More specifically, Christ gave himself for sinners (those who did not

---

[60] Ibid., 295–96.

[61] Ibid., 297.

[62] "Here in this most practical section of his Epistle, when he is talking about our behavior towards others, our speech, and our conduct, down to the minutest detail, suddenly in the midst of it all he introduces this tremendous statement of the doctrine of the Atonement. He cannot leave it alone, because in the Christian life, doctrine and behavior are indissolubly linked together and they must never be separated. It is no use talking about conduct and behavior in a Christian sense without doctrine. And when people neglect doctrine you will always see it in their lives. But on the other hand doctrine alone is of no value. The two things must and will go together. And here, you see, suddenly, as I say, unexpectedly in the midst of this most practical section, he holds before us one of his own greatest and mightiest statements of the doctrine of the Atonement" Ibid., 301.

[63] Ibid., 302.

[64] Ibid., 311; Lloyd-Jones, *Life in Christ*, 365.

deserve it). Only Christians are capable of showing this supernatural type of love. Recall the distinction the Doctor has made between liking and loving. Love surpasses liking (natural and instinctual) and penetrates "beyond the ugliness and the unattractiveness."[65] This type of love goes beyond the golden rule of loving your neighbor as you love yourself and is the Christ-like, gospel love whereby "we do to others what He has done for us."[66] Here is his description:

> When you and I meet difficult people, people who have nothing to recommend them at all, people who are as vile and as objectionable and as foul as they can be, who attack us and persecute us and deal with us spitefully and malign us, we are to deal with them as our Lord dealt with us. Walk in love! Pray for them! Bring yourself to feel sorry for them; so sorry, that you will have a burning desire within you that they may be delivered; so sorry that you will get on your knees and feel deep heart concern for them because they are the victims of sin and of Satan. Love your enemies! Bless them that curse you! Pray for them that persecute you and use you spitefully and malign you.[67]

This is "the ultimate test of our Christian profession."[68] The "yardstick of love" must measure all "our professions and claims and activities."[69] Jesus rebuked Simon the Pharisee at precisely this point. Simon showed no love, but the woman who was forgiven much loved much through many actions. What was the lesson? "Love is always active; if there is no expression, there is no love."[70]

Actions and words are both essential. Words without actions and actions without words both fall short of biblical love. "You can be aware of another's love to you by the actions of that person, but what love craves for always is a personal statement."[71]

Conclusion: By This the World Will Know

This chapter began with a quote concerning the evangelistic impact of faith working through love:

---

[65] Lloyd-Jones, *Life in Christ*, 359.
[66] Lloyd-Jones, *Darkness and Light*, 311.
[67] Ibid., 311–12.
[68] Ibid., 300.
[69] Ibid.
[70] Lloyd-Jones, *Life in Christ*, 364.
[71] Lloyd-Jones, *The Unsearchable Riches of Christ*, 235.

The first Christians conquered the ancient world just by being Christian. It was their love for one another and their type of life that made such an impact upon that pagan world, and there is no question but that this is the greatest need of the hour—the Christian quality of life being demonstrated among men and women. That is something to which we are all called and something which we can all do.[72]

The world needs to see the faith of believers on display through tangible expressions of love. We have no right to be believed if our lives can be explained apart from Christ living in us. The fact that Christ lives in us will certainly impact the world, but it will also produce a sense of joy and privilege within us.

Is there anything in the world which is comparable to the privilege of being a Christian? We are asked and invited and called upon to live as Christ lived; and we are the only people in the world who can live as Christ lived. A man who is not a Christian cannot live like that. He needs to be born again, he must have a new nature and a new life. He must have his eyes opened to the blessed truth of the Gospel. Nothing but *that* can ever enable men and persuade men to walk in love even as Christ did. What a privilege, what an honor, what a high calling, to be imitators of God and of the Lord Jesus Christ![73]

The Christian life catches fire as faith works through love. This fire will be felt in every sphere. The next chapter examines what life in the Spirit looks like in the spheres of home and work.

---

[72] Lloyd-Jones, *The Life of Joy*, 22.
[73] Lloyd-Jones, *Darkness and Light*, 312.

CHAPTER II

LIFE IN THE SPIRIT AT HOME AND WORK

My dear friends, I say again that this is our unique opportunity at this time. That is what we stand for in a world that is so largely non-Christian. The way to convince the world of the truth of that gospel is to let them see that it makes a difference, that it is a power, that we are not mere theorists and philosophers but that we preach the power of God. And we prove that there is a power in the gospel by showing what we are in work, in business, in profession and in the home. Wherever we are, whatever we are, only let our citizenship be worthy of the gospel of Jesus Christ.

D. MARTYN LLOYD-JONES [1]

Introduction

For Lloyd-Jones, Christianity is gloriously invasive: "My Christianity must enter into my married life, into my relationship to parents, into my work, into everything I am, and into everything I do."[2] The world will thus see a difference between Christians and non-Christians in every sphere of life. The difference between the two should be pronounced because "nothing that the Christian does is the same as that which is done by the

---

[1] *The Life of Joy: An Exposition of Philippians 1 and 2* (Grand Rapids: Baker, 1989), 22.
[2] D. Martyn Lloyd-Jones, *Life in the Spirit in Marriage, Home and Work: An Exposition of Ephesians 5:18–6:9* (Grand Rapids: Baker, 1974), 89.

non-Christian."[3] The two different people may do the same things, but they will do them in different ways for different reasons. Christians will put these differences on display in practical ways. The Doctor even goes so far as to claim that "there is nothing more practical in the world than the Christian faith and the Christian teaching."[4]

Is it really true that Christian teaching is more practical than anything else in the world? Many Christians admit that they struggle to know how to take their Christian faith and live it out at home and at work. Why do people struggle to put their faith into practice in these areas? They divorce doctrine from life. One does not need to twist doctrine like a pretzel to make it practical. The practical is an inevitable outworking of the doctrinal.

The Doctor expounded Ephesians 5:18–6:9 in this way on Sunday mornings in 1959–1960. He had these sermons published before certain other volumes in the Ephesians series, because the problems Paul tackled felt so urgent in the Doctor's own day. How did Paul address these problems? He brought doctrine and life together. We must do the same.

> Here, in this most practical of sections, Paul suddenly introduces this tremendous doctrine of the nature of the church, and the relationship of the church to the Lord Jesus Christ. But what we must bear in mind—because it comes out of all that—is that doctrine and practice are so intimately related that they cannot be separated. Anyone, therefore, who says, "I am only interested in the practical," is really denying the essence of the Christian message. This great passage [Eph. 5:18–6:9] demonstrates that in a perfect manner.[5]

We will see how Lloyd-Jones brings doctrine and life together by following the same pattern as in previous chapters. I will allow the Doctor to define his terms, diagnose the difficulty, and then prescribe a path forward.

The Doctor's Definition: A Christian Home and a Christian at Work

First, the Doctor distinguishes a Christian view of marriage from the world's concept. The world regards marriage as purely physical, or a mere human arrangement for the sake of the greater good of society. The purely physical view regards marriage as the "legalizing of physical attraction and

---

[3] Ibid., 305.
[4] Ibid.
[5] Ibid., 92.

physical gratification."[6] The view of marriage as a beneficial human arrangement or social construct depends in large part upon an evolutionary worldview, which suggests that humans used to behave like promiscuous wild animals, and because that created social chaos and confusion, people concluded that monogamy was better for society.[7]

The Doctor defines marriage as an ordinance of God, ordained by him to display the greater marriage between the Lord Jesus Christ and his church. Paul makes more than a passing reference to this doctrine. The Doctor declares that Paul brings out his best doctrinal wine in his marriage discussion. Ephesians 5 represents Paul's "most exalted teaching of all about the nature of the church and the relationship of the church to Christ."[8] When we least expect it, the apostle opens a door through which we are "confronted by the most magnificent and glorious doctrine you have ever met with in your life."[9] If we are not clear on that glorious doctrine, we cannot truly understand or truly appreciate marriage.[10]

Second, the Doctor also distinguishes Christian parenting from worldly parenting. Christian parenting cannot be reduced to a biological partnership between parent and child. Nature teaches that children are dependent upon parents,[11] but the Bible goes further in stressing that parenthood is a picture. God is our Father and Christians are children of God.[12]

Third, the relationship between a worker and a boss is more than a mere financial arrangement. Paul's example deals with the relationship between a slave and a master.[13] Even though the human institution was often unjust and severely flawed, both masters and slaves could portray a greater reality because both master and slave are slaves of Christ.

---

6 Ibid., 95.

7 Ibid.

8 Ibid., 91–92.

9 Ibid.

10 Ibid., 97–98.

11 Lloyd-Jones understood Paul's phrase "for this is right" as a reference to the natural order of things. "This is the order of nature. The young creature in its weakness and ignorance needs the protection and the guidance and the help and the instruction which is given by the parent" (ibid., 243).

12 "So in a very wonderful way the relationship between the parent and the child is a replica and a picture, a portrayal, a preaching of this whole relationship that subsists especially between those who are Christian and God Himself" (ibid., 245).

13 Lloyd-Jones expounds a text on slavery and applies it to many different kinds of work. His argument for this type of application is as follows:

> It would be foolish for someone to say, "Well, if that deals with slavery, what has it to do with me?" The answer is that slavery is only one of the possible relationships of man to man; and what the Apostle is concerned about is the behavior, the conduct and the reaction, of Christian people who are in any position of subservience to others, Christians who are employed in any service. It goes further; we are all subservient to the State, to social enactments and social conditions. So this subject, if we are to look at it truly and thoroughly, will take us into all those various realms. (ibid., 310)

The Doctor's Diagnosis: The Difficulty of Life at Home and Work

Difficulty 1: The Devil

The Doctor cautions us that the spheres of home and work are fragile and fraught with difficulties. The Devil understands how vital and vulnerable relationships are in these contexts, and so he constantly keeps them in his sinister sights, targeting them relentlessly.[14]

Difficulty 2: Sin (Selfishness)

Though the wicked schemes of the Devil are always at play, he is not the greatest threat. Relationships in the home are relationships between sinners. Two sinners say "I do" in marriage. Likewise, parents and children are sinners and will have specific sinful temptations in the ways they relate to each other.

The same is true at work. The effects of the fall are felt in the form of difficulties, tensions, stresses, and strains. People have tried to address these difficulties mainly by improving conditions at work through labor laws and technological advances. But the greatest problem is not outside of us but inside of us. As long as we are self-centered, we will continue to have problems in the workplace.[15]

Difficulty 3: False Teaching and Cultural Captivity

The Doctor warns that some people take the analogy between Jesus and the church "too far." They conflate real submission with absolute submission. They read Paul wrongly to say, "Wives, submit yourselves unto your own husbands *in exactly the same way* as you submit yourselves unto the Lord."[16] The submission of the church to Jesus is absolute; the submission of the wife to her husband is not. Husband and wife are both slaves of Christ; "the wife is not a slave of her husband."[17] Submission to the husband is "an expression" of the wife's absolute "submission to the Lord."[18] The same principle holds true for both Christian children and Christian workers. Obedience is not absolute; our ultimate allegiance is to Christ. A wife or a child or a employee who is asked to compromise his or her Christian faith must refuse and be willing to suffer the consequences.[19]

---

[14] Ibid., 306.
[15] Ibid.
[16] Ibid., 101; my emphasis.
[17] Ibid.
[18] Ibid.
[19] Ibid., 253, 266.

We can also be held captive by the spirit of the age. Parental models in the past were guilty of being carried away by the Victorian pattern of excessive discipline. Authoritarian parenting provokes children and crushes their personalities.[20] This is not discipline; it is "tyranny of the foulest type" and contradicts "the plain teaching of Scripture."[21] The modern age has overcorrected the one error and gone into the opposite ditch by disregarding discipline altogether.[22] Some arguments for eliminating discipline fail to understand grace and law and the biblical doctrine of the loving discipline from God our Father.[23]

Children can also get swept up by the spirit of the age. Children show a great lack of respect for their parents and often rebel against parental authority. The apostle Paul reminded Christians in his own day that in periods of great lawlessness, one characteristic would be "disobedience to parents" (Rom. 1:30; 2 Tim. 3:2).[24] Instead of being conformed to the patterns of the world, Christians must be transformed by Scripture's balanced call for wise, loving, Spirit-filled discipline and obedience.

Difficulty 4: Compartmentalization

The Doctor finds compartmentalization to be a far-too-common diagnosis for the church. The danger is that Christians separate their religious life from marriage, family, and work. This approach is fatal to real Christianity.

> There is nothing so wrong and nothing so fatal, as to be living a life in compartments. Sunday morning comes and I say, "Ah, I am a religious man." So I take up my religious bag. Then Monday morning comes and I say to myself, "I am now a businessman, or something else," and I take up another bag. So I am living my life in compartments; and it is difficult to tell on Monday that I am a Christian at all. Of course I showed it on Sunday when I went to a place of worship. This conception is entirely wrong. The Christian life is a whole; the Christian faith has something to say about every realm and department of life.[25]

Difficulty 5: Change Is Not Automatic

If a Christian calls Jesus "Lord" of his or her entire life, then why is compartmentalization ever an issue? Compartmentalization is a common issue

---

20 Ibid., 281.
21 Ibid.
22 Ibid., 277.
23 Ibid., 268–69.
24 Ibid., 239.
25 Ibid., 88–89.

because change does not automatically take place at conversion. Diagnosing a flaw in the thinking of many Christians, the Doctor places some of the blame on misleading statements made by evangelists that the Christian life is a magical existence where there are no more problems or difficulties.[26] This magical picture is a distortion of Scripture. If it were true, "there would never have been a single epistle in the New Testament."[27]

> The fact that we have become Christians, that the basic matter of our relationship to God has been put right, does not mean that we are now automatically right everywhere in all we think, and in all we say and do. The very paragraph we are looking at is proof, in and of itself, that we need instruction about particular matters.[28]

Conversion does not automatically eliminate the old difficulties. In fact, conversion to Christ often creates new difficulties.

> Not only is it true, as I have been saying, that the Christian is not automatically right about everything, because he is a Christian; we can even say that the fact that a man has become a Christian will probably raise for him new problems which he has never had to confront before. Or if it does not do that, it will certainly present to him problems that he has never faced before in this way.[29]

The Doctor's Prescription: The Lordship of Christ and the Spirit-Filled Life at Home and Work

Christians fail to live out their faith at home and at work because of a fundamental failure to work out biblical teaching. The New Testament teaching on Christian living assumes both the "knowledge of doctrine" and the "ability to work out that doctrine."[30]

> In New Testament teaching we are first of all given the doctrine, the teaching; then we are told that we have to apply that to our personal circumstances. Obviously, if we do not know the doctrine we cannot apply it; if we lack an understanding of the teaching we cannot put it into operation. First of all we have the instruction; we must receive it and understand it;

---

26 Ibid., 87.
27 Ibid.
28 Ibid.
29 Ibid.
30 Ibid., 308.

then we say, "Now in the light of this, this is what I have to do." That is the New Testament doctrine of sanctification; and what we have here is just one practical example and illustration of how we show in a practical way that we are being sanctified.[31]

Paul's discussion of the Christian at home and at work is an application of the atonement, the new birth, and the filling of the Spirit. Christianity at home and in the workplace will look decidedly different from their worldly counterparts because of these doctrinal and experiential realities.

Prescription 1: Head Check (the Lordship of Christ as Slaves of Christ)

How is the doctrine of the atonement to be worked out in the family and on the job? The atonement testifies to the glorious fact that Christians are bought by the blood of Christ and now belong to Christ as slaves of Christ.

> As Christians we are all "slaves of Jesus Christ." He has died for us, His body was broken, His blood was shed for us. He has bought us out of the market, He has ransomed us, he has redeemed us; we belong to Him. I must not think my own thoughts any longer; I am to be controlled by Him in my thinking as well as in my practice. Never forget that you are "slaves of Christ" says the Apostle.[32]

Our identity in Christ defines us more than our social status. The apostle takes up the question of how Christians relate to each other. How does he answer it? By looking all the way up to our relationship to Christ. From that heavenly vantage point, all earthly relationships are redefined and recalibrated. The "secret" of Christian relationships is simple: the lordship of Christ brings everyone to the same position.[33] Suddenly, Christian masters and Christian slaves are both slaves of Christ. Christian husbands and Christian wives are both the bride of Christ. Christian parents and Christian children are both children of God. Therefore, we do not narrowly live for ourselves or for others; we ultimately live "unto the Lord" because we were bought by him and belong to him.

---

[31] Ibid. That is why the Doctor follows Paul's teaching that believers should marry "only in the Lord" (1 Cor. 7:39). He also says that a Christian service at a wedding should be reserved exclusively for Christians. One makes a farce of the whole thing if a Christian wedding service is for non-Christians (ibid., 117).

[32] Ibid., 353. This quote comes from a discussion of slaves and masters, but the Doctor applies it across the board. For example, he says in his discussion on marriage, "We must consider marriage in terms of the doctrine of the atonement" (ibid., 148).

[33] Ibid., 360.

This teaching is the great golden thread of Paul's instructions to spouses, parents, workers, and masters. Wives submit "as to the Lord" (Eph. 5:22). Husbands love their wives "as Christ loved the church" (Eph. 5:25). Children offer obedience to their parents not out of mere duty but "in the Lord" (Eph. 6:1). Fathers bring their children up in the "discipline and instruction of the Lord" (Eph. 6:4). Workers obey masters as "you would Christ" (Eph. 6:5). Masters treat their workers in a certain way because they remember they themselves belong to the same Master in heaven (Eph. 6:9).

The head check leads to an eye exam, and this is the precise point where Christians and non-Christians part ways. They get radically different results on this exam because they are looking in radically different directions. The man of the world looks only at the world, while the slave of Christ looks much higher to the lordship of Christ. What happens when individuals look only at the world? They are truly slaves, controlled by what others think of them. The Doctor has compassion for them when he writes:

> The whole of the life of the unbeliever, poor fellow, is entirely governed and bounded by man. He wants the praise of man, so he always has his eye on men, he is always watching other people. But that should not be true of the Christian—"not as menpleasers." It must not be our ambition to please men.[34]

Christians are not callous. We care about what others think, but we are not controlled by what other people think. The love of Christ controls us. Heavenly vision comes from a new set of eyes received in the new birth. It changes the way we see everything and everyone. The Christian "sees everything in a different way—his work, his wife, his children, his home, his most menial tasks. His entire outlook is changed. Nothing remains the same—'Old things are passed away; behold, all things are become new [2 Cor. 5:17].'"[35]

Therefore, the first diagnostic question comes from the eye exam: Where are you fixing your eyes? Do you have earthly vision or heavenly vision?[36]

Prescription 2: Heart Check (The New Heart from the New Birth)

The head check now moves to a heart check. Has the doctrine gripped the heart? Paul calls for obedience not ultimately from the head but from the

---

34 Ibid., 351.
35 Ibid., 352.
36 Ibid., 351, 367.

heart. The apostle's heart check tests our motives. Is our singular motive to please our Lord?[37]

The Doctor moves closer and asks us if we realize the extent to which this doctrine must be applied. Do children obey their parents in a begrudging way? Do wives submit in a disrespectful way? Do slaves obey in a surly way? Do husbands show half-hearted love? Do parents or masters exercise authority in repressive or harsh ways? If we answer yes, then we are not obeying Christ from the heart.[38] Lloyd-Jones calls this a common failure. Grace at work means that our labor does not need to be "dragged out of us."[39]

Paul calls for obedience from the heart and "the depth of our being."[40] Obedience from the heart is "all out" and "whole-hearted."[41] The Doctor also appeals to the consistency of the biblical witness by pointing to Ecclesiastes 9:10: "Whatever your hand finds to do, do it with your might."

Born-again believers should pass the heart check. Why? God has taken out the heart of stone and put the heart of flesh into every born-again believer. All of Paul's teaching to Christian spouses, children, parents, and slaves or masters presupposes this profound change.

> This teaching assumes that, because we are Christians, we have undergone a profound change at the very center of our lives. I have already said that this teaching is not addressed to the world. It would be utterly pointless to take it and address it to gatherings of working people or of employers who are not Christians. To do that would mean that we do not believe in regeneration; it would mean that we do not believe that man by nature is entirely perverted as the result of sin; it would mean that we do not agree that man is essentially selfish and self-centred. But the whole of the biblical teaching is based upon that supposition.[42]

The heartbeat of the born-again believer is to glorify God. "To please God is the first and chief desire of the Christian."[43] A Christian is a person who realizes he or she is a sinner who has not been following God's will. He or she has refused to glorify God and enjoy him forever. The sinner, under the soul-searching conviction of the Spirit, says:

---

[37] Ibid., 348.
[38] Ibid., 349.
[39] Ibid., 349–50.
[40] Ibid.
[41] Ibid.
[42] Ibid., 307.
[43] Ibid., 352.

"Woe is me! I have never lived for God, and to do the will of God. I have been pleasing everyone but God. I have never thought that to please God should be the first thing in my life." But now he sees it. That is the first thing that is true of a Christian. He is a man who has come to see that his first consideration always in every realm and department of life should be to know, and to do the will of God; and he is determined to live in that way. His first consideration always must be, What is God's will for me? Is it that I continue as I am? Or am I to change to something else? Whatever he believes to be the will of God he proceeds to do.[44]

Prescription 3: The Obedience Check (The Fruit of the Spirit; Filled with the Spirit)

Therefore, once the mind understands the doctrine and God's call to submit or love or show honor or work hard or whatever, the believer will be moved to obey from the heart. This obedience is a work not of the flesh but of the Spirit. Lloyd-Jones frequently reminds his people that in the context of Ephesians all these commands depend on the earlier discussion of being filled with the Spirit. The difference between the lives of believers and unbelievers "is virtually the difference between a man who is drunk and a man who is filled with the Spirit of God."[45] The Holy Spirit will empower and energize our obedience. "The Holy Spirit, I say, does not exhaust; He puts power into us. . . . Alcohol, or any artificial stimulus worked up by man, always leaves us exhausted and tired. Not so the Spirit! Drunkenness exhausts; the Holy Spirit does not exhaust, but energizes."[46]

Therefore, obedience is both an overflow and an outgrowth. First, it is an overflow of being filled with the Spirit. The Doctor says that being filled with the Spirit is the key to parenting, because the person filled with the Spirit will use "disciplined power."[47] The person under the control of the Spirit will have control over his or her temper, unlike the person drunk with wine. The man drunk with wine is easily irritated and provoked to excessive reaction.[48] When disciplining a child, one should first have control over oneself. "If you try to discipline your child when you are in a temper, it is certain that you will do more harm than good. What right have you to say to your child that he needs discipline when

---

44 Ibid., 352–53.
45 Ibid., 236–37.
46 Ibid., 17.
47 Ibid., 278.
48 Ibid.

you obviously need it yourself?"[49] Obedience to Christ is also an organic outgrowth of the Spirit, which is why Paul calls it the "fruit" of the Spirit. Consider, for example, the apostle's call for the husband to love his wife. That love is elsewhere labeled a fruit of the Spirit. "So one of the ways in which I show that I am filled with the Spirit is not so much that I go into ecstasies and manifest certain phenomena; it is the way I behave towards my wife, when I am at home, it is this love which is 'the fruit of the Spirit.'"[50]

Prescription 4: Specific Social and Situational Applications

1. *Wives and husbands.* How does the atonement impact the Christian marriage? The believer, bought with the blood of Christ, has become the bride of Christ. That heavenly marriage union will find a reflection in the earthly one-flesh union of a man and a woman.[51] The spouse is not a partner but the other half. Marriage results not in two units but in "two halves of one."[52] This one-flesh union has many features, though I will restrict myself to three: (1) physical intimacy, (2) relational intimacy, and (3) lifelong commitment.

First, *physical intimacy* is one of the most obvious facets of the one-flesh union. "God has given us these gifts, sex included. There is nothing wrong in the erotic element in and of itself; indeed I go further, I say that it should be present."[53] Denial of the sexual element is a denial of Christian doctrine.[54]

Second, a one-flesh union involves *relational intimacy.* The sexual union is part of the one-flesh union, but not the whole of it. The Doctor says that the one-flesh union means that a husband and wife ought to take a vital interest in each other in every part of life (not just in the bedroom). The wife should take a vital interest in her husband's activities and success just as she does her own.[55] In the same way, the husband will share relational intimacy and not withhold himself emotionally.[56]

---

[49] Ibid., 279.
[50] Ibid., 126.
[51] Ibid., 213.
[52] Ibid.
[53] Ibid., 135.
[54] D. Martyn Lloyd-Jones, *Great Doctrines of the Bible: The Church and the Last Things* (Wheaton, IL: Crossway, 1998), 238.
[55] Lloyd-Jones, *Life in the Spirit*, 205.
[56] "The husband tells his wife everything. She knows his every secret, his every desire, every ambition, every hope, every project that ever enters his mind. She is one with him. He tells her things that he would

Third, union with Christ also reinforces the *depth of commitment* reflected in a Christian marriage. Christ does not divorce his bride, and thus the Christian should enter marriage without a back door in mind.[57]

2. Children and parents. Lloyd-Jones says that Christian children will listen to their parents in a certain way. They don't come alongside their parents to hear them from a horizontal position; they listen as those "under" their parents. Therefore, children are not just looking for what parents have to say; they are looking for directions to follow because, seeing their "position of subservience," they take what their parents say and then "proceed to put it into practice."[58]

But listening and obeying are not distinctively Christian responses in themselves and therefore are not enough. So Paul goes further. Children are to honor their parents. This command calls for far more than "mechanical" or "grudging" obedience. Rather, children should "reverence and respect" their parents and "rejoice" in the great privilege of their position as children.[59] Paul's instructions to Christian children address nature (the natural order), law (the fourth commandment), and grace ("in the Lord"—Eph. 6:1). Grace does not do away with nature or law; grace takes them both higher. "Grace raises the commandment to the highest level, and we are to obey our parents, and to honour them, and to respect them in order to please our Lord and Saviour who is looking down upon us."[60]

The Doctor demonstrates that Paul's instructions to fathers address a specific sinful tendency for parents to provoke their children.[61] Discipline must be administered in balanced, consistent, reasonable ways marked by a spirit of love and self-control. Discipline must never be domineering, capricious, severe, selfish, or mechanical. Such faulty discipline will provoke a powerful reaction of resentment that will only makes matters worse. The end result is worse than if we had never exercised discipline at all.[62]

One may wonder how any parent could possibly show such love, self-control, and long-suffering while avoiding the extremes of domineering or

---

not say to anybody else; she shares everything, there is nothing kept back, nothing is hidden. Such is the relationship of husband and wife" (ibid., 204).

[57] "When two people marry and take their solemn vows and pledges before God and before men they ought to be locking a certain back door that they should never even look at again" (D. Martyn Lloyd-Jones, *Faith on Trial: Studies in Psalm 73* (Grand Rapids: Baker, 1965), 29.

[58] Lloyd-Jones, *Life in the Spirit*, 241.

[59] Ibid., 242.

[60] Ibid., 248.

[61] Ibid., 277.

[62] Ibid.

mechanical discipline. The Doctor's answer is by being filled with the Spirit and the fruit of the Spirit.[63]

3. *Slaves and masters.* The Doctor notes that Paul once again directly addressed the greatest temptations for slaves and masters. A slave will be tempted to serve with "eyeservice," which means working with "his eye always on his masters, to do the minimum and get the most out of it."[64] The master must fight the sinful tendency to use his social position to threaten the slave.[65]

What is the positive application for Christian workers today? The Doctor urges workers to "be the best in every department," because bad work is the "worst possible recommendation for Christianity." Being "the best" does not mean being the "most gifted." Someone else may be more gifted, but here is the difference: the Christian will use whatever powers he or she has to "the maximum."[66]

> The other man may have more powers; that is not the point. If the Christian uses the powers he has to the maximum he is probably doing better work than the other man. That is the exhortation. The Christian should be "all out," always industrious, always honest, always truthful, always reliable, always helpful, always trustworthy. That is what should always stand out in the Christian. You cannot give him new ability, or new propensities; but a Christian, however unintelligent he may be, can be an honest man, an upright man, a reliable man, a man who keeps good time, a trustworthy man, a truthful man, a man whose word is his bond—always, a man upon whom you can rely. And all this, because he is a Christian. That is precisely what the Apostle teaches here.[67]

This is true whether the work feels meaningful or menial. And this is perhaps the most astonishing application. All work, even the most menial, *is* meaningful. What one does is not as important as the One for whom it is done. The exposition of this principle comes in Lloyd-Jones's treatment of Ephesians 6:5–8. Paul urges the slave to obey with "fear and trembling" (6:5) not because he has a slavish fear of his master but because he fears misrepresenting his true Lord and Master.

---

[63] Ibid., 283, 286.
[64] Ibid., 361.
[65] Ibid.
[66] Ibid., 355.
[67] Ibid.

This same phrase ("fear and trembling") appears in 1 Corinthians 2:3 as a description of Paul's preaching in Corinth. Paul preached with fear and trembling not because he was afraid of the Corinthians. It certainly was not stage fright! Rather, Paul feared the One he represented. He feared lest his preaching "might somehow or other misrepresent his Lord and Master."[68] Here is the Doctor's application: a Christian slave is doing a menial task, but he is "told to do it in the same way and in the same spirit as the Apostle himself preached the Gospel."[69] Paul did not elevate himself above the slave in any way. The apostle did all his work as a slave of Christ, and he "reminds these slaves that the same is true of them."[70]

What about the Doctor's application to Christians with authority over others at work? A Christian in authority will lead with great displays of kindness that avoid all forms of threatening. People will perceive a threatening demeanor in a wrong spirit, a harsh look, or words or actions that deliberately put a worker down.[71] The great motive of the earthly master is exactly the same as the best motive of the earthly slave: the desire to please the heavenly Master.[72]

The second motive that controls the earthly master is knowing that, as a slave of Christ, he will give an account to Christ (Eph. 6:9). The master must learn to see the way God sees, because God is not a God of partiality. "He does not look upon our earthly human divisions and distinctions as we do, He is not interested in them as we are."[73] We can focus so much on earthly distinctions in status that we lose sight of reality (God's point of view). The earthly master must keep his eyes on the heavenly Master and the judgment to come.

Life in the Spirit Is Evangelism

Lloyd-Jones stresses that this approach to life will stand out and create opportunities to testify to the power of the gospel. How so? Christ makes all the difference, and that difference will show. The Doctor reflects upon the whole of his pastoral ministry and the difference the gospel makes:

> I think I can say honestly that in my pastoral experience, there has been nothing more wonderful than to see the difference Christianity makes in

---

68 Ibid., 347.
69 Ibid.
70 Ibid., 353.
71 Ibid.
72 Ibid., 361.
73 Ibid., 368.

the husband/wife relationship. Where there was a tendency to part and to drift from one another, and an antagonism and almost a bitterness and a hatred, the two people on becoming Christians have discovered one another for the first time. They have also discovered for the first time what marriage really is, though they may have been married for years. They now see what a beautiful and what a glorious thing it is. You cannot understand marriage unless you are a Christian.[74]

How can Christian children put the power of the gospel on display? Christ came into the world to purchase us with his own blood and give us a new nature. Children can put that difference on display by obeying their parents. It is a wonderful opportunity because Christian children will stand out over against "arrogant, aggressive, proud, boastful, evil-speaking children that are round about you at the present time." So Lloyd-Jones says, "Show you are different, show that the Spirit of God is in you, show that you belong to Christ."[75]

And how can the way we work put the gospel on display? The Doctor closes his sermon on work with this stirring call to evangelism:

Perhaps someone looking at me and seeing me enjoying the drudgery, and doing it with a finesse, and with a glamour and a glory that the world can never produce, may suddenly be convinced and convicted of sin, and may become an enquirer after the way of salvation. Get rid of the notion that you have to be preaching or teaching explicitly in order to evangelize. You can evangelize where you are, just as you are. You do it primarily by your life, by the way in which you do your daily work. You prove that you are a Christian in that way, because only a Christian can possibly do it in that way.[76]

The "secret" of Christian relationships is simple: the lordship of Christ brings everyone to the same position.[77] The Doctor also says that the doctrine of heaven helps orient these relationships in the light of eternity:

So whatever your position is in this life and this world, let me remind you that it is only a temporary arrangement. It is not eternal. . . . This applies not only to servant and master, to husband and wife, to children

---

74 Ibid., 98–99.
75 Ibid., 248.
76 Ibid., 358.
77 Ibid., 360.

and parents, but to all other relationships and circumstances. You may be struggling with some terrible problem that is almost crushing you at this moment; you may be in some situation that is almost impossible for anyone to endure; or your difficulty may be concerned with your health; it matters not what it may be, remember that, whatever your position or problem, it belongs to the temporary order only. It is passing, it is "according to the flesh." It is not eternal. Thank God for that![78]

Conclusion: The Doctor at Home

I can remember reading through the letters of Martyn Lloyd-Jones and being profoundly moved by one letter in particular. It was a love letter sent to his bride, Bethan, in 1939. His family had been evacuated to the countryside during World War II, while Martyn stayed behind in London. He wrote:

> The idea that I shall become used to being without you is really funny. I could speak for a long time on the subject. As I have told you many, many times, the passing of the years does nothing but deepen and intensify my love for you. When I think of those days in London in 1925 and '26, when I thought that no greater love was possible, I could laugh. But honestly, during this last year I had come to believe that it was not possible for a man to love his wife more than I loved you. And yet I see that there is no end to love, and that it is still true that "absence makes the heart grow fonder." I am quite certain that there is no lover, anywhere, writing to his girl who is quite as mad about her as I am. Indeed I pity those lovers who are not married. Well, I had better put a curb on things or I shall spend the night writing to you without a word of any news.[79]

One of the great joys in reading Lloyd-Jones is seeing that he practiced what he preached. The family portraits sketched by grandson Christopher Catherwood testify to the amazing way Lloyd-Jones loved his grandchildren, took an interest in their lives, and seemed to have all the time in the world for them.[80] When I first started reading the biographies of personal heroes like George Whitefield and William Carey, I struggled with their personal examples as husbands or fathers. Therefore, it was refreshing to do a deep dive into the home life of Martyn Lloyd-Jones and come away inspired.

---

[78] Ibid., 365–66.
[79] D. Martyn Lloyd-Jones, *Letters 1919–1981* (Carlisle, PA: Banner of Truth, 1994), 47.
[80] Christopher Catherwood, *Martyn Lloyd-Jones: A Family Portrait* (Grand Rapids: Baker, 1994).

CHAPTER 12

WHY ARE YOU SO DOWNCAST?

Spiritual Depression

Have you realized that most of your unhappiness in life is due to the fact that you are listening to yourself instead of talking to yourself?

D. MARTYN LLOYD-JONES[1]

Introduction

Lloyd-Jones preached a series of twenty-four sermons on spiritual depression at Westminster Chapel in 1954. Some of the sermons were published in 1965 under the title *Spiritual Depression: Its Causes and Its Cure*.[2] Several years later, while lecturing on preaching at Westminster Theological Seminary, the Doctor shared more about the fascinating way the series came into being:

> I had actually determined—it seemed to me that I was being led in that way, but undoubtedly it was my own determination—to start a series of sermons on the Epistle to the Ephesians. However, one morning while dressing, quite suddenly and in an overwhelming manner, it seemed to me that the Spirit of God was urging me to preach a series of sermons on

[1] *Spiritual Depression: Its Causes and Its Cure* (Grand Rapids: Eerdmans, 1965), 20.
[2] Ibid.

"spiritual depression." Quite literally while I was dressing the series took order in my mind, and all I had to do was to rush as quickly as possible to put down on paper the various texts, and the order in which they had come to me, in that way. I had never thought about preaching a series of sermons on spiritual depression; it had never occurred to me to do so; but it came just like that. I always pay attention to such happenings. It is a very wonderful and glorious experience apart from anything else; and I would not dare to disobey what I regard as a very definite injunction coming in that manner. I am quite confident that the preaching of that series of sermons was dictated to me by the Spirit Himself.[3]

While the Doctor believed that the Spirit gave him the *topic* of the series, he would never claim that the Spirit dictated the *content* of the series word for word. He did, however, claim that the Spirit was at work in the process of organizing the series. Lloyd-Jones had been in the habit of writing outlines for sermons that could be preached on later occasions. He claimed that the Spirit showed him that some of those sermon skeletons in the pile would constitute a series on spiritual depression.

I was more or less able there and then, if I remember rightly, to put down on paper some twenty-one outlines of sermons. I had got the skeletons there, and all that seemed to happen at that moment was that the Spirit put them into order for me. So all I had to do was to go to the bundle of skeletons and pull out the particular ones indicated and look at them. It seemed to me immediately that this suggested arrangement was a perfect one, and I dared not vary it in any way. I added one or two at the end—but even the skeletons of those were also in the pile.[4]

Before looking at the Doctor's definition, diagnosis, and prescription regarding depression, let's start with an overview of *Spiritual Depression*. One could trace the flow of the book in three basic sections. The first section is an introductory sermon/chapter in which he establishes the overarching principle of "taking yourself in hand" and "preaching to yourself instead of listening to yourself." These general considerations are largely drawn from an exposition of Psalm 42.

The second section covers seventeen causes of spiritual depression and a corresponding cure for each. These sermons are wide-ranging discus-

---

[3] D. Martyn Lloyd-Jones, *Preaching and Preachers* (Grand Rapids: Zondervan, 1971), 189–90.
[4] Ibid., 194–95.

sions that move from causes such as shallow or flawed understandings of the doctrines of sin, justification, and the new birth. The sermons also address practical causes such as past guilt, fear of the future, false teaching, and suffering.

The third and final section looks at Paul's prescription for joy in the book of Philippians. The Doctor unpacks three key concepts from Philippians: (1) the peace of God, (2) contentment in Christ, and (3) the final cure of Christ's all-sufficiency.

One more introductory point must be made. Some would claim that *Spiritual Depression* is one of the Doctor's most controversial books, because he does not sufficiently distinguish between spiritual depression and physical depression. He does not expound upon the medical or chemical causes of physical depression and the need for medication or other treatments. He addresses spiritual depression, and thus he mainly puts forth spiritual cures. He also stresses that "a depressed Christian is a contradiction in terms, and he is a very poor recommendation for the gospel."[5] One Lloyd-Jones scholar believes that this is perhaps the most notorious thing that Lloyd-Jones has written.[6] It can have the effect of heaping a heavy burden of guilt upon an already depressed and dejected believer.

Therefore, this book must be read with a proper understanding of the nuanced differences between physical depression and spiritual depression. The next step is to define what Lloyd-Jones is addressing.

The Doctor's Definition: The Essence of Spiritual Depression

Spiritual depression is a debilitating condition of feeling cast down, dejected, and disquieted. Instead of composing a specific definition, the Doctor unpacks Psalm 42 as an overall portrayal of this condition. A spiritually depressed person is someone "tearful and weeping, who does not want to eat, or to see anybody, and who is so preoccupied with all his miseries that the kind of picture and impression that he presents is one of gloom and depression."[7]

Psalm 42 makes it quite clear that our countenance will reflect our relationship with God. Someone who feels far from God will show it in his or her face and look "dejected and disquieted and miserable." But the psalmist

---

[5] Lloyd-Jones, *Spiritual Depression*, 11.
[6] Andrew Atherstone, personal correspondence with the author, February 28, 2017.
[7] Lloyd-Jones, *Spiritual Depression*, 14.

also says that when he really looks at God, his countenance improves, because God is the "health of my countenance."

> I lose that drawn, haggard, vexed, troubled, perplexed, introspective appearance and begin to look composed and calm, balanced and bright. This is not the putting on of a mask, but something that is inevitable. If we are depressed or unhappy, whether we like it or not, we will show it in our face. On the other hand, if we are in the right relationship to God, and in a true spiritual condition, that again quite inevitably must express itself in our countenance.[8]

Lloyd-Jones is also careful to comfort downcast Christians. The New Testament Epistles testify to Christians who needed the authoritative teaching of the apostles to help them through innumerable troubles. That fact gives a strange kind of comfort to us today.

> If anyone reading my words is in trouble, let me say this: The fact that you are unhappy or troubled is no indication that you are not a Christian; indeed, I would go further and say that if you have never had any trouble in your Christian life I should very much doubt whether you are a Christian at all.[9]

Having loosely defined the condition, the Doctor next diagnoses the causes before moving to his prescription.

The Doctor's Diagnosis: The Causes of Spiritual Depression

What are some of the underlying causes of spiritual depression? The Doctor detects several interrelated factors: (1) temperament, (2) physical health issues, (3) Satanic attacks, (4) unbelief, and (5) a lack of doctrinal clarity and balance.

Diagnosis 1: A Susceptible Temperament

Some people are susceptible to spiritual depression because of their temperaments. Lloyd-Jones begins with two basic categories of people: introverts (people who generally look inward) and extroverts (people who generally look outward). Some introverts cross the line from self-

---

[8] Ibid., 13–14.
[9] Ibid., 66.

examination to morbid introspection. "I suggest that we cross the line from self-examination to introspection when, in a sense, we do nothing but examine ourselves periodically, but if we are always doing it, always, as it were, putting our soul on a plate and dissecting it, that is introspection."[10] Spiritual depression not only afflicts overly introspective introverts. Temperament may make one susceptible to a variety of other sinful responses, which Lloyd-Jones calls our own "special problems":

> You are always yourself, and, though you become Christian, you are still yourself. You have your own peculiar temperament, your own peculiar characteristics, and the result is that we all have our special problems. There are certain problems that are fundamental and common to us all, and even our particular problem comes under the general category of sin and the results of the Fall, but it comes to us in different ways, in several ways. . . . We all have certain things about which we have to be particularly and exceptionally careful. Other people are not troubled by these things at all. Ah, yes, but they have other things about which they have to be careful. The hot-tempered person has to watch that temper very closely, and equally the phlegmatic and lethargic person has to be careful, because he is so flabby in his whole mentality that he tends not to stand when he should stand. In other words, we all have our particular temperament which God has given us.[11]

Lloyd-Jones points to Peter as an illuminating example of what happens when our strengths quickly turn into sore spots of temptation and failure: "Peter's great characteristic was his energy, his capacity for quick decision, his active personality," but this energetic enthusiasm could lead to problems like impulsive or rash decisions. Therefore, Peter had to watch over this area of strength because it "was constantly leading him into trouble."[12]

Spiritual depression is a complex reality because many other factors compound the problem. Physical factors like diet and overall health add another layer of complexity.

Diagnosis 2: Physical Health Issues

One must not separate temperament too sharply from physical factors because temperament and physiology are intertwined. But it is clear that

---

10 Ibid., 17.
11 Ibid., 151.
12 Ibid., 152.

health issues can make someone even more susceptible to spiritual depression. Lloyd-Jones puts various health issues into this category, such
as fatigue, overstrain, and any form of illness. He asks a probing question:
"Does someone hold the view that as long as you are a Christian it does not
matter what the condition of your body is?" And he gives this pointed reply:
"Well, you will soon be disillusioned if you believe that."[13]

The Doctor takes a holistic view of Christianity that combines body,
mind, and spirit. Therefore, physical and spiritual issues can be distin-
guishable but not separable. He lays down a clear principle for how physical
and spiritual factors come together in spiritual depression: "The greatest
and the best Christians when they are physically weak are more prone to
an attack of spiritual depression than at any other time and there are great
illustrations of this in the Scriptures."[14]

These first two factors are mainly physical, but the problem takes
a decidedly supernatural and spiritual turn with the third factor of satanic attacks.

Diagnosis 3: Satanic Attacks

It is impossible to separate the earlier doctrinal discussion from this practical discussion of spiritual depression. The doctrine of angels and demons
comes to the forefront here. Do we believe in Satan and his malevolent spiritual forces or not? As Lloyd-Jones argues in his doctrinal lectures, "I do not
hesitate to say that the devil turns men and women in upon themselves,
knowing that when they are looking at themselves they are not looking at
God, and so he produces all these moods and depressions within us."[15]

The book *Spiritual Depression* identifies several subtle ways Satan
tempts us to take our eyes off of Christ by focusing on a variety of other
things. The Devil is a powerful and subtle foe who will ceaselessly change
his tactics until he can successfully tempt the saints to put Jesus on the
periphery and anything else at the center in his place. Satan will tempt us to
focus on our feelings, past sins, or future difficulties. In some cases, he will
bring false teaching forward with a full frontal attack on the doctrine of
Jesus's deity or humanity, but at other times he will cunningly suggest we
fixate upon secondary issues and make them central. The Devil will tempt

---

13 Ibid., 18.
14 Ibid., 19.
15 D. Martyn Lloyd-Jones, *Great Doctrines of the Bible: God the Father, God the Son* (Wheaton, IL: Crossway, 1996), 124–25.

weak Christians to conclude that they are not really Christians if they lack elevated emotions or overwhelming amounts of good works, or if they suffer from low levels of hope because of difficult trials or anxious doubts.[16]

Lloyd-Jones expertly lists various factors while showing how they combine and intersect with a fourth factor: unbelief.

Diagnosis 4: Unbelief

The Doctor makes the stunning statement that "unbelief is always the root reason or ultimate cause for spiritual depression."[17] How does this statement square with the previous discussion concerning satanic influence? Lloyd-Jones asserts that "if it were not for unbelief even the devil could do nothing."[18] The battle lines are clearly drawn between listening to the Devil or to God. "It is because we listen to the devil instead of listening to God that we go down before him and fall before his attacks."[19] The Christian life is a fight for sight. Spiritual depression happens when we lose sight of God. The psalmist's relationship with God and trust in God's power were weak because he had forgotten God and thus was depressed and downcast.[20]

Diagnosis 5: Lack of Doctrinal Clarity and Certainty

The fifth diagnosis builds upon the previous point. Christians may struggle with spiritual depression because they have only partial sight. They have faith, but it is also shot through with unbelief. They lack the complete sight and faith of doctrinal clarity and certainty.

Lloyd-Jones says that some people who suffer from spiritual depression are like the man in Mark 8:22–26 who was half healed of his blindness. He is difficult to describe. One cannot say he is blind any longer, but neither can he truly see because he sees people as trees walking. He is blind and yet not blind. People who are disquieted and unhappy and miserable share this same lack of clarity. Are they Christians or not? One day they feel it, and the next they do not. They have come to see the shallowness and emptiness of the world and its pleasures. They realize that they cannot save themselves, and they have come to see that Jesus Christ is "somehow" their only hope. But what don't they see? They are often unclear about the absolute necessity

---

[16] Lloyd-Jones, *Spiritual Depression*, 117.
[17] Ibid., 20.
[18] Ibid.
[19] Ibid.
[20] Ibid.

of Christ's death and the new birth. They lack balance and wholeness because they are half-hearted and have a divided will. Christianity moves them somehow, but they do not find real joy in it. They strain to pull themselves up to it and remind themselves of it, but their minds, hearts, and wills are not engaged fully. They do not like Jesus's narrow teaching. They have not learned to embrace it all, every word.

The Doctor lists various causes for this lack of clarity. Sometimes it is the fault of the evangelist or preacher for preaching a truncated gospel. "Lop-sided Christians are generally produced by preachers or evangelists whose doctrine lacks balance, or rotundity, or wholeness."[21] This lack of balance inevitably brings trouble "because man has been made by God in this balanced way."[22] For example, perhaps one's pastor preaches with only a shallow understanding of the gospel and never strengthens the flock with the faith-fortifying doctrine of God's sovereign and loving control over trials and suffering in this fallen world. False expectations can be fatal to joy and assurance. "The kind of person who thinks that once you believe on the Lord Jesus Christ all your problems are left behind and the story will be 'they all lived happily ever after' is certain sooner or later to suffer from this spiritual depression."[23]

Other times the fault lies with the people themselves. They do not like the demands that come with clarity and rigorous precision. They prefer a nebulous, vague system that gives them more control in the particulars. Perhaps they have never accepted the full teaching and authority of the Scriptures. They despise doctrine because it makes demands on them and insists upon self-examination and submission to the authority of God's Word.

The Doctor's Prescription: The Cure Is Preaching to Yourself

Reading the Doctor's prescription requires spiritual honesty—the kind pictured in the story of the man partially healed of his blindness (Mark 8:22–26). When Jesus asked him if he could see, he admitted that he could only see partially. We must not fall into the ditch of declaring that we see clearly if we only see partially, and we must not fall into the other ditch of cynically saying we don't see at all, when in fact we see some. After being honest

---

[21] Ibid., 53.
[22] Ibid., 60.
[23] Ibid., 51.

with Jesus concerning our condition, we must humbly yield to whatever he says. We must come to him in "utter submission as a little child," and confidently believe that "he never leaves anything incomplete."[24]

Prescription 1: Take Yourself in Hand

The first cure that Lloyd-Jones gives for the condition of spiritual depression is mastering the art of handling yourself or taking yourself in hand. Here is what he means:

> The main art in the matter of spiritual living is to know how to handle yourself. You have to take yourself in hand, you have to address yourself, preach to yourself, question yourself. You must say to your soul: "Why are thou cast down"—what business have you to be disquieted? You must turn on yourself, and say to yourself: "Hope thou in God"—instead of muttering in this depressed, unhappy way. And then you must go on to remind yourself of God, Who God is, and what God is and what God has done, and what God has pledged Himself to do. Then having done that, end on this great note: defy yourself, and defy other people, and defy the devil and the whole world, and say with this man: "I shall yet praise Him for the help of His countenance, who is also the health of my countenance and my God."[25]

The art of handling yourself means not passively listening to yourself, but actively preaching to yourself. Preach what? Notice how the doctrine of God immediately comes to the forefront. Preach God to your whole person. Preach all of God: his person, attributes, and promises. Hope in God! Passive listening must be replaced with active preaching. We must not placidly give this "other man within us" control so that the Devil uses him to drag us down and depress us.[26] Where do these thoughts originate, and who is this other man? Listen to Lloyd-Jones's answer:

> Have you realized that most of your unhappiness in life is due to the fact that you are listening to yourself instead of talking to yourself? Take those thoughts that come to you the moment you wake up in the morning. You have not originated them, but they start in the morning. You have not originated them, but they start talking to you, they bring back the

24 Ibid., 46–48.
25 Ibid., 21.
26 Ibid.

problems of yesterday, etc. Somebody is talking. Who is talking to you? Your self is talking to you.[27]

Taking yourself in hand means standing up and saying, "Self, listen for a moment, I will speak to you."[28] The next chapter in *Spiritual Depression* provides the next topic of conversation that we should have with ourselves: the depth of our sin.

Prescription 2: See the Staggering Depth of Our Sin Problem

Doctrinal and experiential clarity concerning the essence of sin is vital for spiritual health. Many symptoms show up when conviction of sin is shallow or absent altogether. It may seem strange that one would try to produce a deeper conviction of sin in those who are spiritually depressed, but Lloyd-Jones believes this approach is absolutely necessary and loving.

> "You say your object is to make us happy but if you are going to preach to us about conviction of sin, surely that is going to make us still more un-happy. Are you deliberately trying to make us miserable and wretched?" To which the simple reply is, Yes! That is the teaching of the great Apostle in these chapters [Romans 1–4]. It may sound paradoxical—the term does not matter—but beyond any question that is the rule, and there are no exceptions. You must be made miserable before you can know true Chris-tian joy. Indeed the real trouble with the miserable Christian is that he has never been truly made miserable because of conviction of sin. He has by-passed the essential preliminary to joy, he has been assuming some-thing he has no right to assume.[29]

Instead of simplistically equating sins with certain notorious acts like drunkenness or fornication, look at sin in its terrible essence. A negative test looks at external actions and asks which ones are obviously sinful. Lloyd-Jones proposed a positive test:

> My test is a positive one: "Do I know God? Is Jesus Christ real to me?" I am not asking whether you know things about Him but do you know God, are you enjoying God, is God the center of your life, the soul of your being, the source of your greatest joy? He is meant to be. He made man in such

---

27 Ibid., 20–21.
28 Ibid., 21.
29 Ibid., 28.

a way that that was to be the position, that man might dwell in communion with God and enjoy God and walk with God. You and I are meant to
be like that, and if we are not like that, it is sin. That is the essence of sin.
We have no right not to be like that. That is sin of the deepest and worst
type. The essence of sin, in other words, is that we do not live entirely to
the glory of God.[30]

If that exposition of the ugliness of sin hits close to home, then we are
ready for the high doctrine of justification.

Prescription 3: Glory in the High Doctrine of Justification

When conviction of sin makes one feel the darkness of condemnation, then
the gospel of justification by faith shines in its bright declaration of "no
condemnation." Justification by faith means that we look for salvation in
nothing else and no one else but Christ.

His being the propitiation for our sins means that God has made Him
responsible for our sins. They have been placed upon Him and God has
dealt with them and punished them there, and therefore because He has
punished ours sins in Christ, in His body upon the Cross, He can justly
forgive us. You see this is high doctrine. It is a daring thing for the Apostle
to say, but it has to be said and I repeat it. God, because He is righteous
and holy and eternal, could not forgive the sin of man without punishing
it. He said He would punish it, so He must punish it, and, blessed be His
name, He has punished it. He is just, therefore, and the justifier of them
that believe in Jesus. The sin has been punished, so God, Who is just and
righteous, can forgive sin.[31]

The declaration of justification comes through the gift of the righteousness of Christ received by faith. "He [the Father] imputes the righteousness of Christ to us who believe in Him, and regards us as righteous,
and declares and pronounces us to be righteous in Him. . . . So that it comes
to this. That I see and I believe and I look to nothing and to no one except to
the Lord Jesus Christ."[32] Lloyd-Jones makes it very practical. He describes
encounters in which he explains justification by faith to people and then
asks them if they believe it. When they say yes, he responds, "Well, then,

---

[30] Ibid., 31.
[31] Ibid., 32–33.
[32] Ibid., 33.

you are now ready to say that you are a Christian." But they hesitate. And when he asks them why, their response is often, "I do not feel that I am good enough." Reflecting on this, the Doctor offers his expert opinion:

> At once I know that in a sense I have been wasting my breath. They are still thinking in terms of themselves; their idea still is that they have to make themselves good enough to be a Christian, good enough to be accepted with Christ. They have to do it! "I am not good enough." It sounds very modest, but it is the lie of the devil, it is a denial of the faith. You think that you are being humble. But you will never be good enough; nobody has ever been good enough. The essence of the Christian salvation is to say that He is good enough and that I am in Him.[33]

Believing the lie that you have to be good enough is a denial of the promises of God and a denial of the completed work of Christ. There can be no joy without justification by faith!

> You will continue to be cast down and disquieted in your soul. You will think you are better at times and then again you will find that you are not as good as you thought you were. . . . Forget yourself, forget all about yourself. Of course you are not good enough, you never will be good enough. The Christian way of salvation tells you this, that it does not matter what you have been, it does not matter what you have done. How can I put this plainly? I try to say it from the pulpit every Sunday because I think it is the thing that is robbing most people of the joy of the Lord. It does not matter if you have almost entered into the depths of hell, if you are guilty of murder as well as every other vile sin, it does not matter from the standpoint of being justified with God. You are no more hopeless than the most respectable self-righteous person in the world.[34]

The glory of the gospel is not merely a judicial glory in the justifying declaration of "not guilty." The gospel is a complete gospel that captures the whole person.

Prescription 4: Come to Grips with the Greatness of the Gospel

In Lloyd-Jones's sermon on Romans 6:17, one witnesses the way the gospel captivates and satisfies the whole person. There Paul rejoices, "But

---

[33] Ibid., 34.
[34] Ibid.

thanks be to God, that you who were once slaves of sin have become obedient from the heart to the standard of teaching to which you were committed."

The "standard of teaching" or pattern of doctrine in this text is a total gospel. The Doctor asserts that the gospel is a "tremendous presentation of truth," which is not "partial or piecemeal"; rather it "takes in the whole life, the whole of history, the whole world."[35] How complete is this gospel? The Doctor glories in the fact that "there is no aspect of life but that the gospel has something to say about it."[36]

Failure to receive the totality of the gospel will cause people to miss the glory and greatness of the gospel. Lloyd-Jones says, "Spiritual depression or unhappiness in the Christian life is very often due to our failure to realize the greatness of the gospel."[37]

Why does depression or unhappiness flow from this failure? Unless one grasps the greatness of the gospel, its teaching will not reach the whole person: "the mind, the heart and the will."[38] Lloyd-Jones calls this complete capture "one of the greatest glories of the gospel": "Now one of the greatest glories of the gospel is this, that it takes up the whole man. Indeed, I go so far as to assert that there is nothing else that does that; it is only this complete gospel, this complete view of life and death and eternity, that is big enough to include the whole man."[39] Lloyd-Jones can scarcely find language to express the exalted nature of this threefold capture of the mind, the heart, and the will.

> The Christian position is three-fold; it is the three together, and the three at the same time, and the three always. A great gospel like this takes up the whole man, and if the whole man is not taken up, think again as to where you stand. "You have obeyed from the heart the form of doctrine delivered unto you." What a gospel! What a glorious message! It can satisfy man's mind completely, it can move his heart entirely, and it can lead to wholehearted obedience in the realm of the will. That is the gospel. Christ has died that we might be complete men, not merely that parts of us may be saved; not that we might be lop-sided Christians, but that there may be a balanced finality about us.[40]

---

35 Ibid., 54.
36 Ibid., 56.
37 Ibid., 54.
38 Ibid., 52.
39 Ibid., 56.
40 Ibid., 60.

It will come as no surprise that the Doctor stresses a particular sequence: (1) doctrine comes to the mind, then (2) the truth captures the heart, which (3) moves the will to act. He merely wants his order to match the order of the apostle Paul in Romans 6:17. "We must always put these things in the right order, and it is Truth first. It is doctrine first, it is the standard of teaching first, it is the message of the gospel first."[41]

Second, the truth grasped by the mind moves the heart in two directions: loving truth and hating falsehood. "Then having seen the truth the Christian loves it. . . . He sees what he was, he sees the life he was living, and he hates it."[42]

Third, when the mind and heart are in the grip of truth, the will wholeheartedly acts. A person "obeys, not grudgingly or unwillingly, but with the whole heart."[43] Therefore, the three come together because of the greatness of the gospel. "If you see the truth clearly, you must feel it. Then that in turn leads to this, that your greatest desire will be to practice it and live it."[44]

Seeing the full greatness of the gospel (chap. 4 of *Spiritual Depression*) frees us from our partial blindness and lopsidedness (chap. 3) whereby people look like trees walking. The greatness of the gospel now emboldens us to say goodbye to our past.

Prescription 5: Don't Look Away from Jesus

How does one respond to the subtle suggestions of Satan to fixate upon something other than Jesus? It is not enough to "just say no." Willpower alone is too weak to resist temptations. Why? Each temptation pulls at us. Each one feels right even though it is wrong. We must understand both the enticement and the right way to fight it.

First, *Satan can tempt us with our past.* Anyone who loves holiness has a holy hatred and shame for a sinful past. Satan's trap is sprung when we get stuck in the past, relive the sin, and feel paralyzed and condemned. Fixation upon the past paralyzes people when they are overwhelmed by the crushing weight of guilt. Lloyd-Jones says that he addressed this situation in pastoral ministry more than any other difficulty.[45]

What is the cure? Doctrine! Faith in the finished work of Christ means

---

41 Ibid., 61.
42 Ibid.
43 Ibid., 62.
44 Ibid., 61.
45 Ibid., 66.

saying farewell to our sinful past. The gospel puts your past under the blood so that it is buried in the sea of forgetfulness. Therefore, quit taking trips back in time to wallow in regret. What a miserable time machine the mind can be! A settled rest in the present reality of forgiveness requires active preaching that grabs your past by the throat and says, "Listen up!" When confronting our sinful past, we must preach the finished work of Christ. The dam will break and "immediately you will begin to experience a joy and a release that you have never known in your life before."[46]

Now we come to a life-changing lesson. Looking at the past should result not in depression but in praise for a blood-bought believer.

> Let me sum it up in this way, therefore. You and I—and to me this is one of the great discoveries of the Christian life; I shall never forget the release which realizing this for the first time brought to me—you and I must never look at our past lives; we must never look at any sin in our past life in any way except that which leads us to praise God and to magnify His grace in Christ Jesus. I challenge you to do that.[47]

The only way a backward glance at past guilt can produce praise is to go all the way back to the cross. We must avoid getting stuck at the moment of guilt; go all the way back to Christ's cross and see our guilt decisively dealt with there. At the cross, if we can say, "'Thank God His grace was more abundant, He was more than sufficient and His love and mercy came upon me in such a way that it is all forgiven, I am a new man,' then all is well."[48]

Second, if Satan cannot tempt us with the past, *he will tempt us with the future.* Anxiety comes from an overactive heart and mind. Lloyd-Jones walks us through an example. When someone we love is sick, notice how hard the mind and heart and imagination begin to work, causing a sleepless night.

> What a prolific cause of anxiety is the imagination. You are confronted with a situation, but if it were merely that, you would probably be able to lie down and go to sleep. But the imagination comes in and you begin to think: 'What if this or that should happen? Everything is fairly under control tonight, but what if by tomorrow morning the temperature should be up, or what if this condition should arise and lead to

---

46 Ibid., 35.
47 Ibid., 75.
48 Ibid.

that? You go on thinking for hours, agitated by these imaginations.
Thus your heart keeps you awake. [49]

The mind keeps us awake as well.

You find yourself beginning to consider possibilities and you put up
positions and deal with them and analyze them and you say: "If that
should take place we shall have to make this arrangement, or we shall
have to do that." You see how it works. The heart and mind are in control. We are the victims of thoughts; in this condition of anxiety we are
the victims; it is the heart and the mind, these powers that are within
us and which are outside our control that are mastering us and tyran-
nizing over us. [50]

The cure for anxiety is the outworking of doctrine. The Doctor notes
Paul's prescription of prayer in Philippians 4:6–7: "Do not be anxious about
anything, but in everything by prayer and supplication with thanksgiving
let your requests be made known to God. And the peace of God, which surpasses all understanding, will guard your hearts and your minds in Christ
Jesus."

We start with communion with God, enjoying his presence in prayer.
Only then do we come to the particulars of our petition. But we do not bring
our petitions without thanksgiving. In other words, we do not doubt the
goodness of God while bringing these petitions to God. We call to mind
what a glorious, blessed Father we have. Finally, we trust God's promise of
peace. The promise is not that God will remove the difficult circumstances,
but that he will guard our hearts and minds in Christ.

To me that is one of the most thrilling things about the Christian life. The
glory of the gospel is this, that whatever our circumstances, we ourselves
can be put right and maintained. It does not mention our condition, it
does not talk about these things that are harassing and perplexing, it does
not say a single word about them. They may or may not happen, I do not
know. Paul does not say that the thing feared is not going to take place,
he says that we shall be kept whether it happens or whether it does not
happen. Thank God, that is the victory. I am taken above these circumstances, I am triumphant in spite of them. [51]

---

49 Ibid., 265.
50 Ibid., 264–65.
51 Ibid., 269.

Third, *Satan can tempt us to believe that our emotions for Christ are not elevated enough to qualify as Christian.* This temptation has some pull because feelings have a place in the Christian life. "If you and I have never been moved by our feelings, well, we had better examine the foundations again. . . . You cannot read through your New Testament without seeing at a glance that joy is meant to be an essential part of the Christian experience."[52]

The cure is to start with faith, not feelings. If the Devil tempts us with our lack of feelings, we should say, "No, I do not feel anything, but whether I feel or not, I believe the Scriptures. I believe God's Word is true and I will stay my soul on it, I will believe in it come what may."[53]

Fourth, *Satan can use our trials to tempt us.* He can whisper that our trials prove that God does not love us. It is true that God permits painful circumstances to come into our lives. But that is not the most painful part. The biggest pill to swallow is that "He often appears to be quite unconcerned about it."[54] Lloyd-Jones calls the pain and the apparent lack of concern the "trial of faith."[55] The disciples faced one such painful test when they questioned Jesus's care for them in the story of the stilling of the storm.

What is the cure? Doctrine! We must understand the doctrine of God's sovereignty and his loving, sanctifying purposes for his children in suffering.

> Let us then be clear about this. We must start by understanding that we may well find ourselves in a position in which our faith is going to be tried. Storms and trials are allowed by God. If we are living the Christian life, or trying to live the Christian life, at the moment, on the assumption that it means just come to Christ and you will never have any more worry in the whole of your life, we are harbouring a terrible fallacy.[56]

Storms and painful circumstances come into our lives as a chastening, sanctifying grace. "A most prolific cause of this condition of spiritual depression is the failure to realize that God uses varied methods in the process of our sanctification."[57] Failure to understand God's purposes for our sanctification through varied methods like painful circumstances has severe consequences.

---

52 Ibid., 110.
53 Ibid., 117.
54 Ibid., 141.
55 Ibid.
56 Ibid., 140.
57 Ibid., 235.

Our failure to realize that often causes us to stumble and, in our sin and folly, at times even to misunderstand completely some of God's dealings with us. Like foolish children we feel that our heavenly Father is unkind to us and we pity ourselves and feel sorry for ourselves and feel that we are being dealt with harshly. That, of course, leads to depression and it is all due to our failure to realize God's glorious purposes with respect to us.[58]

The greatest answer to Satan's temptation to doubt that we are children of God because we suffer is to turn the argument on its head. Lloyd-Jones makes much of the fact that the author of Hebrews says we suffer discipline *because* we are the children of God.[59] The precise reason God's children should not grow weary when disciplined by God is this:

> For the Lord disciplines the one he loves,
>   and chastises every son whom he receives. (Heb. 12:6)

Prescription 6: Don't Separate Seeking Jesus from Obeying Jesus!

Satan's temptations to take our eyes off Jesus will fail only when we see enough of Jesus to fill up our sight and truly satisfy us. In other words, the cure for spiritual distraction and depression is a direct look at Jesus.

> There is only one thing to do, really seek Him, seek Him Himself, turn to the Lord Jesus Christ Himself. If you find that your feelings are depressed do not sit down and commiserate with yourself, do not try to work something up but—this is the simple essence of it—go directly to Him and seek His face, as the little child who is miserable and unhappy because somebody else has taken or broken his toy, runs to its father or its mother.[60]

Treasuring Jesus produces a hunger and thirst for Christlikeness. Holiness and happiness are not at odds at all. They find a blessed union together.

> If you want to be truly happy and blessed, if you would like to know true joy as a Christian, here is the prescription—"Blessed (truly happy) are they who do not go on seeking thrills; seek righteousness. Turn to yourself, turn to your feelings and say: 'I have no time to worry about

---

[58] Ibid.
[59] Ibid.
[60] Ibid., 117.

feelings, I am interested in something else. I want to be happy but still more I want to be righteous, I want to be holy. . . .'" Seek for happiness and you will never find it, seek righteousness and you will discover you are happy—it will be there without your knowing it, without your seeking it.[61]

Scripture commands us to pursue our ultimate joy and delight in Christ. We are called to rejoice in the Lord always (Phil. 4:4). This pursuit of delight in the Lord will never be an end run around holiness. Rather, "everlasting joy" (Isa. 35:10) belongs only to those who take the highway of holiness (Isa. 35:8).

We do not run on the highway of holiness in our own strength. The secret of the Christian life is to seek the power of Christ.

> The secret of power is to discover and to learn from the New Testament what is possible for us in Christ. What I have to do is to go to Christ. I must spend my time with Him, I must meditate upon Him, I must get to know Him. That was Paul's ambition—"that I might know Him." I must maintain my contact and communion with Christ and I must concentrate on knowing Him. . . . What else? I must do exactly what He tells me. I must avoid things that would hamper. . . . If we do not keep the spiritual rules we may pray endlessly for power but we shall never get it. There are no short cuts in the Christian life.[62]

The Doctor believes that the power often comes as one steps forward in obedience, not while waiting in prayer before obedience. Seeking the power of Jesus should not be separated from obedience to Jesus.

> That, then, is the prescription. Do not agonize in prayer beseeching Him for power. Do what He has told you to do. Live the Christian life. Pray, and meditate upon Him. Spend time with Him and ask Him to manifest Himself to you. And as long as you do that you can leave the rest to Him. He will give you strength—"as thy days so shall thy strength be." He knows us better than we know ourselves, and according to our need so will be our supply. Do that and you will be able to say with the apostle: "I am able (made strong) for all things through the One who is constantly infusing strength into me."[63]

---

61 Ibid.
62 Ibid., 298–99.
63 Ibid., 300.

Conclusion: The Sun Hidden but for a Season

Martyn Lloyd-Jones's preaching on spiritual depression can be a healing balm for struggling saints, but only if one can properly distinguish between physical and spiritual depression.

The Doctor's prescriptions are not a step-by-step self-help program. The power to break the black chains of spiritual depression comes only from the Holy Spirit, not from our ability to keep a prescription with precision. Dark shadows may come over the soul and not lift for a season, but by faith we know that the sun still shines, even when hidden behind the clouds. The next chapter will look at a dark shadow that every Christian will face: the valley of the shadow of death.

CHAPTER 13

THE ACID TEST

The Hope of Glory

The acid test of our profession is this: What do you feel like when you are sitting in an air-raid shelter and you can hear the bombs dropping round and about you, and you know that the next bomb may land on you and may be the end of you? That is the test. How do you feel when you are face-to-face with the ultimate, with the end?

D. MARTYN LLOYD-JONES [1]

Introduction

The apostle Paul counsels Christians, "Examine yourselves, to see whether you are in the faith" (2 Cor. 13:5). Of the many different criteria one could utilize to determine whether someone is a true Christian, is any one test better than the rest? Lloyd-Jones believes that one is. He calls it the "acid test" of Christianity: "the most delicate, the most sensitive test, the test of tests." [2]

The Doctor's Definition: The Acid Test

The Doctor begins by considering three different tests of genuine faith: (1) the doctrinal test, (2) the morality test, and (3) the experience test. [3]

---

[1] *Setting Our Affections upon Glory: Nine Sermons on the Gospel and the Church* (Wheaton, IL: Crossway, 2013), 16.
[2] Ibid., 13.
[3] Ibid., 13–15.

The first, *the doctrinal test*, Lloyd-Jones calls "the test of orthodoxy." He argues that orthodoxy is vitally important, and one cannot be a Christian without it, but it is inadequate by itself because one can have dead orthodoxy.

The second, *the morality test*, says that moral living is what matters because what people do is more important than what they say. Once again, the Doctor says that morality and conduct are absolutely essential; one cannot be a Christian without holy conduct. Yet one can live a moral life and not be a Christian. Nonbelievers can live highly ethical and moral lives. The test of conduct is not a test that can stand on its own.

The third test is *the test of experience*. Once again Lloyd-Jones agrees that experience is a vital part of the whole Christian position. One must be born again to be a Christian. But the cults also stress experience, and thus experience by itself is not a reliable guide. Lloyd-Jones mentions that one of the most dramatic changes he ever saw in a person's life happened when a woman he knew joined the cult of Christian Science. "She was entirely changed and transformed—a great experience!"[4] If we put up experience as the ultimate standard, the acid test, we are left without any reply to these various cults.

In the end, the Doctor evaluates each test and pronounces that each one is essential but not sufficient to stand on its own. The three are not "delicate and sensitive enough to merit the term *acid test*."[5] But the Doctor puts forth one great standard of analysis that does incorporate all the other assessments (mind, heart, and actions): *the hope of glory*. He argues that 2 Corinthians 4:17–18 is the acid test of Christianity: "For this light momentary affliction is preparing for us an eternal weight of glory beyond all comparison, as we look not to the things that are seen but to the things that are unseen. For the things that are seen are transient, but the things that are unseen are eternal."

The particular sermon in which he makes this point was preached and recorded in 1969 in Pensacola, Florida, during a hurricane warning. The organizers moved up the Sunday evening service to 2:00 p.m. so that congregants could be in their homes by the time Hurricane Camille struck the city. The Doctor proclaimed that the ultimate proof of a Christian profession comes in moments that bring us face-to-face with time and eternity,

---

4 Ibid., 15.
5 Ibid.

life and death. Therefore, he addressed the impending danger of the hurricane in a direct way. One man present for the sermon said he had a sense that "the sermon was not in the Doctor's plan but was one he had used during the Blitz and thought appropriate for the occasion."[6]

Lloyd-Jones's sermon references the Nazi *Blitzkrieg* upon London in World War II. The Nazis conducted an air strike in which they ruthlessly and relentlessly dropped bombs on London. The whole nation was ready to lose heart. People could find no hope in what they saw outside their windows. They could see no reasons to rejoice in the rubble. The Doctor says that the true criterion of Christianity is not how you feel in pleasant circumstances or while you are reading theology. It is how you respond to the worst circumstances.

> The acid test of our profession is this: What do you feel like when you are sitting in an air-raid shelter and you can hear the bombs dropping round and about you, and you know that the next bomb may land on you and may be the end of you? That is the test. How do you feel when you are face-to-face with the ultimate, with the end?[7]

Next, Lloyd-Jones works back through the three assessments one by one to show that the hope of glory in the face of death is a sufficient answer to guarantee all of the others.

> I suggest that this is the acid test because, you see, it covers my orthodoxy. The only people who can speak like this are those who know whom they have believed, those who are certain of their faith. Nobody else can. Other people can turn their backs upon disasters and whistle to keep up their courage in the dark, they can do many things, but they cannot speak like this without being orthodox.[8]

The hope of glory also covers the criterion of morality. "This test also guarantees conduct and morality, because the trouble with people who merely have an intellectual belief is that in the moment of crisis their faith does not help them. They feel condemned. Their consciences accuse them. They are in trouble because they know they are frauds."[9]

---

6 John Schultz, forward to Lloyd-Jones, *Setting Our Affections upon Glory*, 9.
7 Lloyd-Jones, *Setting Our Affections upon Glory*, 16.
8 Ibid.
9 Ibid.

The hope of glory also incorporates the proof of experience.

> And in the same way this test also guarantees the experiential element, the life, the power, the vigor. People cannot speak like this unless these truths are living realities to them. They are the only ones who are able to look upon calamity and smile at it and refer to it as "our light affliction, which is but for a moment," which "worketh for us a far more exceeding and eternal weight of glory."[10]

The hope of glory gives probing proof of a true Christian profession because calamity will cause other, counterfeit hopes to come crashing down. When all earthly hopes are lost, a Christian still has hope because his hope is fixed not upon this passing world but upon the world to come.

But why do we find it so difficult to live out the truth of 2 Corinthians 4:17–18?

The Doctor's Diagnosis: The Problem of Pain and the Tyranny of Time

The first difficulty is the *problem of pain*. We are not able to call our painful afflictions and trials "light," as Paul does in 2 Corinthians 4:17. They feel crushing and consuming. We feel defeated and drained by them.

The second difficulty is the *tyranny of time*. We are not able to call our afflictions "momentary," the way Paul does in verse 17. "Time! Most people today are defeated by the time element. . . . It is time that defeats people."[11] Life feels painfully slow. Sometimes a week can feel eight or ten days long. Life in a fallen world is full of problems, and when we face them on a daily basis, such afflictions do not feel momentary.

The challenge is compounded when the problem of pain and the tyranny of time both weigh on us at once. Lloyd-Jones gives an example of how they work together against us:

> Take a man and his wife who suddenly lose their only child. All their affection and interest had been settled on this child, and, oh, how happy they were together! Suddenly their son is killed in a war or drowned in the sea. Someone who is dearer to them than life is suddenly taken away, and they are bereft. And this is what they say: "How can we go on? How can we bear it? How can we face it? Six months, oh, how terrible. A year. Ten years.

---

[10] Ibid., 16–17.
[11] Ibid., 23.

Twenty years. It's impossible. How can we keep going? We've lost the thing that made life worth living." The tyranny of time. Time is so long. But Paul puts it like this: "Our light affliction, which is but for a moment."[12]

The third difficulty is that life feels "long and arduous," not "momentary and light."[13] "The difficulty with us," Lloyd-Jones diagnoses, "is that we are all so immersed in the petty problems of life that we do not see life as a whole."[14] He shows that Christianity brings a prescription to bear that changes everything with one essential contrast: "the grand context of eternity."[15]

The Doctor's Prescription: The Hope of Glory

The hope of glory gives us exactly what we need to avoid getting buried beneath the problems of this present age.

> I sometimes like to think of the Christian faith as something that takes people up in an airplane or up to the top of a high mountain and enables them to view the whole landscape, the great panorama. Christians have a complete, a perfect, a whole view of life. "The world is too much with us." That is our trouble. And we are beaten by it and defeated and immersed in it and lost. The Christian faith takes us up out of this world, and we look down upon it and see it from a different perspective.[16]

Doctrine makes all the difference in dealing with the tyranny of time when it feels unbearably long, not "momentary."

> There is only one thing to do with time, and that is to take it and put it into the grand context of eternity. When you and I look forward, ten years seems like a terribly long time. A hundred years? Impossible. A thousand? A million? We cannot envisage it. But try to think of endless time, millions upon millions upon millions of years. That is eternity. Take time and put it into that context. What is it? It is only a moment. If you look at time merely from the standpoint of your calendars and your almanacs and life as you know it in this world, it is an impossible tyranny. But put it into God's eternity and it is nothing.[17]

---

12 Ibid.
13 Ibid., 24.
14 Ibid.
15 Ibid.
16 Ibid., 23. Lloyd-Jones here quotes William Wordsworth: "The world is too much with us."
17 Lloyd-Jones, *Setting Our Affections upon Glory*, 24.

Christian doctrine also teaches us what to do with trials that seem unbearably heavy, not "light." Lloyd-Jones shows that Paul is careful not to say that our trials are light in and of themselves. They are counted as light only when contrasted with something else: the weight of glory.

> The apostle Paul has a picture. Do you see it? Here he is with a table in front of him, and on the table is a balance, a pair of scales. There is a pan on one side and a pan on the other side, and he puts in one pan his toils, troubles, problems, and tribulations. And down goes the pan, with all that unbearable weight. But then he does a most amazing thing. He takes hold of what he calls "a far more exceeding and eternal weight of glory." The learned commentators will tell you that at this point Paul's language fails him. He piles superlative on top of superlative, and still he cannot say it. A "far more," an "exceeding," an exceedingly abundant "weight of glory." He puts that on the other side. What happens? Down goes the pan, and that first weight was nothing. He does not say that it was light in and of itself but that when you contrast it with this "far more exceeding and eternal weight of glory" on the other side it becomes nothing. Put fifty-six pounds on one side—and it is a great weight. Yes, but put the "far more exceeding and eternal weight of glory" on the other side and your ton becomes a feather.[18]

But someone could object that all this talk about the doctrine of eternity is intellectual, not experiential. One can intellectualize about eternity, but how can someone experience eternity while being bound by time in the body? Doctrine and life find a blessed union through our spiritual resurrection, whereby we are already raised and seated with Christ. "Christians are already seated 'in heavenly places in Christ Jesus' (Eph. 2:6). They belong to eternity, and they are free from the tyranny of time."[19]

This intellectual and experiential knowledge of eternity (i.e., doctrine) is the key to a vibrant Christian life, because the doctrine of heaven and our heavenly inheritance helps us not just die well but also live well. Everything that the world can give can be gone in a second: cars, homes, fame, fortune. If we lose them all, we will not lose heart, because we have a better heavenly inheritance, which is incorruptible, undefiled, unfading, and kept safely in heaven for us (1 Pet. 1:4).

This heavenly hope puts earthly tragedies in eternal perspective. "Let your hurricanes come one after the other, and all together it will make no

---

[18] Ibid., 25.
[19] Ibid., 24.

difference. Let men set off all their bombs in the whole universe at the same time, this inheritance remains solid, durable, everlasting, and eternal."[20]

This hope of glory is also essential for our Christian witness and evangelism. We are living in a context where the Christian hope of glory can stand out against the black backdrop of despair. When a Christian hope of glory shines in the dark circumstances, people whose hopes have all been dashed will ask us for a reason for the hope that lies within us.

> Very many people give the impression of having inward peace and tranquillity when everything is going well. We can, most of us, put up a very good show when we are well and hale and hearty and young, and everything is prospering, and the sun is shining in the heavens; most of us are fairly good under such conditions. We have wonderful theories and say we will do this, that, and the other. But the test comes when everything goes wrong. Then people find that they have nothing at all, and they break down. That is where the opportunity for the Christian comes in at the present time because never have the outward stresses and strains been greater than they are at this moment.[21]

The trials of this present world are like smelling salts that jolt us awake after we have been lulled to sleep by the passing pleasures of this world. What do we wake up and see? The hope of glory! The hope of a new heaven and new earth! "Heaven on earth—that is where we shall spend our eternity, and not as disembodied spirits, for the whole man will be redeemed, the body included. A concrete body must have a concrete world in which to live; and we are told that that will be the case. The whole creation is going to be delivered."[22] The hope is a perfect hope of perfect harmony that cannot disappoint, because it will exceed all of our expectations.

> The perfect harmony that will be restored will be harmony in man, and between men. Harmony on the earth and in the brute creation! Harmony in heaven, and all under this blessed Lord Jesus Christ, who will be the Head of all! Everything will again be united in Him. And wonder of wonders, marvelous beyond compare, when all this happens it will never be undone again.[23]

---

20 Ibid., 26.
21 D. Martyn Lloyd-Jones, *Living Water: Studies in John 4* (Wheaton, IL: Crossway, 2009), 720.
22 D. Martyn Lloyd-Jones, *The Final Perseverance of the Saints: An Exposition of Romans 8:17–39* (Carlisle, PA: Banner of Truth, 1975), 89.
23 D. Martyn Lloyd-Jones, *God's Ultimate Purpose: An Exposition of Ephesians 1* (Grand Rapids: Baker, 1978), 206–7.

Language fails all fallen people at this point. We do not have the words or the capacity to comprehend fully the glory that awaits. The New Testament does not say more about heaven, because our language would fail us, and even if our vocabulary were "adequate," the description "would be so baffling we could not tolerate it, the thing is so glorious and wonderful."[24]

Lloyd-Jones teaches clearly that we are not to look forward to death as an escape from our problems, because that is a morbid and pagan view of the afterlife. The Christian view is always positive and triumphant. We look forward not to death but to eternal life. What do we anticipate most in a positive sense? Rest, freedom from trouble, peace, joy, reunion with loved ones? All those things are found in heaven, but they all fall short of our greatest desire: the face of God. "The Vision Splendid, the *Summum Bonum*, to stand in the very presence of God—'To gaze and gaze on Thee.' Do we long for that? Is that heaven to us?"[25]

The world to come is a place where disappointment is impossible. All our expectations are finite. If God is infinite, then it will be impossible for finite beings to be disappointed with what an infinite being of pure love, perfect wisdom, and almighty power would prepare for us. You can dial your hopes as high as possible, and you will find that they were child's play compared to what God has prepared. And the greatest gift of all is the Lord. Indeed, Lloyd-Jones says it well: "As we advance in faith and in knowledge and in experience, we shall more and more desire God Himself."[26]

Conclusion: Passing the Test

It is good to hold authors to the same standard they set for others. Did Martyn Lloyd-Jones pass the acid test? As the moment of death neared, he reached a point where he asked people not to pray for his healing; he could not handle the thought of being held back from "the glory." His eldest daughter, Elizabeth Catherwood, was reading her Bible by his bedside when the Doctor—who had lost all ability to talk—pointed excitedly to the passage about the eternal weight of glory (2 Cor. 4:17–18). When confronted with death, the hope of glory came roaring to life.

The Doctor has a probing question for us all in the conclusion of his sermon on the hope of glory:

---

24 D. Martyn Lloyd-Jones, *Children of God: Studies in 1 John* (Wheaton, IL: Crossway, 1994), 34.
25 D. Martyn Lloyd-Jones, *Faith on Trial: Studies in Psalm 73* (Grand Rapids: Baker, 1965), 111.
26 D. Martyn Lloyd-Jones, *Revival* (Wheaton, IL: Crossway, 1987), 216.

My dear friends, orthodoxy is not enough, morality is not enough, experiences are not enough. The one question for each of us is this: do we know something about this glory? Do we set our affections upon it? Do we live for it? Do we live in the light of it? Do we seek to know more about it? That is the secret of the Christian.[27]

There is one hope that is immune to any illness, indestructible in the face of calamity, and outside the range of any weapon: the hope of glory. The Doctor heralds the truth that it is not enough to know the test; we must also pass the test.

---

[27] Lloyd-Jones, *Setting Our Affections upon Glory*, 26.

PART 4

THE DOCTOR'S LEGACY

CHAPTER 14

THE LEGACY OF MARTYN LLOYD-JONES

Martyn Lloyd-Jones was one of the titanic figures of twentieth-century Christianity. What now sets him apart is the fact that his writings, sermons, and other messages are even more influential now, more than two decades after his death, than when he engaged in such a massive ministry at Westminster Chapel and beyond.

R. ALBERT MOHLER JR. [1]

Introducing the Disease of the Modern Church

Unbelief

Lloyd-Jones diagnoses the root disease in the world as unbelief. The church's influence in and impact on the world has declined because historically the church has become infected with the same disease.

> The Church and her own leaders began to criticise this book [the Bible], to set themselves up as authorities, to deny certain aspects of the teaching. They deny the God of the Old Testament, they do not believe in him, they say. They made a mere man out of the Lord of glory, they denied his virgin birth, they denied his miracles, they denied his atonement, they denied the person of the Holy Spirit, and they reduced this Bible to a book

---

[1] Endorsement of Martyn Lloyd-Jones, *The Cross: God's Way of Salvation* (Wheaton, IL: Crossway, 1986).

of ethics, and of morals. That is why the Church is as she is. The Church
rebelled in her doctrine and in her belief. She set up the wisdom of men in
the place of the wisdom of God. She became proud of her learning, and of
her knowledge, and what she asked about her preachers and her servants
was not any longer, "Is he filled with the Spirit? Has he a living experience
of God?" but, "Is he cultivated? Is he cultured? What are his degrees?" Now,
I am not romancing, am I? This is literal history.[2]

Proposed "Cures" in the Doctor's Day: Denigrate, Defend, or Downplay the Word

In chapter 1 we saw how the Doctor's confidence in the Scriptures stood
in stark contrast to the dominant approach in his day. Liberals (modern-
ists) took a very *cynical* view of the Scriptures, while many fundamentalists
took a *defensive* view that sounded like a retreat. Many evangelicals did not
retreat but surrendered, making peace with this low view of Scripture and
adopting a *lowest-common-denominator* view. They reasoned that the best
way to come together was to water down evangelical doctrinal distinctives
in order to become a bigger, broader ecumenical force that would have a
greater impact on the world.

The Doctor's Prescription: Preach the Word in the Power of the Spirit

Lloyd-Jones strongly believes that the risen Christ—not the world—needs
to set the agenda for his church. Christ's commission is to preach the gospel. God's pleasure is to save the world through the foolishness of the message preached (not the gospel merely discussed or defended). God always
has created and always will create his people by his Word. In this regard,
the Doctor points out that a revival of biblical preaching has been the defining mark of every true reformation and revival in church history.[3] True
preaching is "the most urgent need in the Christian Church" and therefore
"the greatest need of the world also."[4]

Therefore, the Doctor does not take a defensive posture. He sees himself as an evangelist, not an apologist. He believes in preaching the gospel,
not defending it. He agrees with Spurgeon that the gospel is like a caged
lion: you don't have to defend it so much as just let it out of the cage. Lloyd-

---

[2] D. Martyn Lloyd-Jones, *Revival* (Wheaton, IL: Crossway, 1987), 286–87.
[3] D. Martyn Lloyd-Jones, *Preaching and Preachers* (Grand Rapids: Zondervan, 1971), 24–25.
[4] Ibid., 9.

Jones let the lion out of the cage with biblical preaching that was (1) expository, (2) doctrinal, (3) experiential, (4) evangelistic, and (5) anointed.

Impact in His Own Day: Bringing Together the Word and the Spirit

1. *Expository.* Lloyd-Jones practiced expository preaching in a day where it was almost completely forgotten. His ministry caused many in the church to wake up not just to the necessity but also the beauty of biblical exposition. It must be crystal clear to the people that "what we are saying comes out of the Bible, and always comes out of it. That is the origin of our message."[5] The Doctor stresses that all preaching must be expository. An expository sermon will honor what he calls the golden rule of preaching: be honest with the text. "At this point there is one golden rule, one absolute demand—honesty. You have got to be honest with your text. I mean by that, that you do not go to a text just to pick out an idea which interests you and then deal with that idea yourself. That is to be dishonest with the text."[6] All expository preaching must have both the doctrinal and the experiential, and avoid the either–or ditch of emphasizing one over the other.

2. *Doctrinal.* Expository preaching is not a running commentary on a passage. Nor is it a transfer of information in which the people understand a mass of details in a text. It is not enough to show the grammatical fine points of a passage; one must draw out the eternal doctrines.

The people must know these doctrines and grasp them firmly with their minds. The doctrinal (in the mind) must come before the experiential (in the heart). The doctrines must be known (to the mind), then experienced (in the heart), and then applied (by the will).

3. *Experiential.* Once the doctrines are clear from the text, the work of direct address and application begins. The Doctor's Sunday morning sermons were more pastoral and experiential in terms of pressing home doctrines into one's heart and life. An expository sermon must not merely fill the head (as doctrinal/instructional) or warm the heart (as devotional) or move the will (as motivational). It must bring the three together in that order: head, heart, and will. The glory of the gospel is that all three are filled and inflamed.

---

[5] Ibid., 75.
[6] Ibid., 199.

4. *Evangelistic.* The focus of the Doctor's Sunday evening sermon was exclusively evangelistic. He celebrated scriptural authority and brought the claims of Christ to bear upon modern man clearly, passionately, and powerfully in his preaching. His evangelistic sermons would start with a common problem in society. He would then survey the world's answers to that problem and show how invariably shallow they were; they addressed the symptoms, not the root disease (sin). The Doctor would then examine the disease of sin and herald the gospel cure. He would clearly call for sinners to come to Christ. These sermons were expository, doctrinal, and experiential in nature, like his Sunday morning pastoral preaching—with one major difference. The morning sermons could have many points of application. The evening evangelistic sermons had only one point of application: repent and believe the gospel.

5. *Anointed.* The Doctor's weekly pattern was to focus his preaching on three kinds of need: (1) doctrinal/instructional (Friday night), pastoral (Sunday morning), and evangelistic (Sunday night). His overarching prayer was that all three messages would be logic on fire. Like Elijah on Mount Carmel, he could prepare the sacrifice in an orderly way, but only God could bring down the fire. The sermon must catch fire to be true preaching.

Lloyd-Jones believed that many people tried to supplement preaching with more drama or more music or worldly attractions because they had never heard or experienced true preaching. Biblical preaching must follow Paul's model for preaching, which insisted on the demonstration of the Spirit and power (1 Cor. 2:4). Without the Spirit, a preacher is only reading his notes or repeating words in reliance upon human oratory. Therefore, the Doctor celebrated the primacy of preaching in the demonstrable power of the Spirit. Some said that the result was that his preaching would come at the hearer with all the force of an electric shock.

One witness to his preaching, the noted theologian J. I. Packer, first heard the Doctor when Packer was a twenty-two-year-old student in London. Recalling his initial visit to Westminster Chapel in 1948, he describes his first encounter with the Doctor:

> The preacher was a small man with a big head and evidently thinning hair, wearing a shapeless-looking black gown. His great domed forehead caught the eye at once. He walked briskly to the little pulpit desk in the centre of the balcony, said "Let us pray" in a rather pinched, deep, Welsh-

inflected, microphone-magnified voice, and at once began pleading with God to visit us during the service. The blend of reverence and intimacy, adoration and dependence, fluency and simplicity in his praying was remarkable: he had a great gift in prayer. Soon he was reading a Bible chapter (Matthew 11), briskly and intelligently rather than dramatically or weightily; and in due course the auditorium lights went out and he launched into a 45-minute sermon. . . . The sermon (as we say nowadays) blew me away.[7]

Packer reflects upon the sermon's impact on him:

What was special about it? It was simple, clear, straightforward man-to-man stuff. It was expository, apologetic, and evangelistic on the grand scale. It was both the planned performance of a magnetic orator and the passionate, compassionate outflow of a man with a message from God that he knew his hearers needed. He worked up to a dramatic growling shout about God's sovereign grace a few minutes before the end; then from that he worked down to businesslike persuasion, calling on needy souls to come to Christ. It was the old, old story, but it had been made wonderfully new. I went out full of awe and joy, with a more vivid sense of the greatness of God in my heart than I had known before.[8]

Packer summarizes the legacy of Lloyd-Jones in personal terms: "I have never heard another preacher with so much of God about him."[9] And right there is the heart of Lloyd-Jones's legacy. The Doctor left people with a sense of God. When one encountered the Doctor himself, there was not much there that made an immediate, powerful impression. Quite the opposite. But the whole secret of his ministry comes at this very point. The goal was not to arrange an encounter with him but to encounter God through him.

Another visitor to Westminster Chapel during World War II describes the very same experience. When he arrived, he found a note posted on the front door. It said that the damage suffered from German bombings necessitated moving the worship service to a hall at another location. The visitor found the temporary location and took his seat among the small congregation. The service began and, the visitor later commented,

---

[7] J. I. Packer, foreword to Martyn Lloyd-Jones, *The Heart of the Gospel* (Wheaton, IL: Crossway, 1991), 7–8.
[8] Ibid., 8.
[9] Iain H. Murray, *D. Martyn Lloyd-Jones: The Fight of Faith, 1939–1981* (Carlisle, PA: Banner of Truth, 1990), 325.

A small man in a collar and tie walked almost apologetically to the platform and called the people to worship. I remember thinking that Lloyd-Jones must be ill and that his place was being taken by one of his office-bearers.

This illusion [of weakness] was not dispelled during the first part of the service, though I was impressed by the quiet reverence of the man's prayers and his reading of the Bible. The man seemed introverted and almost monotone. Surely he must be a last-minute stand-in.

When it came time for the sermon, the same mild man stepped into the pulpit with a quiet demeanor and voice. The sermon began and the illusion of weakness continued.

Then a curious thing happened. For the next forty minutes I became completely unconscious of everything except the word that this man was speaking—not his words, mark you, but someone behind them and in them and through them. I didn't realize it then, but I had been in the presence of the mystery of preaching, when a man is lost in the message he proclaims.[10]

The recovery of the role of the Spirit: The romance of a supernatural ministry. Lloyd-Jones prized the power of the Spirit in his preaching, but he knew he could not control the power or even forecast precisely when and how the Spirit would move in power.

The most romantic place on earth is the pulpit. I ascend the pulpit stairs Sunday after Sunday; I never know what is going to happen. I confess that I come expecting nothing; but suddenly the power is given. At other times I think I have a great deal because of my preparation; but, alas, I find there is no power in it. Thank God it is like that. I do my utmost, but he controls the supply and the power, he infuses it.[11]

The Doctor describes the impact of the Holy Spirit's presence, first on the preacher:

It gives clarity of thought, clarity of speech, ease of utterance, a great sense of authority and confidence as you are preaching, an awareness of power not your own thrilling through the whole of your being, and an indescribable sense of joy. You are a man "possessed," you are taken hold

10 Iain H. Murray, *Lloyd-Jones: Messenger of Grace* (Carlisle, PA: Banner of Truth, 2008), 30.
11 D. Martyn Lloyd-Jones, *Spiritual Depression: Its Causes and Its Cure* (Grand Rapids: Eerdmans, 1965), 299–300.

of and taken up. I like to put it like this—and I know of nothing on earth that is comparable to this feeling—that when this happens you have a feeling that you are not actually doing the preaching, you are looking on. You are looking on at yourself in amazement as this is happening. It is not your effort; you are just the instrument, the channel, the vehicle: and the Spirit is using you, and you are looking on in great enjoyment and astonishment.[12]

He then describes the impact of the Spirit upon the people:

What about the people? They sense it at once; they can tell the difference immediately. They are gripped, they become serious, they are convicted, they are moved, they are humbled. Some are convicted of sin, others are lifted up to the heavens, anything may happen to any one of them. They know at once that something quite unusual and exceptional is happening. As a result they begin to delight in the things of God and they want more and more teaching.[13]

The Doctor declares that true preaching cannot be divorced from the Spirit's power. What is preaching without the Spirit? We are merely reading our notes and repeating words. That is not true preaching.

True preaching, after all, is God acting. It is not just a man uttering words; it is God using him. He is being used of God. He is under the influence of the Holy Spirit; it is what Paul calls in 1 Corinthians 2 "preaching in demonstration of the Spirit of power." Or as he puts it in 1 Thessalonians 1:5: "Our gospel came not unto you in word only, but also in power, and in the Holy Ghost, and in much assurance."[14]

Lloyd-Jones longed for others to get caught up into the very presence of God through the eternal truth of his Word. A student from Jamaica describes his experience at Westminster Chapel in the same way: "It was as if I lost all count of time and space. The eternal truth that I hungered for so deeply was being revealed, and I was caught up body, mind and spirit in the sublime experience of receiving, finding, understanding, knowing."[15] This process of seeking the Spirit's power does not start when the sermon

---

12 Lloyd-Jones, *Preaching and Preachers*, 324.
13 Ibid., 325.
14 Ibid., 95.
15 Quoted in Philip H. Eveson, *Travel with Martyn Lloyd-Jones* (Leominster, UK: Day One, 2004), 86.

manuscript is complete; it must be the focus from the first moment of the preacher's preparations. The Doctor urges us to seek, expect, and yield to this power as the "supreme thing" and to "be content with nothing less."[16] Without this emphasis, there is "always a very real danger of our putting our faith in our sermon rather than in the Spirit."[17]

Doctrine on fire: Combining the best of the seventeenth and eighteenth centuries. Another way to talk about the holistic impact of Lloyd-Jones is to say that he was able to bring together the best of the seventeenth and eighteenth centuries. "I draw a great distinction between the preaching of the Puritans and the preaching of the eighteenth-century men. I myself am an eighteenth-century man, not seventeenth-century; but I believe in using the seventeenth-century men as the eighteenth-century men used them."[18] In fact, many of his lectures at the yearly Puritan and Westminster Conferences were not directly on the Puritans but on the eighteenth-century men like George Whitefield, Howell Harris, Daniel Rowland, and William Williams, who were marked by the influence of the Puritans.[19] Lloyd-Jones modeled his ministry mostly after the Calvinistic Methodist preachers of the eighteenth-century Great Awakening. The only kind of Calvinism that the Doctor believed in was Calvinism on fire.

> The more powerful Calvinism is the more likely you are to have a genuine revival and reawakening. It follows of necessity from doctrine. . . . I regard the term "dead Calvinism" as a contradiction in terms. I say that a dead Calvinism is impossible and that if your Calvinism appears to be dead it is not Calvinism.[20]

Continued Impact in Our Day

We have discussed the life and ministry of Lloyd-Jones as it was experienced in his own day, but what about his impact in our day? The things that shaped him are the same things that continue to shape the evangelical church today through him. His life was a rediscovery of expository preaching, the Puritans and the Great Awakening, and the fire of the Holy Spirit. His rediscovery of these three things caused a reawakening of all three in our day. God has brought these things to fuller bloom today, and so Lloyd-

---

[16] Lloyd-Jones, *Preaching and Preachers*, 325.
[17] Ibid., 230.
[18] Ibid., 120.
[19] Lloyd-Jones, *The Puritans: Their Origins and Successors* (Carlisle, PA: Banner of Truth, 2014).
[20] Ibid., 210–11.

Jones's ministry is even more influential now than it was more than three decades ago in his day.[21]

1. *Revival of expository preaching.* The Doctor's life and ministry have led to a reawakened interest in expository preaching. Not only do his sermons model expositional preaching; his preaching book has instructed and inspired many to follow his model.[22] In fact, John MacArthur says that the expository example of Lloyd-Jones is one of the greatest in the history of the church: "Martyn Lloyd-Jones was without question the finest biblical expositor of the twentieth century. In fact, when the final chapter of church history is written, I believe the Doctor will stand as one of the greatest preachers of all time."[23] All his books began as sermons or lectures he gave. He himself labored to edit most of them into books during his retirement years. The rest have been published after his death because of the labor of love of his family members. These sermons continue to speak long after his death.

Some people initially questioned the wisdom of publishing whole sermon series instead of shorter books and abridged sermons. John Stott once wondered if there would even be a market for such massive sets of unabridged sermons—such as the fourteen volumes on Romans. History has shown that the appetite is great. In fact, as Albert Mohler says, the Doctor's ministry is more influential today than it was during his own lifetime because of "his profound commitment to biblical exposition and the great skill with which he preached and taught the Word of God."[24]

Lloyd-Jones's sermons continue to speak in both print and audio formats. The MLJ Trust has over 1,600 sermons available to play or download (https://www.mljtrust.org/).

Lloyd-Jones had a unique ability to address the hearts and minds of his hearers. He believed that his books spoke directly to people because every book began as sermons originally designed to speak in that direct way. The rare unction that marked his original ministry still attends the

---

[21] Recall R. Albert Mohler's words at the beginning of this chapter. The Doctor is more influential today than he was in his own day. Endorsement of Lloyd-Jones, *The Cross.*

[22] As noted earlier, *Preaching and Preachers* was a series of lectures delivered at Westminster Theological Seminary in 1969 and then published in 1971. In the preface, Lloyd-Jones claims that this series of lectures is really his understanding of "expository preaching." Many have asked him to give a lecture on expository preaching, but he believes it is impossible in that "such a subject demanded a whole series of lectures because there was no magical formula that one could pass on to others" (Lloyd-Jones, *Preaching and Preachers*, 3).

[23] Endorsement of Martyn Lloyd-Jones, *Life in Christ: Studies in 1 John* (Wheaton, IL: Crossway, 2002).

[24] Endorsement of Lloyd-Jones, *The Cross.*

reading or hearing of those sermons. The sermons still convey a sense of the greatness of God, the wonder of the gospel, and the nearness of eternity. The Doctor's books continue to be read because his writings are so piercing and profound.

2. *Revival of interest in the Puritans, Reformed theology, and the Great Awakening.* Lloyd-Jones has also contributed to a revival of interest in the Puritans, Reformed theology, and the Great Awakening. He blew the historical dust off of these spiritual giants and reintroduced them to others so that they could shape a new generation. One practical thing the Doctor did was to help establish the Banner of Truth Trust and thus reawaken interest in the Puritans by republishing their works. One must not separate expository preaching and the Puritan movement. The Doctor testifies to the way they came together historically:

> We must ever remember that the Truth of God while meant primarily for the mind is also meant to grip and influence the entire personality. Truth must always be applied, and to handle a portion of Scripture as one might handle a play of Shakespeare in a purely intellectual and analytical manner is to abuse it. People have often complained that commentaries are "as dry as dust." There is surely something seriously wrong if that is the case. Any kind of exposition of "the glorious gospel of the blessed God" should ever produce such an impression. It is my opinion that we have had far too many brief commentaries on and studies in the Scriptures. The greatest need today is a return to expository preaching. That is what happened in the time of the Reformation and the Puritan Revival and the Evangelical Awakening of the 18th Century. It is only as we return to this that we shall be able to show people the grandeur, glory and majesty of the Scriptures and their message.[25]

No one could ever label the Doctor's ministry "dry as dust." We need to close this book by once again striking the glorious note as to what set his ministry apart.

3. *Courage in the face of criticism.* The holistic way the Doctor brought doctrine and life together like fuel and fire continues to challenge the church today. Some still fall into the trap of either–or thinking when it

---

[25] D. Martyn Lloyd-Jones, *Atonement and Justification: An Exposition of Romans 3:20–4:25* (Carlisle, PA: Banner of Truth, 1998), xii.

comes to Reformed theology and the presence and power of the Holy Spirit. One of the hallmarks of the Doctor's ministry is the blessed union of these two realities. He brought together what so many ministers tear asunder. With the Lord's help, he was able to keep his ministry on the straight and narrow and out of the ditches of overreaction. He avoided "the excesses of the Pentecostal and charismatic movements," in the one ditch, and a "cold non-emotional Calvinism," in the other.[26] The reader may remember the Doctor's own testimony about trying to steer clear of both errors—and the criticism that came as a result:

> It seems to me that we have a right to be fairly happy about ourselves as long as we have criticism from both sides. . . . For myself, as long as I am charged by certain people with being nothing but a Pentecostalist and on the other hand charged by others with being an intellectual, a man who is always preaching doctrine, as long as the two criticisms come, I am very happy. But if one or the other of the two criticisms should ever cease, then, I say, is the time to be careful and to begin to examine the very foundations.[27]

We must be willing to open ourselves to this kind of criticism because our need is so dire to banish this kind of either–or thinking. Let us go back further in time than the Reformers, the Puritans, or the Great Awakening—back to the early church prior to Pentecost. Pause for a moment to take inventory of all that the disciples had before Pentecost. It staggers the imagination. They saw, heard, and touched Jesus in the flesh. They witnessed his miracles and heard his teaching. They were already practiced in ministry as Jesus had sent them out to heal and to preach. They even witnessed his death and resurrection!

Furthermore, he opened their minds to understand the Scriptures after his resurrection so that they could see him in all the Law, Prophets, and Writings. And thus it is all the more striking that they are told to wait. They were still missing something: the power of the Spirit. The Doctor powerfully brings this point home:

> You would have thought these men therefore were now in a perfect position to go out to preach; but according to our Lord's teaching they were

---

[26] Eveson, *Travel with Martyn Lloyd-Jones*, 86.
[27] D. Martyn Lloyd-Jones, *The Love of God: Studies in 1 John* (Wheaton, IL: Crossway, 1994), 18.

not. They seem to have all the necessary knowledge, but that knowledge is not sufficient, something further is needed, is indeed essential. The knowledge indeed is vital for you cannot be witnesses without it, but to be effective witnesses you need the power and the unction and the demonstration of the Spirit in addition. Now if this was necessary for these men, how much more is it necessary for all others who try to preach these things?[28]

Conclusion: An Enduring Legacy

Martyn Lloyd-Jones believed that the Spirit is often neglected, quenched, or minimized in both preaching and Christian living. One of the Doctor's lasting legacies is his insistence on the blessed union of Word and Spirit. He spoke often against reductionism in the Christian life that would stress mind, heart, or will in a segmented or segregated way. He would counsel us to pursue the "balanced finality" of doctrine on fire in the mind, heart, and will.[29] The Christian life is doctrine on fire in which the glorious gospel takes up the whole person.

---

[28] Lloyd-Jones, *Preaching and Preachers*, 307–8.
[29] Ibid., 60.

THE CHARISMATIC CONTROVERSY

Introduction: Did the Doctor Become a Charismatic?

Christopher Catherwood describes two kinds of experiences he endured as a grandson of Martyn Lloyd-Jones. One involved people asking whether the Doctor had become a Pentecostal. The other involved whether someone had tampered with his books to make them sound Pentecostal. Had he become a Pentecostal, or had his books been hijacked by the Pentecostals?[1]

The answer is neither. Catherwood says that his grandfather's views are crystal clear in print:

> Yes, he believed in the baptism of the Spirit as an experience separate from conversion, although sometimes quite close to it. Yes, he also believed that all Christians received the Holy Spirit on conversion. What he calls baptism with the Holy Spirit was something different. Yes, he did believe in the continuation of spiritual gifts. But, no, he did not believe that they could be claimed, on demand as it were, nor did he believe that the gift of tongues was the necessary evidence of baptism with the Spirit. As for whether something was genuine, we have seen that he also believed all phenomena must be tested.[2]

Was the Doctor Pentecostal? No. He distinguished himself from the Pentecostalism *of his day* in four very important respects: in his view, (1) every Christian receives the Holy Spirit at conversion;[3] (2) it is possible to be baptized with the Spirit and never speak in tongues;[4] (3) no one today can transmit the blessing of baptism with the Spirit through the laying on of hands;[5] and (4) it is always wrong to divorce doctrine and experience.[6]

---

[1] Christopher Catherwood, *Martyn Lloyd-Jones: A Family Portrait* (Grand Rapids: Baker, 1994), 123.
[2] Ibid.
[3] D. Martyn Lloyd-Jones, *Joy Unspeakable: Power and Renewal in the Holy Spirit* (Wheaton, IL: Shaw, 1984), 34. "So while a Christian, by definition, is a man who has the Holy Spirit dwelling in him, that does not mean he is baptized with the Holy Spirit" (ibid.).
[4] D. Martyn Lloyd-Jones, *The Sovereign Spirit: Discerning His Gifts* (Wheaton, IL: Shaw, 1985), 53–54.
[5] Lloyd-Jones, *Joy Unspeakable*, 50.
[6] D. Martyn Lloyd-Jones, *Knowing the Times: Addresses Delivered on Various Occasions* (Carlisle, PA: Banner of Truth, 1989), 14, 312.

In 1971, Lloyd-Jones spoke strongly against what he witnessed in the charismatic or Pentecostal movement:[7]

> There is a factor which to me is a very serious one at the present time, and that is what is known as the charismatic movement. I am sure you are familiar with this. This is a phenomenon that has been confronting us for the last fifteen years or so, and it is very remarkable. It began in America and it has spread to many other countries, most countries probably by now. . . . The teaching of this movement is that nothing matters but "the baptism of the Spirit." . . . They have their congresses and their conferences, and they are virtually proclaiming that doctrine does not matter at all.[8]

In a letter, he warned against "the gross dangers and thoroughly unscriptural character of the whole thing."[9] In fact, Lloyd-Jones was appalled at the way Pentecostal teaching so brazenly departed from classic Christian orthodoxy. "They are virtually saying that truth has only come by them and that for 1,900 years the Church has dwelt in ignorance and in darkness. The thing is monstrous."[10]

Therefore, it is clear that Lloyd-Jones did not line up with traditional Pentecostal teachings in his day. But it is easy to understand why he was so hard to categorize as either charismatic or Reformed. His unique take on the baptism of the Holy Spirit did not align with classic Reformed theology either. What were his unique views on this matter?

Summarizing the Doctor's Position on the Baptism of the Spirit

It is essential to see that the Doctor addressed this subject many times at Westminster Chapel. He laid out his views on it in his lectures on Christian doctrine in 1954. He preached on it in his sermons on Ephesians 1:13 in 1955.[11] It appeared again in his sermons on Romans 5:5 in 1958[12] and his sermons on Romans 8:16 in 1961.[13] Then he preached on the subject again

---

[7] I am not lumping together all forms of continuationism in our day. I am adhering to the Doctor's words about the charismatic movement that emerged in his day.

[8] Lloyd-Jones, *Knowing the Times*, 312, 14.

[9] D. Martyn Lloyd-Jones, *Letters 1919–1981* (Carlisle, PA: Banner of Truth, 1994), 204.

[10] D. Martyn Lloyd-Jones, *Spiritual Depression: Its Causes and Its Cure* (Grand Rapids: Eerdmans, 1965), 188.

[11] D. Martyn Lloyd-Jones, *God's Ultimate Purpose: An Exposition of Ephesians 1* (Grand Rapids: Baker, 1978).

[12] D. Martyn Lloyd-Jones, *Assurance: An Exposition of Romans 5* (Carlisle, PA: Banner of Truth, 1998).

[13] D. Martyn Lloyd-Jones, *The Sons of God: An Exposition of Romans 8:5–17* (Carlisle, PA: Banner of Truth, 1974).

in 1964–1965 in his expositions of John 1:26–33. These sermons were published as two books in 1984–1985.[14]

Lloyd-Jones consistently stressed the same three things in these expositions: (1) the "witness" (Rom. 8:16), the "sealing" (Eph. 1:13), and the "baptism" (Acts 8:14–17; 10:44–46; 19:6) of the Spirit all refer to the same reality; (2) the witness/sealing/baptism of the Spirit is the highest form of assurance one can have; and (3) this work of the Spirit cannot be identified as regeneration.

First, *the three terms (witness, sealing, and baptism of the Spirit) all refer to the same reality.* Iain Murray agrees that Lloyd-Jones believed all "refer to the same experience and were therefore terms that he used interchangeably."[15] Lloyd-Jones did make a distinction when it came to different types of "filling" with the Spirit. He saw two different types in the Epistles (Eph. 5:18) and the book of Acts. He believed being filled with the Spirit in Ephesians 5:18 deals with sanctification. It is a command and thus, presumably, under our control.[16] The examples in Acts (of both being baptized and being filled with the Spirit) are all direct and therefore cannot be controlled. "The whole essential difference is this: in Ephesians there is an exhortation to do something, whereas in every single instance of the baptism with the Spirit it is something that happens to us, which we do not control."[17] The Doctor made the case that the terms "baptized" and "filled" are "used interchangeably" in the book of Acts.[18] He suggested the difference was that "baptism" is the word used to describe the first occurrence, while "filled" is the word used to describe subsequent occurrences.[19]

Christopher Catherwood argues that the book *Joy Unspeakable* led to greater controversy because that is where Lloyd-Jones more consistently utilized the language of *baptism* with the Spirit (a controversial code word) rather than terms like the *witness* or *sealing* of the Spirit.[20]

Second, *all three terms (witness, baptism, sealing) directly relate to the doctrine of assurance.* In fact, the Doctor said that the direct giving of assurance by the Spirit is "the greatest and most essential characteristic of the baptism with the Spirit."[21] The Doctor taught that the Bible testifies to

---

14 Lloyd-Jones, *Joy Unspeakable*. The second book was published the following year, Lloyd-Jones, *The Sovereign Spirit: Discerning His Gifts* (Wheaton, IL: Shaw, 1985).
15 Iain H. Murray, *Lloyd-Jones: Messenger of Grace* (Carlisle, PA: Banner of Truth, 2008), 129.
16 Lloyd-Jones, *God's Ultimate Purpose*, 263.
17 Lloyd-Jones, *Joy Unspeakable*, 77. See also Lloyd-Jones, *Sons of God*, 273.
18 Lloyd-Jones, *God's Ultimate Purpose*, 264.
19 Murray, *Messenger of Grace*, 141.
20 Catherwood, *Lloyd-Jones: A Family Portrait*, 124.
21 Lloyd-Jones, *Joy Unspeakable*, 90.

"three types of assurance" that are possible for the Christian.[22] The first type of assurance comes from trusting the promises that God makes to his children concerning their ultimate security. The second type comes from observing the objective changes that God has wrought in the life of the believer. He or she passes the tests laid out in 1 John for assurance. This second type of assurance strengthens and reinforces the first.[23]

These first two come from a process of deduction, but the third type is different in that it comes directly from the Spirit. Lloyd-Jones called it "the highest form of assurance."[24] He was very clear that directness is the defining characteristic of this work of the Spirit. "No longer indirect, but direct . . . this is entirely the action of the Holy Spirit—not our action."[25] The "glory" of this third type of assurance is "that it is neither anything that we do nor any deduction that we draw, but an assurance that is given to us by the blessed Spirit himself.[26]

Third, *this direct work of the Spirit is experiential and must not be confused with what happens at regeneration.* "The baptism of the Holy Ghost is not identical with regeneration; it is something separate."[27] This follows inescapably from the directness of the Spirit's work. The believer will be very aware that this work has been performed. It is not something that happens unconsciously or subconsciously (like the Spirit's work in regeneration). The Doctor cared deeply about keeping these two doctrinal realities (regeneration and baptism with the Spirit) distinct.

> It is said that the baptism of the Holy Spirit is "nonexperimental," that it happens to every one at regeneration. So we say, "Ah well, I am already baptized with the Spirit; it happened when I was born again, at my conversion; there is nothing for me to seek, I have got it all." Got it all? Well, if you have "got it all," I simply ask in the Name of God, why are you as you are? If you have "got it all," why are you so unlike the Apostles, why are you so unlike the New Testament Christians?[28]

Why did the Doctor care so much about this distinction? Without this post-conversion experience of baptism with the Spirit, Christians will lack

---

22 Ibid., 91.
23 Ibid., 92.
24 Ibid., 91.
25 Lloyd-Jones, *The Sons of God*, 304.
26 Lloyd-Jones, *Joy Unspeakable*, 93.
27 D. Martyn Lloyd-Jones, *The Christian Warfare: An Exposition of Ephesians 6:10–13* (Carlisle, PA: Banner of Truth, 1976), 281.
28 Ibid., 280.

assurance. Lloyd-Jones went so far as to say that the "greatest need at the present time is for Christian people who are assured of their salvation."[29] Lack of assurance hurts the witness of the church in the world.

Furthermore, if people "say that they [regeneration and baptism of the Spirit] are identical, you do not expect anything further."[30] He strongly asserted that believers quench the Spirit when they fail to keep these doctrines distinct:

> I am convinced that there are large numbers of Christian people who are quenching the Spirit unconsciously by denying these possibilities in their very understanding of the doctrine of the Spirit. There is nothing, I am convinced, that so "quenches" the Spirit as the teaching which identifies the baptism of the Holy Ghost with regeneration.[31]

The charismatic camp fell into the ditch of *fanaticism*. They divorced experience from doctrine by becoming "so interested in the experimental side that they become indifferent to The Scripture." "Now that is fanaticism, and it is a terrible danger which we must always bear in mind. It arises from a divorce between Scripture and experience, where we put experience above Scripture, claiming things that are not sanctioned by Scripture, or are perhaps even prohibited by it." The Reformed camp fell into the opposite error, "as these things generally go from one violent extreme to the other."[32] The Reformed camp divorced doctrine from experience and thus fell into the ditch of *intellectualism*. They reacted so strongly to fanaticism that they went "right over to the other side without facing what is offered in the New Testament."[33] The Reformed camp fell into the error of "being satisfied with something very much less than what is offered in the Scripture, and the danger of interpreting Scripture by our experiences and reducing its teaching to the level of what we know and experience."[34] The Doctor regarded the second danger as even greater than the first.

He concluded that the Reformed camp did not arrive at its position from an exposition of the Scriptures. But people were "so terrified of the supernatural that they were in danger of quenching the Spirit." They drove into that ditch because their fear of the charismatics caused them

---

29 Lloyd-Jones, *Joy Unspeakable*, 39.
30 Lloyd-Jones, *The Christian Warfare*, 281.
31 Ibid., 280.
32 Lloyd-Jones, *Joy Unspeakable*, 18.
33 Ibid., 19.
34 Ibid.

to overreact and overcorrect. They did so not because they were following Scripture but because they were duped by the wiles of the Devil.

> The devil does not want us to know this; he would keep us trembling and unhappy and miserable. He succeeds with some even with respect to the very doctrine of the Spirit. He keeps them in a state of uncertainty. He says, "To claim that the Spirit has given you direct assurance is presumption. You say you are a child of God, that you know that God is your Father, and that the Spirit has testified to it. That is enthusiasm! Ecstasy! Be careful; that is not the humility of the Christian man." Christians are so much afraid of excesses and enthusiasm that they are only satisfied that they are Christians when they are really miserable. What a tragedy! What blindness, what misunderstanding of Christian doctrine![35]

So Lloyd-Jones called for a combination of doctrine and experience:

> This is New Testament Christianity! New Testament Christianity is not just a formal, polite, correct and orthodox kind of faith and belief. No! What characterizes it is this element of love and passion, this pneumatic element, this life, this vigor, this abandon, this exuberance—and, as I say, it has ever characterized the life of the church in all periods of revival and of re-awakening. That is what we must seek—not experiences, not power, not gifts. If he chooses to give them to us, thank God for them, exercise them to his glory, but the only safe way of receiving gifts is that you love him and that you know him.[36]

This teaching on the baptism of the Spirit dovetails with the Doctor's emphasis on revival. In fact, revival is what happens when many people experience this reality of the Spirit's baptism at the same time.[37] Failing to keep regeneration distinct from the baptism of the Spirit quenches the Spirit and hinders revival. This reality informed how Lloyd-Jones spoke to fellow ministers about seeking the Spirit's power. He never urged ministers to follow charismatic practice. Rather, he exhorted them to "seek the Lord without setting limits on what he might do or what we would allow him to do, asking him to turn to us and visit us in gracious revival."[38]

---

[35] Lloyd-Jones, *The Christian Warfare*, 281–82.
[36] Lloyd-Jones, *Joy Unspeakable*, 203.
[37] Ibid., 51. See also D. Martyn Lloyd-Jones, *Revival* (Wheaton, IL: Crossway, 1987).
[38] Hywel Jones, "The Pastor's Pastor," in *Chosen by God*, ed. Christopher Catherwood (Crowborough: Highland, 1986), 24–25.

Evaluating the Doctor's Position on the Baptism of the Spirit

I applaud and commend Lloyd-Jones's concern that Christian people not be content with low expectations that prevent them from pursuing fuller measures of the Spirit. At the same time, I believe he took an experience (his own and what he read about in church history) and then read that experience into certain texts (which is eisegesis, not exegesis).

The Doctor's emphasis on experience caused him to ignore some key textual and terminological factors. Very few scholars have followed him in his understanding of the pertinent texts. Take his reading of Ephesians 1:13–14 as a case in point: "In him you also, when you heard the word of truth, the gospel of your salvation, and believed in him, were sealed with the promised Holy Spirit, who is the guarantee of our inheritance until we acquire possession of it, to the praise of his glory." The Doctor believed that the sealing of the Spirit is a post-conversion work of the Spirit that directly gives the believer a profound sense of assurance. This would mean that some believers experience this reality decades after conversion based on the sovereign timing of the Spirit.

I am not aware of any New Testament scholar today who adopts the Doctor's view. New Testament commentators argue that the aorist participles ("when you heard" and "believed") occur in the same time frame as the main verb ("were sealed").[39] These commentators all read Paul's words as stressing that the sealing of the Spirit is something that happens to every Christian when he or she believes. The Spirit is the seal of ownership stating that every believer belongs to God, and thus the Spirit is also the guarantee of the inheritance to come.[40]

Furthermore, the entire context works against the Doctor's reading of the text. The language seems to speak of a conversion experience of hearing and believing the gospel ("the word of truth, the gospel of your salvation"). The text itself does not give any hint whatsoever that this reality is for some Christians and not others. The whole point of this passage is that it is describing *all* the spiritual blessings that believers have in Christ (Eph. 1:3). It would go against the grain of Paul's stated purpose (expounding all

---

[39] The participles are coincident temporal participles. See for example, C. E. Arnold, *Ephesians*, Zondervan Exegetical Commentary on the New Testament (Grand Rapids: Zondervan, 2010), 92; A. T. Lincoln, *Ephesians*, Word Biblical Commentary (Dallas: Word, 1990), 39; F. F. Bruce, *The Epistles to the Colossians, to Philemon, and to the Ephesians*, The New International Commentary on the New Testament (Grand Rapids: Eerdmans, 1984), 265.

[40] Arnold, *Ephesians*, 92; Lincoln, *Ephesians*, 39–40; Bruce, *The Epistles to the Colossians, to Philemon, and to the Ephesians*, 265.

the blessings that are ours in Christ) if he were to cite a blessing that some believers have in Christ, but not others.

The Doctor was inconsistent when it came to why the Epistles do not give instructions on baptism with the Spirit. He said that it was not necessary for the doctrine to be taught in the Epistles because "all those addressed already possessed the experience";[41] today the experience is less common for believers, but every believer ought to pursue it patiently and passionately, even if they have to wait for decades.[42] But then why did the Epistles (like 1 John) have to teach about the lower forms of assurance (the first two types), if early believers had already experienced the higher and greatest form of assurance (the third)?

Yet another difficulty with the Doctor's view is the context of the Acts passages he cited. Is it true that assurance is what believers receive directly from the Spirit in Acts 1, 8, 9, and 19? The emphasis that the Doctor put on assurance as the defining mark of the baptism of the Spirit does not fit the context or content of the passages under discussion.

Conclusion: Seeking Fuller Measures of the Spirit's Presence

Lloyd-Jones cited the post-conversion experiences of people like Thomas Goodwin, Jonathan Edwards, George Whitefield, D. L. Moody, and many others.[43] I am not discounting their experience; I am only casting doubt on calling it "baptism with the Spirit." Why not simply call it a fresh "filling" with the Spirit? The book of Acts testifies to many experiences of being filled with the Spirit (e.g., Acts 2:4; 4:31).

I believe the Doctor overstated his case that linking the baptism of the Spirit with what happens at conversion will quench the Spirit and lead to low expectations for experiencing the Spirit's power and presence. I agree with Iain Murray that one can hold to the traditional Reformed view that the baptism of the Spirit happens at conversion and still yearn for fuller measures of the Spirit's presence.

> I think the danger he wanted to meet can be addressed by understanding that Christ's giving of the Spirit to the churches and to individuals is not uniform; there are variations, measures, and degrees of the Spirit's work, and thus always cause for believers to seek more. . . . There are cor-

---

[41] Lloyd-Jones, *Joy Unspeakable*, 36, 38, 43.
[42] Ibid., 225.
[43] Ibid., 86–96.

responding variations in the Christian experience. Sometimes blessings are deeper and more intensely felt, but there is no warrant to say that one of these should be counted as *the* blessing.[44]

The Doctor's insistence on the blessed union of Word and Spirit can be upheld without embracing his precise formulation of baptism with the Spirit and its specific connection to the doctrine of assurance.

---

[44] Murray, *Messenger of Grace*, 144.

THE SECESSION CONTROVERSY

Introduction

Before turning to Lloyd-Jones's famous speech in 1966 and its aftermath, it is necessary to sketch a bit of the background. The Doctor had a growing sense that a crisis was on the horizon regarding the nature and unity of the church. He shared this sense with Anglican clergyman and New Testament scholar Philip Edgcumbe Hughes (1915–1990) already in December of 1965. Lloyd-Jones put the crisis in the form of a question: "Do we believe in a territorial church or in a gathered church of saints?"[1] How one works for the unity of the church will directly depend on one's definition of the nature of the church, whether it is fundamentally viewed as "territorial" (like the church of England) or local (a gathered assembly of the saints).

A group called the Evangelical Alliance organized an event called the Second National Assembly of Evangelicals on October 18, 1966. This event became something of a turning point for evangelicalism in the United Kingdom. The ripple effect of this meeting would be felt far and wide.

The Event and Its Aftermath

Lloyd-Jones addressed the assembly with a message entitled "Evangelical Unity: An Appeal." The leadership committee had invited the Doctor to speak on this theme. They knew almost exactly what he would say but had not counted on its powerful effect on his listeners. In fact, the chairman for the assembly, the Rev. John R. W. Stott (1921–2011), became concerned that the message was so compelling that it would cause impressionable young evangelicals to pull out of mixed denominations (like the Anglican church) instead of laboring to renew them from within. Therefore, Stott made an impromptu decision. Instead of closing the meeting as scheduled, he thanked the Doctor for his talk and then, "with much nervousness and

---

[1] D. Martyn Lloyd-Jones, *Letters 1919–1981* (Carlisle, PA: Banner of Truth, 1994), 167.

diffidence," offered a few remarks in reply to make plain that he did not agree with the Doctor's address. Christopher Catherwood (Lloyd-Jones's grandson) believes that Stott's words "came over far more forcefully than he had intended."[2] Stott said: "I believe history is against what Dr. Lloyd-Jones has said. . . . Scripture is against him. . . . I hope no one will act precipitately. . . . We are all concerned with the same ultimate issues and with the glory of God."[3]

This event has been revisited many times in the five decades since it happened. Nothing close to a consensus has emerged on what Lloyd-Jones actually meant or what happened next, or who is to blame for what happened next.[4] The tragic irony of the Doctor's speech and Stott's response is that it "prompted a crisis in itself, in that it exposed a major division within evangelicalism on the opening day of a conference which was intended to foster evangelical unity."[5]

Unfortunately, the relational fallout from this event can be clearly documented. The Doctor's friend, J. I. Packer (b. 1926), was not present at the meeting but heard the report of it and eventually sided with Stott. This decision served to damage his long-standing friendship with Lloyd-Jones. Packer summarized the positional separation between them as follows:

> The Doctor believed that his summons to separation was a call for evangelical unity as such, and that he was not a denominationalist in any sense. In continuing to combat error, commend truth, and strengthen evangelical ministry as best I could in the church of England, he thought I was showing myself a denominationalist and obstructing evangelical unity, besides being caught in a hopelessly compromised position. By contrast, I believed that the claims of evangelical unity do not require ecclesiastical separation where the faith is not actually being denied and renewal remains possible; that the action for which the Doctor called would be, in effect, the founding of a new, loose-knit, professedly undenominational denomination; and that he, rather than I, was the denominationalist for insisting that evangelicals must all belong to this grouping and no other.[6]

[2] Christopher Catherwood, *Martyn Lloyd-Jones: A Family Portrait* (Grand Rapids: Baker, 1994), 145.
[3] Quoted in Iain H. Murray, *D. Martyn Lloyd-Jones: The Fight of Faith, 1939–1981* (Carlisle, PA: Banner of Truth, 1990), 525.
[4] See Iain H. Murray, "Divisive Unity," *The Masters Theological Journal* 12, no. 2 (2001): 231–47. Murray provides an apt summary: "What were Lloyd-Jones and John Stott disagreeing about? Asking this question leads us immediately into the controversy, because, strange as it may sound, to this day there is no agreement over what the difference actually was!" (ibid., 233).
[5] Alister McGrath, *J. I. Packer: A Biography* (Grand Rapids: Baker, 1997), 125.
[6] J. I. Packer, "David Martyn Lloyd-Jones," in *Honouring the People of God*, vol. 4 of *The Collected Shorter Writings of J. I. Packer* (Carlisle, UK: Paternoster, 1999), 79.

Packer continued to speak about Lloyd-Jones with the utmost respect and admiration, saying that "he was the greatest man I have ever known and that there is more of him under my skin than there is of any other of my human teachers."[7] The close friendship between Fred and Elizabeth Catherwood (Lloyd-Jones's son-in-law and daughter) and Jim and Kit Packer—which went back to undergraduate days at Oxford—also continued.[8]

Stott did later apologize to Lloyd-Jones, and the two men continued to enjoy a warm personal relationship. Christopher Catherwood stressed how Stott went out of his way to show kindness to both Martyn and Bethan two years later when Martyn was in the hospital.[9]

Sam Storms says, "Some believe that Lloyd-Jones destroyed evangelical unity and that Packer and Stott together followed the pathway of compromise. These judgments are almost certainly wrong."[10] A more balanced assessment would recognize that both sides responded in unhelpful ways. Christopher Catherwood points to the experience of Francis Schaeffer in this connection. Schaeffer himself had to break with a denomination over doctrinal matters in the 1930s, and his experience taught him to identify two tragic tendencies when such a break occurs. First, "a sense of spiritual superiority" can infiltrate the ranks of those who leave, and they can in turn cultivate a kind of bitterness toward those who refuse to leave. Second, among those who stay in mixed denominations, there can be an increasing tendency to compromise. Once the decision to stay has been made, it can become a fixed resolve never to leave, even when things get worse and worse. Catherwood believes that both of these things happened in the aftermath of the Doctor's speech.[11]

Bob Horn is probably correct in his summary of the drift that took place between denominational evangelicals and independent evangelicals:

Before 1966, evangelicals had been more conscious of their ties to each other than their links to denominations. . . . We were in general militantly defensive—battling for the truth against the ecumenical monoliths, with a simple clarity and a robust cohesion. After 1966, evangelicalism drifted into various camps. . . . Denominational affairs took up time and energy

---

7 Ibid., 77.
8 Christopher Catherwood, *Martyn Lloyd-Jones: His Life and Relevance for the 21st Century* (Wheaton, IL: Crossway, 2015), 89.
9 Catherwood, *Lloyd-Jones: A Family Portrait*, 145.
10 Sam Storms, *J. I. Packer on the Christian Life: Knowing God in Christ, Walking by the Spirit* (Wheaton, IL: Crossway, 2015), 20.
11 Catherwood, *Lloyd-Jones: His Life and Relevance*, 90.

that could have (and previously had) gone to inter-evangelical relationships. Evangelicals, denominational and independent, drifted apart.[12]

How should we assess this moment and its aftermath with respect to the life and legacy of Lloyd-Jones? In what follows, I will briefly summarize the substance of his speech and then offer a short assessment.

Summarizing the Doctor's Address

What did the Doctor actually say or stress in this speech? Christopher Catherwood asks those who go back and read the speech to take careful note of the *way* the Doctor crafted his plea. Lloyd-Jones himself put the emphasis on the positive call to unite, not a negative call to divide. Why does that finely tuned nuance matter? It means that the address was not a call against Anglicans in particular, but rather a positive call to *all* evangelicals from every denominational affiliation (e.g., Baptist Union, Congregationalists, Welsh Presbyterians).

The substance of the Doctor's conviction was that schism was already happening. Evangelicals were wrongly divided. That disunity must be addressed. Denominations, he believed, are man-made constructs that wrongly lump together true believers with people who merely claim to be Christians. Therefore, man-made, mixed denominations are to blame for breaking the fellowship of true believers from visible expressions of unity. Leaving a mixed denomination would not make someone guilty of schism. Schism does not happen when evangelicals divide from those who deny the faith. Instead, schism happens when those who embrace the essentials of the faith are divided among themselves. What is at stake in such division?

First, the church holds up a confusing picture for the watching world concerning what it means to be a church and a Christian.[13] The church cannot afford to be confused or confusing on these matters. Lloyd-Jones believed that if evangelicals continued as they were, it would have a corrosive effect, like a universal acid that would eat away trust in the gospel and robust doctrinal identity.

One must remember that the ecumenical movement did not challenge

---

12 Bob Horn, "His Place in Evangelicalism," in *Chosen by God*, ed. Christopher Catherwood (Crowborough: Highland, 1986), 24–25.
13 Martyn Lloyd-Jones, "Evangelical Unity: An Appeal," in *Knowing the Times: Addresses Delivered on Various Occasions* (Carlisle, PA: Banner of Truth, 1989), 254.

someone's profession of faith. If a person professed to be a Christian, then it was assumed that he or she was (regardless of denomination or faith position). Therefore, the ecumenical movement was mainly concerned with bringing together people who already claimed to be Christian. The movement was not interested in defining or defending the gospel and did not devote time or attention to discerning biblically what a legitimate Christian confession really is.

Therefore, the far-reaching issue, for the Doctor, was defining and preserving the gospel so that it could be clearly proclaimed to a lost world. This was the point he consistently stressed when speaking on these matters at other times.

> There are those who seem to think that the one problem in the Church today is the problem of unity. So they give all their time and attention to this. That people are going to hell does not seem to matter to them, they are always preaching about unity, and writing books about it. "The Unity of the Church" is their gospel. But that has never saved anyone. If all the Churches in the world, including the Roman Catholic Church, became amalgamated and you could say that now we had one great world Church, I venture to prophesy that it would not make the slightest difference to the man in the street. He is not outside the Churches because the Churches are disunited, he is outside because he likes his sin, because he is a sinner, because he is ignorant of spiritual realities. He is no more interested in this problem of unity than is the man in the moon! And yet the Church is talking about the problem of unity as if it were the central problem.[14]

Second, this division of evangelicals quenches the Spirit and prevents an outpouring of revival. The Doctor believed that evangelicals who stayed in mixed denominations were trusting in the power of man-made structures and man-made methods, like influence and position and numbers. The church should not try to do the Lord's work and win the world using the world's methods. The church needs to rely upon the power of the Spirit to win the world.[15] Therefore, evangelicals should come together as "a fellowship, or an association, of evangelical churches."[16]

---

[14] D. Martyn Lloyd-Jones, *The Christian Soldier: An Exposition of Ephesians 6:10–20* (Grand Rapids: Baker, 1977), 292.
[15] Lloyd-Jones, "Evangelical Unity," 256.
[16] Ibid., 257.

Evaluating the Doctor's Address and Its Aftermath

Lloyd-Jones was clearly right to be concerned about the state of the church and the doctrinal decline that was underway in his day. Iain Murray, in his landmark book *Evangelicalism Divided*, delivers a powerful exposé of what was happening.[17] Murray rightly shows that liberalism's war cry that "Christianity is life, not doctrine" would destroy evangelical identity if followed. But there was no compromise, at one level, because the battle lines were clearly drawn. By saying that the church did not need to insist on doctrine and orthodox beliefs, liberalism created an entirely new definition of a Christian. One did not need to believe in the fall of man, the atonement, or the deity of Christ to be a Christian. Therefore, the ecumenical movement was based on one important ground rule: "All who say they are Christians are to be accepted as such." But Murray identifies the problem for evangelicals clearly and forcefully:

> If agreeing to the ground rule "we are all Christians" was necessary to gain ecumenical and denominational acceptance, how could such agreement be consistent with the uniqueness of their beliefs? If evangelical belief is, in essence, gospel belief, how can Christian fellowship exist independently of any common commitment to that belief?[18]

The reason the Doctor chose to stress evangelical unity at this time was the belief that the ecumenical movement, the World Council of Churches, and the doctrinal decline he witnessed everywhere had simply gone too far. In essence, this speech marked the moment he crossed the Rubicon.[19] It is truly stirring to witness the lionhearted way the Doctor not only heralded the gospel but also defended it from the corrosive acid of modernism. He was surely right on that point.

Evangelical identity was at stake and needed to be defended. The question then became one of strategy, not principle. What was the best strategy for contending for the evangelical faith? Christopher Catherwood has made an important point concerning how denominational affiliation directly impacts the interpretation of the Doctor's call for unity. In particular, the Free Church tradition and the state church tradition operate on totally different wavelengths because they begin with vastly different commitments and assumptions.

---

[17] Iain H. Murray, *Evangelicalism Divided: A Record of Crucial Change in the Years 1950 to 2000* (Carlisle, PA: Banner of Truth, 2000).

[18] Murray, "Divisive Unity," 238.

[19] Catherwood, *Lloyd-Jones: A Family Portrait*, 142.

The Doctor, as a Congregationalist, believed that a true church is a local body of believers where the Word is rightly preached, the ordinances are rightly administered, and church discipline is rightly practiced. Therefore, the idea of a national church or territorial church did not make biblical sense to him. He defined the church as independent congregations. These independent congregations would share a loose affiliation for the purpose of Christian witness to the world and thereby display true evangelical unity, not false ecumenical unity.

Those from the state-church ecclesial tradition would hear the call very differently. People in a state church have more of a territorial vision for the church than a Congregationalist would have. Evangelical Anglicans chose to stay within that denomination for gospel reasons because they sincerely viewed the church of England as "God's means of proclaiming biblical truth to the English, the country in which God had put them."[20] The belief was not in a territorial church first and foremost, but in "using the existence of a territorial church as a means created by God to enable the evangelization of England."[21]

It is also vital to observe that Lloyd-Jones did not have a clearly defined denominational plan. He spoke more prophetically than structurally. J. I. Packer has noted this same dynamic:

> He never gave substance to his vision by producing, or getting others to produce, a blueprint for the new para-denomination. . . . Probably the truest thing to say about his campaign of words without plans is that he was testing the waters, looking to see if the Holy Spirit would use what he said to evoke major support and a widespread desire for action, and he would not risk prejudicing his own prophetic role in the process by any appearance of wanting to be a denominational boss. And who will blame him for that.[22]

Most of the initial responses to the controversy came from either Stott and Packer supporters or Lloyd-Jones supporters.[23] The passing of time has now brought many excellent scholarly treatments of this momentous

---

20 Catherwood, *Lloyd-Jones: His Life and Relevance*, 87; my emphasis.

21 Ibid., 88.

22 J. I. Packer, "David Martyn Lloyd-Jones," in Catherwood, *Chosen by God*, 49–50.

23 The best place to start may be with the respective biographers of the persons involved. For the perspective of Lloyd-Jones, see Iain H. Murray, *The Life of Martyn Lloyd-Jones, 1899–1981* (Carlisle, PA: Banner of Truth, 2013), 375–408. For the perspective of John Stott, see Timothy Dudley-Smith, *John Stott: A Global Ministry: A Biography: The Later Years* (Downers Grove, IL: InterVarsity Press, 2001), 65–71. For the perspective of J. I. Packer, see Alister McGrath, *J. I. Packer*.

event.[24] John Brencher's biography of Lloyd-Jones claims that only two Anglican evangelical ministers seceded from the Anglican Church in response to Lloyd-Jones.[25] Andrew Atherstone shows that the actual number was "nearly ten times as large."[26] He demonstrates that evangelical ministers routinely left the Anglican Church "almost every year between 1964 and 1974, sometimes two or three within the space of a few months. It is no exaggeration to speak of an Anglican 'secession crisis.'"[27] Many ministers had already left the Anglican church prior to 1966 for exactly the reasons the Doctor referenced in the speech itself.

The evangelical landscape has changed in the five decades since the speech. New opportunities and challenges have arisen that call for new responses. Christopher Catherwood believes that the "global situation has shifted in the direction that the Doctor wished in his speech in October 1966—before his words became twisted by both sides."[28] He also points out that Packer has more recently seen the need to leave the territorial dioceses of the Anglican Church and find unity with the evangelical expressions of Anglicanism. The argument is that "territorial dioceses are man-made institutions," and thus it is possible to stay in the Anglican Communion and affiliate with evangelical Anglican dioceses in Latin America or Africa.[29] Catherwood also documents the presence of more and more gospel partnerships in the United Kingdom that cut across denominational lines.[30] Together for the Gospel or the Gospel Coalition would be good examples of expressions of evangelical unity today in the United States.

Is there any evidence that the Doctor had such gospel partnerships in mind in his speech? Catherwood suggests that the International Fellowship of Evangelical Students (which the Doctor loved and supported for decades) "was surely closest to the heart of what Martyn Lloyd-Jones perceived Christ-centered, Bible-believing unity to be all about."[31] Lloyd-Jones was the chair of this group of evangelicals who met to craft the IFES

---

[24] Perhaps the best all-around treatment is Andrew Atherstone, "Lloyd-Jones and the Anglican Succession Crisis," in *Engaging with Martyn Lloyd-Jones: The Life and Legacy of the Doctor*, ed. Andrew Atherstone and David Ceri Jones (Nottingham, UK: Apollos, 2011). See also chaps. 4–5 of John J. Brencher, *Martyn Lloyd-Jones (1899–1981) and Twentieth-Century Evangelicalism*, Studies in Evangelical History and Thought (Carlisle, UK: Paternoster, 2002). Another excellent resource is Alister Chapman, *Godly Ambition: John Stott and the Evangelical Movement* (New York: Oxford University Press, 2012), 90–111.
[25] Brencher, *Martyn Lloyd-Jones*, 100.
[26] Atherstone, "Lloyd-Jones and the Anglican Succession Crisis," 262.
[27] Ibid.
[28] Catherwood, *Lloyd-Jones: His Life and Relevance*, 92–93.
[29] Ibid., 94.
[30] Ibid., 95.
[31] Ibid., 99.

statement of faith in 1945–1947. It was a statement that evangelicals from every denomination could sign, but only because they were evangelical. The statement stressed the primary evangelical doctrines, not the secondary matters of difference that should not divide them.

Conclusion: Building on the True Foundation

Carl R. Trueman says that the Doctor's address has attained a "legendary, perhaps even mythical" status in our day.[32] One could devote a tremendous amount of time researching this important event.

I approach the issue as a convinced Baptist, and thus I interpret these matters through a certain grid. I do not claim to be unbiased. I believe that church unity finds expression first and foremost in a local body of believers. Calls to address divisiveness (like Titus 3:10) are church discipline matters for a local assembly. The New Testament is simply not clear in laying out details about how local churches should relate to other local churches. There seems to be no authoritative instruction for how local churches should assemble into *governing* relationships with each other. Therefore, I share the sentiments of Mark Dever on this controversy with respect to the true nature of church unity: "Mayhem ensues as biblical imperatives to unity are applied to relationships *between congregations*, relationships that are nowhere defined in Scripture, and about which there is and should be Christian liberty."[33]

This controversy does highlight something important about Lloyd-Jones: his commitment to doctrine. True unity can be built only on a true doctrinal foundation. Therefore, this whole discussion reinforces the Doctor's commitment to the essential role of doctrine in defining the life of the church and, as we have seen throughout these chapters, the essential role of doctrine in living the Christian life.

---

[32] Carl R. Trueman, "J. I. Packer: An English Nonconformist Perspective," in *J. I. Packer and the Evangelical Future: The Impact of His Life and Thought*, ed. Timothy George (Grand Rapids: Baker, 2009), 120.
[33] Mark Dever, "MLJ—Man of the Church" (presentation at the Martyn Lloyd-Jones conference in Herne, England, March 21, 2006).

BIBLIOGRAPHY

Martyn Lloyd-Jones never technically set out to write a book. All his books began as sermons or addresses that were later gathered for publication. His books are listed here in near chronological order based on when they were delivered. Secondary sources are listed in alphabetical order.

Works of Martyn Lloyd-Jones

1927–1938

Evangelistic Sermons at Aberavon. Carlisle, PA: Banner of Truth, 1983.

Old Testament Evangelistic Sermons. Carlisle, PA: Banner of Truth, 1996. Eleven of the twenty-one sermons were preached at Aberavon.

1939

Why Does God Allow War? Wheaton, IL: Crossway, 2003. Five sermons preached in October 1939. This was the Doctor's first published book (London: Hodder & Stoughton, 1939).

1941–1950

The Christian in an Age of Terror: Selected Sermons of Dr Martyn Lloyd-Jones, 1941–1950. Edited by Michael Eaton. Grand Rapids: Kregel, 2008. Features expositions of Acts 12, Romans 8:9–15, 1 Corinthians 16:13–14, Hebrews 1:1–3, and Revelation 4.

The Plight of Man and the Power of God. Fearn, Ross-shire, UK: Christian Heritage, 2013. The Doctor's second book, this consists of five expositions/lectures on Romans 1 delivered at Edinburgh in March 1941.

Expository Sermons on 2 Peter. Carlisle, PA: Banner of Truth, 1983. Twenty-five expositions during 1946–1947.

Truth Unchanged, Unchanging. Wheaton, IL: Crossway, 1950. Five lectures given at Wheaton College in 1947.

The Life of Joy: An Exposition of Philippians 1 and 2. Grand Rapids: Baker, 1989. This and *The Life of Peace* constitute an expository series of sermons through Philippians preached in 1947–1948.

The Life of Peace: An Exposition of Philippians 3 and 4. Grand Rapids: Baker, 1993.

The Heart of the Gospel. Wheaton, IL: Crossway, 1991. Sunday evening sermons on Matthew 11:2–30 preached in 1948–1949.

Life in Christ: Studies in 1 John. Wheaton, IL: Crossway, 2002. Sixty-seven Sunday morning sermons preached in 1948–1950 and originally published by Crossway in five volumes: *Fellowship with God* (1992); *Walking with God* (1993); *Children of God* (1994); *The Love of God* (1994); and *Life in God* (1995).

1950–1954

Studies in the Sermon on the Mount. 2 vols. in 1. Grand Rapids: Eerdmans, 1974. Sixty sermons preached from Matthew 5–7 in 1950–1952.

From Fear to Faith: Rejoicing in the Lord in Turbulent Times. Downers Grove, IL: InterVarsity Press, 1953. Eight sermons on Habakkuk preached in 1950.

Out of the Depths: Psalm 51. Fearn, Ross-shire, UK: Christian Heritage, 2011. Four Sunday evening sermons on Psalm 51 preached in 1950.

Let Not Your Hearts Be Troubled. Wheaton, IL: Crossway, 2009. Eight sermons on John 14:1–12 preached in 1951.

Great Doctrines of the Bible: God the Father, God the Son. Wheaton, IL: Crossway, 1996. This and the following two *Great Doctrines of the Bible* titles consist of Friday night lectures delivered in 1952–1953.

Great Doctrines of the Bible: God the Holy Spirit. Wheaton, IL: Crossway, 1997.

Great Doctrines of the Bible: The Church and the Last Things. Wheaton, IL: Crossway, 1998.

The Assurance of Our Salvation: Studies in John 17. Wheaton, IL: Crossway, 2000. Forty-eight sermons preached in 1952–1953.

Faith on Trial: Studies on Psalm 73. Grand Rapids: Baker, 1965. Eleven sermons preached in 1953.

Spiritual Depression: Its Causes and Its Cure. Grand Rapids: Eerdmans, 1965. Twenty-one sermons preached in 1954.

The All-Sufficient God: Sermons on Isaiah 40. Carlisle, PA: Banner of Truth, 2005. Nine Sunday evening sermons preached on Isaiah 40 in 1954.

1954–1968

▪ *1954–1962*

God's Ultimate Purpose: An Exposition of Ephesians 1. Grand Rapids: Baker, 1978. Lloyd-Jones preached an expository series of 361 sermons on Ephesians in 1954–1962. Baker Book House, along with Banner of Truth, published them under this and the following seven titles.

God's Way of Reconciliation: An Exposition of Ephesians 2. Grand Rapids: Baker, 1972.

The Unsearchable Riches of Christ: An Exposition of Ephesians 3. Grand Rapids: Baker, 1979.

Christian Unity: An Exposition of Ephesians 4:1–16. Grand Rapids: Baker, 1981.

Darkness and Light: An Exposition of Ephesians 4:17–5:17. Grand Rapids: Baker, 1982.

Life in the Spirit in Marriage, Home and Work: An Exposition of Ephesians 5:18–6:9. Grand Rapids: Baker, 1974.

The Christian Warfare: An Exposition of Ephesians 6:10–13. Grand Rapids: Baker, 1976.

The Christian Soldier: An Exposition of Ephesians 6:10–20. Grand Rapids: Baker, 1977.

The Gospel in Genesis: From Fig Leaves to Faith. Wheaton, IL: Crossway, 2009. Six Sunday evening sermons on Genesis 3 preached in 1955.

Seeking the Face of God: Nine Reflections on the Psalms. Wheaton, IL: Crossway, 2005. Two Sunday evening sermons from Psalm 84 and seven other texts in Psalms. Lloyd-Jones preached five Sunday evening sermons on Psalm 84 in 1957.

Authority. Carlisle, PA: Banner of Truth, 1984. Three addresses Lloyd-Jones delivered at a conference of the general committee of the International Fellowship of Evangelical Students, Ontario, September 1957.

Revival. Wheaton, IL: Crossway, 1987. Twenty-four sermons, preached in 1959, which celebrated the centennial of the great Welsh revival.

Magnify the Lord: Luke 1:46–55. Fearn, Ross-shire, UK: Christian Heritage, 2011. Four Sunday evening sermons preached in 1959.

Love So Amazing: Exposition of Colossians 1. Grand Rapids: Baker, 1995. Fourteen Sunday evening sermons preached in 1962.

A Merciful and Faithful High Priest: Studies in the Book of Hebrews. Wheaton, IL: Crossway, 2017. Nineteen sermons on the book of Hebrews preached at various times.

▪ *1955–1968*

The Gospel of God: An Exposition of Romans 1. Carlisle, PA: Banner of Truth, 1985. The Romans volumes listed here and below grew out of a Friday night lecture series from 1955 until the Doctor's retirement in 1968. By then he had reached Romans 14:17.

The Righteous Judgment of God: An Exposition of Romans 2:1–3:20. Carlisle, PA: Banner of Truth, 1985.

Atonement and Justification: An Exposition of Romans 3:20–4:25. Carlisle, PA: Banner of Truth, 1998.

Assurance: An Exposition of Romans 5. Carlisle, PA: Banner of Truth, 1998.

The New Man: An Exposition of Romans 6. Carlisle, PA: Banner of Truth, 1972.

The Law: Its Function and Limits. An Exposition of Romans 7:1–8:4. Carlisle, PA: Banner of Truth, 1973.

The Sons of God: An Exposition of Romans 8:5–17. Carlisle, PA: Banner of Truth, 1974.

The Final Perseverance of the Saints: An Exposition of Romans 8:17–39. Carlisle, PA: Banner of Truth, 1975.

God's Sovereign Purpose: An Exposition of Romans 9. Carlisle, PA: Banner of Truth, 1991.

Saving Faith: An Exposition of Romans 10. Carlisle, PA: Banner of Truth, 1998.

To God's Glory: An Exposition of Romans 11. Carlisle, PA: Banner of Truth, 1999.

Christian Conduct: An Exposition of Romans 12. Carlisle, PA: Banner of Truth, 2000.

Life in Two Kingdoms: An Exposition of Romans 13. Carlisle, PA: Banner of Truth, 2003.

Liberty and Conscience: An Exposition of Romans 14:1–17. Carlisle, PA: Banner of Truth, 2003.

■ *1962–1964*

The Basis of Christian Unity: An Exposition of John 17 and Ephesians 4. Grand Rapids: Eerdmans, 1962. Two addresses the Doctor delivered to a gathering of ministers in June 1962.

Born of God: Sermons on John 1. Carlisle, PA: Banner of Truth, 2011. Sermons preached on John 1 in 1962–1963.

True Happiness: Psalms 1 and 107. Wheaton, IL: Crossway, 2001. Eight evangelistic sermons on Psalm 107 preached in 1955, and four evangelistic sermons on Psalm 1 preached in 1963.

God's Way, Not Ours: Isaiah 1. Grand Rapids: Baker, 1999. Nine evangelistic sermons preached in 1963.

The Kingdom of God. Wheaton, IL: Crossway, 2010. Twelve evangelistic sermons from Mark 1:14–15 and various other texts preached in 1963.

The Cross: God's Way of Salvation. Wheaton, IL: Crossway, 1986. Nine evangelistic sermons on Galatians 6:7–15 preached in 1963–1964. Lloyd-Jones actually preached fifteen sermons in the original series, but only nine were published here.

A Nation under Wrath: Studies in Isaiah 5. Grand Rapids: Baker, 1998. Nine evangelistic sermons on Isaiah 5 preached in 1964.

I Am Not Ashamed: Advice to Timothy. Grand Rapids: Baker, 1986. Eleven evangelistic sermons on 2 Timothy 1:12 delivered in 1964.

■ *1964–1965*

Joy Unspeakable: Power and Renewal in the Holy Spirit. Wheaton, IL: Shaw, 1984. This volume and *The Sovereign Spirit* constitute a series of twenty-four sermons on John 1:26–33 preached in 1964–1965.

The Sovereign Spirit: Discerning His Gifts. Wheaton, IL: Shaw, 1985.

The Path to True Happiness: John 2. Grand Rapids: Baker, 1999. Twelve sermons preached from John 2 in 1965.

■ *1965–1968*

Authentic Christianity: Studies in the Book of Acts. Wheaton, IL: Crossway, 2000. This and the following five volumes represent the 120 Sunday evening sermons on Acts 1:1–8:35 that Lloyd-Jones preached from 1965 until his retirement in 1968.

Courageous Christianity: Studies in the Book of Acts. Wheaton, IL: Crossway, 2001.

Victorious Christianity: Studies in the Book of Acts. Wheaton, IL: Crossway, 2003.

Glorious Christianity: Studies in the Book of Acts. Wheaton, IL: Crossway, 2004.

Triumphant Christianity: Studies in the Book of Acts. Wheaton, IL: Crossway, 2006.

Compelling Christianity: Studies in the Book of Acts. Wheaton, IL: Crossway, 2007.

Experiencing the New Birth: Studies in John 3. Wheaton, IL: Crossway, 2015. Twenty-six sermons preached in 1966.

Living Water: Studies in John 4. Wheaton, IL: Crossway, 2009. Thirty-seven sermons preached in 1966–1968.

1969

Preaching and Preachers. Grand Rapids: Zondervan, 1971. Lectures that Lloyd-Jones gave at Westminster Theological Seminary in Philadelphia in the spring of 1969.

Setting Our Affections upon Glory: Nine Sermons on the Gospel and the Church. Wheaton, IL: Crossway, 2013. Sermons preached in Pensacola, Florida, during the Doctor's final visit to America in 1969.

1977

Jesus Christ and Him Crucified. Carlisle, PA: Banner of Truth, 2000. A sermon that Lloyd-Jones preached in February 1977 in the same Aberavon pulpit where he first preached the same text when he started his ministry in 1926.

Various Times

Knowing the Times: Addresses Delivered on Various Occasions. Carlisle, PA: Banner of Truth, 1989.

Letters 1919–1981. Carlisle, PA: Banner of Truth, 1994.

Not against Flesh and Blood. Fearn, Ross-shire, UK: Christian Heritage, 2013.

The Puritans: Their Origins and Successors. Carlisle, PA: Banner of Truth, 2014.

Secondary Sources

Atherstone, Andrew, and David Ceri Jones, eds. *Engaging with Martyn Lloyd-Jones: The Life and Legacy of the Doctor.* Nottingham, UK: Apollos, 2011.

Brencher, John J. *Martyn Lloyd-Jones (1899–1981) and Twentieth-Century Evangelicalism.* Studies in Evangelical History and Thought. Carlisle, UK: Paternoster, 2002.

Catherwood, Christopher, ed. *Chosen by God.* Crowborough, UK: Highland, 1986.

———. *Martyn Lloyd-Jones: A Family Portrait.* Grand Rapids: Baker, 1994.

———. *Martyn Lloyd-Jones: His Life and Relevance for the 21st Century.* Wheaton, IL: Crossway, 2015.

Clark, Lynette G. *Far above Rubies: The Life of Bethan Lloyd-Jones.* Fearn, Ross-shire, UK: Christian Focus, 2015.

Eaton, Michael A. *Baptism with the Spirit: The Teaching of Martyn Lloyd-Jones.* Downers Grove, IL: InterVarsity Press, 1989.

Eveson, Philip H. *Travel with Martyn Lloyd-Jones.* Leominster, UK: Day One, 2004.

Lawson, Steven J. *The Passionate Preaching of Martyn Lloyd-Jones.* Sanford, FL: Reformation Trust, 2016.

Lloyd-Jones, Bethan. *Memories of Sandfields.* Carlisle, PA: Banner of Truth, 2008.

Lynch, J. E. Hazlett. *Lamb of God—The Saviour of the World: The Soteriology of Rev. Dr. Martyn Lloyd-Jones.* Bloomington, IN: Westbow, 2015.

Murray, Iain H. *D. Martyn Lloyd-Jones: The Fight of Faith, 1939–1981.* Carlisle, PA: Banner of Truth, 1990.

———. *D. Martyn Lloyd-Jones: The First Forty Years, 1899–1939.* Carlisle, PA: Banner of Truth, 1982.

———. *Evangelicalism Divided: A Record of Crucial Change in the Years 1950 to 2000.* Carlisle, PA: Banner of Truth, 2000.

———. *The Life of Martyn Lloyd-Jones, 1899–1981.* Carlisle, PA: Banner of Truth, 2013.

———. *Lloyd-Jones: Messenger of Grace.* Carlisle, PA: Banner of Truth, 2008.

Sargent, Tony. *The Sacred Anointing: The Preaching of Dr. Martyn Lloyd-Jones.* Wheaton, IL: Crossway, 1994.

GENERAL INDEX

SCRIPTURE INDEX

WISDOM FROM THE PAST
FOR LIFE IN THE PRESENT

Theologians on the Christian Life

AUGUSTINE
by GERALD BRAY

BAVINCK
by JOHN BOLT

BONHOEFFER
by STEPHEN J. NICHOLS

CALVIN
by MICHAEL HORTON

EDWARDS
by DANE C. ORTLUND

LEWIS
by JOE RIGNEY

LLOYD-JONES
by JASON MEYER

LUTHER
by CARL R. TRUEMAN

NEWTON
by TONY REINKE

OWEN
by MATTHEW BARRETT &
MICHAEL A. G. HAYKIN

PACKER
by SAM STORMS

SCHAEFFER
by WILLIAM EDGAR

SPURGEON
by MICHAEL REEVES

WARFIELD
by FRED G. ZASPEL

WESLEY
by FRED SANDERS

The Theologians on the Christian Life series provides accessible
introductions to the great teachers on the Christian life, exploring their
personal lives and writings, especially as they pertain to the walk of faith.

Visit crossway.org/TOCL for more information.